Oracle® Solaris 11 System Virtualization Essentials

Second Edition

Oracle® Solaris 11 System Virtualization Essentials

Second Edition

Jeff Victor, Jeff Savit,
Gary Combs, Bob Netherton

PRENTICE
HALL

Boston • Columbus • Indianapolis • New York • San Francisco • Amsterdam • Cape Town
Dubai • London • Madrid • Milan • Munich • Paris • Montreal • Toronto • Delhi • Mexico City
São Paulo • Sydney • Hong Kong • Seoul • Singapore • Taipei • Tokyo

For information about buying this title in bulk quantities, or for special sales opportunities (which may include electronic versions; custom cover designs; and content particular to your business, training goals, marketing focus, or branding interests), please contact our corporate sales department at corpsales@pearsoned.com or (800) 382-3419.

For government sales inquiries, please contact governmentsales@pearsoned.com.

For questions about sales outside the U.S., please contact intlcs@pearson.com.

Visit us on the Web: informit.com/ph

Library of Congress Control Number: 2016959409

ISBN-13: 978-0-13-431087-9
ISBN-10: 0-13-431087-X

1   17

Jeff Victor dedicates this book to the memory of his sister, Diana Lyn Victor.

Contents

Foreword to the First Edition

I'm no longer sure when I first became hooked. Was it when I overheard a casual conversation about running a "test" copy of MVS in parallel with the real copy of MVS on a new 390 mainframe? Or was it the idea of Zarniwoop researching the *Hitchhiker's Guide to the Galaxy* in an electronically synthesized copy of the entire universe he kept in his office? Whatever the cause, I'm still addicted to virtual machine technology.

Fooling a whole stack of software to run correctly on a software simulation of the platform it was designed to run on has been a recurring interest in my career. Poring through the history of VM/370 as a graduate student, absorbing James Gosling's audacious idea of the Java VM, spending a few weeks building an experimental machine emulator to run SPARC applications on Solaris for PowerPC, the "aha!" moment when we realized how useful it would be if we arranged that a set of processes could behave as a little OS within an OS (the idea that became Solaris Zones), the first bring-up of OpenSolaris running as a paravirtualized guest on Xen—those are just a few of the highlights for me.

This book began as a project within Sun in mid-2009 during Oracle's acquisition of the company, so it both explores aspects of Sun's virtualization technology portfolio, and—now that the acquisition is complete—peers a little into 2010. Sun's unique position as a systems company allowed it to deliver a full set of integrated virtualization technologies. These solutions span the different trade-offs between maximizing utilization for efficiency and maximizing isolation for availability, while enabling the system to be managed at a large scale and up and down the layers of the systems architecture. Because that systems perspective informs everything we do, we have a wealth of solutions to match the diverse needs of modern enterprise architectures. Many of these tools are interoperable, enabling solutions that are otherwise impossible or impractical. Oracle's acquisition of Sun provides two further benefits to that portfolio: a secure future for these technologies and the exciting potential for integration with Oracle VM, Oracle Enterprise Manager, and the wealth of Oracle applications.

Here are some examples from the Sun portfolio. ZFS is a key storage virtualization technology at the core of the future of the Solaris operating system as well as the appliance products we build from Solaris technology today. Solaris networking virtualization technologies allow cutting-edge network hardware to be exploited and managed efficiently while providing a natural virtual network interface abstraction. For server virtualization, Solaris Zones (also known as Solaris Containers) have turned out to be very popular and very successful—a natural fit for the needs of many customers. The logical domains hypervisor is an extremely efficient design, and enables customers to get the most out of the tremendous throughput capability of SPARC CMT platforms. Our work with the Xen community enables a high-performance Solaris x64 guest for Oracle VM. For client virtualization, look no further than VirtualBox—for the laptop and desktop, both as a developer utility, and as a virtual appliance developer tool for the cloud. And it's not just a client technology: VirtualBox is the server component of Sun's virtual desktop infrastructure product, and it continues to grow more server-class features with every release. As well as infrastructure virtualization platforms, we have created infrastructure management software—Ops Center—intended to reduce the complexity that comes with using the new capabilities in large-scale deployments.

Virtual machines in one form or another have been around for a long time. Yet virtualization is such a fundamental idea that it remains associated with many developing fields. In the past decade, the runaway success of hypervisor-based virtualization on x64 platforms has largely been driven by the operational savings achieved by consolidating Microsoft Windows guests. But now this layer of the system architecture is just part of the way infrastructure is done—a new raft of capabilities can be built on top of it.

Recently we've seen the emergence of the Infrastructure as a Service (IaaS) style of cloud computing. Enabled by the combination of ever-increasing Internet connectivity and bandwidth, coupled with Moore's law about providing more and more computational power per dollar, users of an IaaS service send their entire software stacks to remote data centers. Virtualization decouples the software from the hardware to enable those data centers to be operated almost as a utility. This approach promises to revolutionize the fundamental economics across the IT industry. The capital expenditures currently devoted to under-utilized equipment can be shifted to pay-as-you-go operating expenses, both within large enterprises and between service providers and their customers.

This new layer of the systems architecture brings new opportunities and new problems to solve—in terms of security, observability, performance, networking, utilization, power management, migration, scheduling, manageability, and so on. While both industry and the academic research community are busily responding to many of those challenges, much remains to be done. The fundamentals remain important, and will continue to differentiate the various virtualization solutions in the marketplace.

This book is a deep exploration of virtualization products and technologies provided by or for Solaris, written by experienced practitioners in the art of delivering real solutions to data center problems. It provides a holistic view of virtualization, encompassing all of the different models used in the industry. That breadth itself is rare: No other organization has as complete a view of the entire range of system virtualization possibilities. A comprehensive background chapter leads neophytes into virtualization. Experienced data center architects will appreciate the individual chapters explaining the technologies and suggesting ways to use them to solve real problems—a critical resource in a rapidly changing world. I hope you find it as fascinating as I do!

Tim Marsland
Vice President and Fellow, Sun Microsystems, Inc.
Menlo Park
February 18, 2010

Preface

Computer virtualization has become a core component of the server industry; many organizations use virtualization in more than 75% of their servers. The portion of workloads running in virtual environments has increased in tandem with the maturity, number, and flexibility of virtualization options. Further, virtualization has become a required enabler of cloud computing.

Oracle® Solaris 11 System Virtualization Essentials presents the multiple technologies that the Oracle Solaris operating system uses to virtualize and consolidate computing resources, from hardware partitioning to virtual machines and hypervisors to operating system virtualization, commonly called "containers." The intent of *Oracle® Solaris 11 System Virtualization Essentials* is to discuss computer virtualization in general and to focus on those system virtualization technologies provided by, or that provide support to, the Oracle Solaris operating system. Oracle Solaris 11 supports a rich collection of virtualization technologies:

- Physical domains
- Oracle VM Server for SPARC (previously called Logical Domains)
- Oracle VM VirtualBox
- Oracle Solaris Zones (previously called Solaris Containers)

Virtualization offers a tremendous opportunity to add computing workloads while controlling operational costs and adding computing flexibility. For the system administrator, this new knowledge area requires skills with new technologies such as hypervisors, which create virtual machines on a single hardware machine, and containers (also known as zones), which create virtual operating systems running on a single complete operating system.

Oracle® Solaris 11 System Virtualization Essentials describes the factors that affect your choice of technologies. Along the way, it explains how to achieve the following goals:

- Use physical domains to maximize workload isolation on Oracle SPARC systems
- Use Oracle VM Server for SPARC to deploy different Oracle Solaris 11 environments on SPARC systems
- Use Oracle VM VirtualBox to develop and test software in heterogeneous environments
- Use Oracle Solaris Zones to maximize the efficiency and scalability of workloads
- Use Oracle Solaris Zones to migrate Solaris 10 workloads to new hardware systems
- Mix virtualization technologies so as to maximize workload density

Oracle® Solaris 11 System Virtualization Essentials contains nine chapters. Chapter 1 discusses system virtualization in general terms. This material includes the needs driving consolidation, the value and benefits of virtualization, and the most common types of computer virtualization. In addition, Chapter 1 also describes many of the concepts, features, and methods shared by many implementations of system virtualization. The concepts introduced in Chapter 1 are subsequently explored in much more detail in the other chapters.

Modern virtualization has been put to many varied uses. Chapter 2 introduces a few of those uses from a generic standpoint, tying benefits to features and providing simplified examples.

Chapters 3 through 6 hone in on Oracle's computer virtualization technologies that are directly related to the Oracle Solaris operating system. The large-scale deployment of virtual environments has created new system management challenges. In two different contexts, Chapter 7 reviews automation and management tools that can ease the pain of adopting virtualization solutions. Chapter 8 discusses the factors that should be considered when choosing a virtualization technology or combination of technologies, and suggests a process of analysis that can be used to choose a virtualization technology or combination of technologies. Assembling all of the pieces, Chapter 9 walks you through several real-world applications of those technologies. Finally, the Appendix offers a whirlwind tour of the history of virtualization.

Because this book focuses on system virtualization technologies, technologies and methods that do not virtualize a computer system are not discussed. These topics include, for example, storage virtualization and application virtualization.

Intended Audience

This book can benefit anyone who wants to learn more about Oracle Solaris 11. It is written to be particularly accessible to system administrators who are new to Solaris—people who are perhaps already serving as administrators of Linux, Windows, or other UNIX systems.

If you are not presently a practicing system administrator but want to become one, this book provides an excellent introduction to virtualization. In fact, most of the examples used in this book are suited to or can be adapted to small learning environments such as a home computer. Thus, even before you venture into corporate system administration or deploy Oracle Solaris 11 in your existing IT installation, this book will help you experiment in a small test environment.

Oracle® Solaris 11 System Virtualization Essentials is especially valuable to several specific audiences. A primary group is generalists who desire knowledge of the entire system virtualization space. The only assumed knowledge is general UNIX or Linux administrative experience. Another key audience is current and future data center staff who need an understanding of virtualization and use of such technologies in real-world situations.

- Data center architects will benefit from the broad coverage of virtualization models and technologies, enabling them to optimize system and network architectures that employ virtualization. The extensive coverage of resource controls can lead to better stability and more consistent performance of workloads in virtualized systems.

- Computer science students with UNIX or Linux experience will gain a holistic understanding of the history and current state of the system virtualization industry. The breadth of virtualization models discussed provides a framework for further discovery, and the real-world examples prepare students for data center careers.

- Technical support staff who troubleshoot virtualized systems will gain an introduction to system virtualization and interactions between virtualized systems. This background can shorten the time needed to diagnose problems, and enable personnel to readily distinguish between problems related to virtualization and ones that are independent of virtualization.

How to Use This Book

Readers who wish to learn about one specific Oracle Solaris virtualization technology should read Chapters 1 and 2, and the appropriate sections of Chapters 3 through 6, 7, and 9. If you would like to understand all of the virtualization technologies that use Oracle Solaris as a core component and determine how to choose among them, read all of the chapters in this book.

If you already understand virtualization but want to learn about virtualization using Oracle Solaris, you should skim through Chapter 1 to understand the context of the rest of the book as well as the definitions of terms used throughout the book, and then read Chapter 2 and the introductory sections of Chapters 3 through 6. Chapters 8 and 9 will also be especially useful.

If you are implementing virtualization technologies on many systems, you should read Chapter 9 to understand the unique problems that must be addressed as part of this work and to identify software that can significantly reduce the complexity of large virtualization farms.

Register your copy of *Oracle® Solaris 11 System Virtualization Essentials, Second Edition,* at informit.com for convenient access to downloads, updates, and corrections as they become available. To start the registration process, go to informit.com/register and log in or create an account. Enter the product ISBN (9780134310879) and click Submit. Once the process is complete, you will find any available bonus content under "Registered Products."

Acknowledgments

The authors would like to thank Detlef Drewanz and Doug Schwabauer for writing the two sections of Chapter 7 in the second edition. Bill Calkins entered late in the game to update the chapter dedicated to VirtualBox. The authors appreciate these valuable contributions.

The authors also appreciate the expertise and hard work of Prentice Hall executive editor Greg Doench, as well as freelance project manager Rachel Paul and copy editor Jill Hobbs.

Jeff Victor would like to thank his wife Cara and their daughter Kathryn for their patience and support during this endeavor. He also thanks John Fowler, Markus Flierl, and Dawit Bereket for their support during the production of the second edition.

Jeff Savit thanks his wife Vicky for her support during this effort. He also thanks Honglin Su, John Falkenthal, and the Oracle VM Server for SPARC organization for creating and growing this powerful virtualization platform.

About the Authors

This book is made possible by the hard work and expertise of the following contributing authors.

Jeff Victor is the principal author of *Oracle® Solaris 11 System Virtualization Essentials* and a Principal Sales Engineer at Oracle Corporation. Prior to joining Oracle, Jeff was a Principal Engineer at Sun Microsystems. He leverages his expertise in computer virtualization, operating systems, and network architecture to help organizations run more efficiently. He is a regular author, contributor, and speaker at corporate and industry events. His blog can be found at http://blogs.oracle.com/JeffV. Jeff received a bachelor of science degree in computer science from Rensselaer Polytechnic Institute. In his spare time, he travels with his family, leads an automated wildlife photography project, and investigates STEM topics with his daughter. Jeff lives in New York with his wife and daughter.

Jeff Savit is a product manager in the Oracle VM Server organization and specializes in operating systems, virtualization, and performance. Prior to Oracle, he was a Principal Field Technologist at Sun. Previously he was a Vice President at Merrill Lynch, with roles in systems programming, software development, market data, and web applications.

Gary Combs is a Sales Performance Designer in the Oracle Sales and Partner Academy at Oracle Corporation. He specializes in creating field sales training programs covering SPARC servers, and all Engineered Systems. Prior to joining Oracle, Gary was with Sun Microsystems. He has more than 15 years of direct sales support experience as a systems engineer, and more than 15 years of experience in marketing positions in product management, product definition, and technical marketing.

Bob Netherton is a Master Principal Sales Consultant at Oracle Corporation specializing in Oracle Solaris, virtualization, open-source software, and Engineered Systems. Prior to joining Oracle, Bob was a Principal Field Technologist for Sun Microsystems, and was one of the architects and content developers of the Solaris Boot Camp and Deep Dive seminar series. In addition, he has developed several best practices guides for Solaris as well as an advanced Solaris training curriculum. Bob received a bachelor of science degree in applied mathematics from the University of Missouri, and he is a regular blogger on Solaris, virtualization, and open-source technologies.

1

Introduction to Virtualization

Virtualization is a maturing technology. This chapter provides an introduction to basic virtualization concepts and issues. It begins by defining virtualization and examining the motivations for using it, then turns to system virtualization models.

1.1 Definitions and Motivations

Technology is developed in response to a need. Virtualization technologies were invented to address gaps in the functionality of existing computer systems. Let's take a look at the meaning of computer virtualization and consider the various needs that it fulfills.

1.1.1 What Is Virtualization?

System virtualization is technology that creates "virtual environments," which allow multiple applications to run on one computer as if each has its own private computer. Virtualization is achieved by creating a virtual computer or virtual operating system that behaves like a real one, but isn't. Workload isolation is the primary goal of system virtualization.

Three virtualization models are commonly used. The first model is based on the ability to provide multiple isolated execution environments in one operating system (OS) instance—an approach called operating system virtualization (OSV). In this model, each environment contains what appears to be a private copy of the operating system in a container (a similar technology calls them jails). In the second model of virtualization, multiple operating system instances run on one set of hardware resources. This model takes advantage of virtual machines (VMs), which may run the same or different operating systems. Virtual machines are provided by hardware and/or software called a hypervisor, which creates the illusion of a private machine for each "guest" OS instance. In the third model, hardware partitioning ensures the electrical segregation of computer hardware resources—CPUs, RAM, and I/O components—so as to create multiple independent computers within one computer. Each isolated grouping of hardware is called a partition or domain.

Through the course of this book, we will describe different forms of computer virtualization in detail. We will use the phrase "virtual environment" (VE) to refer to any of these three models of virtualization.

1.1.2 Why Virtualize?

The original and most common reason to virtualize is to facilitate server consolidation, although the implementation of compute clouds is emerging as an important alternative type of consolidation. Today's data center managers face a series of extreme challenges: They must continue to add to compute workloads while minimizing operational costs, which include the electricity to power and cool those computing systems. In data centers with little empty rack space, this requirement necessitates squeezing existing workloads into unused compute capacity on existing systems and increasing the workload density of new systems.

Virtualization also provides a convenient layer of separation. This greatly simplifies the provisioning of a workload into a pool of compute resources, as well as the movement of workloads among compute nodes in a pool. These abilities greatly increase the flexibility and ease of creating compute clouds such as Database as a Service (DBaaS), Platform as a Service (PaaS), and Infrastructure as a Service (IaaS).

New servers are better able to handle this task than older ones. In many cases, data centers have achieved consolidation ratios of 20:1 or even 100:1, thereby reducing annual costs by hundreds of thousands or millions of dollars.

How can you achieve such savings? Workload consolidation is the process of implementing several computer workloads on one computer. This type of consolidation is not the same as the concept exemplified by installing multiple programs on a desktop computer, where you are actively using only one program at a time.

Instead, a server with consolidated workloads will run multiple programs on the same CPU(s) at the same time.

Most computers that are running only one workload are under-utilized, meaning that more hardware resources are available than the workload needs. The result is inefficient use of an organization's financial resources. Which costs more: five computers to run five workloads, or one computer that can run all five workloads? Of course, it is impossible to purchase exactly the right amount of "computer." For example, it is not possible to purchase a computer with half of a CPU for a workload that needs only half of the compute power of a single CPU.

Figure 1.1 shows the amount of CPU capacity used by two workloads, each residing on its own system. Approximately 70% of the investment in the first system's CPU is wasted, and 60% of the second system's CPU goes unused. In this arrangement, the cost of a CPU—not to mention other components, such as the frame and power supplies—is wasted.

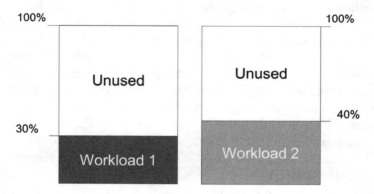

Figure 1.1 Two Under-utilized Systems

It is possible—and often desirable—to run another workload on the same system instead of purchasing a second computer to handle the second workload. Figure 1.2 shows the CPU consumption for the same two workloads after consolidation onto one system. As you can see, the amount of wasted investment has decreased by an entire CPU. In this system, the OS will spend some compute cycles managing resource usage of the two workloads and reducing the impact that one workload has on the other. This mediation increases CPU utilization, thereby reducing available CPU capacity, but we will ignore this effect for now.

Of course, these examples use average values, and real-world computers do not run well at 100% CPU utilization. Given this fact of life, you must avoid being overly aggressive when consolidating workloads.

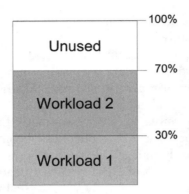

Figure 1.2   A Consolidated System

In the early days of the computer industry, computers were often so expensive that a corporation might be able to own only one of these machines. Given the precious nature of this resource, it was important for an organization to make the most of a computer by keeping it as busy as possible doing useful work.

At first, computers could run only one program at a time. This arrangement was unwieldy when a group of users sought to use the same computer, creating a need for a multiuser operating system. Software engineers designed such operating systems with features that prevented one program from affecting another program in a harmful way and prevented one user from causing harm to the other users' programs and data. Other features were designed to prevent one program from consuming more system resources—CPU cycles, physical memory (RAM), or network bandwidth—than it should. This consideration was important for early batch systems like OS/360 on early mainframes, but it became even more important for influential early time-sharing systems such as CTSS and Multics.

A further issue was that computers, prior to the development of virtualization, were able to run only one operating system at a time. This constraint created operational problems and increased costs if different users of a system needed different operating systems for their applications. Some operating systems were good for time-sharing and others were oriented toward batch processing, but applications during that era were inevitably written for a specific operating system or for a specific version. Without virtualization, companies had to purchase additional systems to run the different operating systems, or schedule dedicated time for each group of users needing their own OS version.

For example, an IBM mainframe customer in the 1970s might want to upgrade from an older IBM operating system like OS/360 to the newly released MVS. This change required the purchase of additional, very expensive hardware, and perhaps created the need to schedule system conversion and test times on weekends and late at night. VM/370—one of the first virtualization technologies—became very popular with systems programmers because they were able to run both the old and new operating systems at the same time, during normal working hours. The same programmers found that VM/370 provided a time-sharing environment that was pleasant and efficient compared to the batch-oriented operating systems otherwise in use. Different operating systems with different strengths could run side by side on the same hardware without incurring the capital expense needed to acquire another system.

Later, computer manufacturers developed inexpensive microcomputers, which were more affordable than the relatively expensive minicomputers and mainframes. Unfortunately, these microcomputers and their early operating systems were not well suited to running multiple production applications. This led to a common practice of running one application per computer.

Some early virtualization approaches offered little choice of operating systems for guests. Although the current virtual machine platforms typically support multiple operating system types in their virtual machines, hardware partitioning and operating system virtualization approaches do not.

More recently, progress in computer performance has led to a desirable problem: too much compute capacity. Many servers in data centers run at a very low average CPU utilization rate. Many users would like to put most of the rest of this capacity to work—a feat that can be achieved by consolidating workloads.

1.1.3 Virtualization Improves Consolidation

Operating systems designed for use by multiple users (e.g., most UNIX derivatives) have a long history of running multiple applications simultaneously. These operating systems include sophisticated features that isolate running programs, thereby preventing them from interfering with one another and attempting to provide each program with its fair share of system resources. Even these systems have limitations, however. For example, the application might assume that only one instance of that application will be running on the system, and it might acquire exclusive access to a singular, non-shareable system resource, such as a lock file with a fixed name. The first instance of such an application would lock the file to ensure that it is the only application modifying data files. A second instance of that application might then attempt to lock that same file, but the attempt would inevitably fail. Put simply, multiple instances of that application cannot coexist unless they can be isolated from each other.

Even if multiple workloads can coexist, other obstacles to consolidation may be present. Corporate security or regulatory rules might dictate that one group of users must not be able to know anything about programs being run by a different group of users. Either a software barrier is needed to prevent undesired observation and interaction, or those two user groups must be restricted to the use of different systems. The different user groups might also require different OS patch levels for their applications, or require the applications to operate with different system availability and maintenance windows. In general, however, UNIX-like operating systems are good platforms for consolidation because they provide user separation and resource management capabilities and scale well on large platforms.

Some other operating systems—particularly those that were originally designed to be single-user systems—cannot be used as a base for consolidated workloads quite so easily. Their architecture can make coexistence of similar workloads impossible and coexistence of different workloads difficult. Modifying a single-user OS so that it can run multiple workloads concurrently can be much more difficult than designing this capability into the system at the beginning. The use of these platforms as single-application servers led to the industry mindset of one application per server, even on systems that can effectively run multiple applications simultaneously.

Another solution is needed: the ability—or apparent ability—to run multiple copies of the operating system concurrently with one workload in each OS, as shown in Figure 1.3. To the hardware, this arrangement does not differ dramatically from previous ones: The two workloads have become slightly more complex, but they are still two workloads.

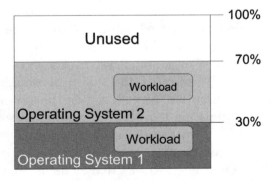

Figure 1.3   Multiple Operating System Instances on One Computer

To achieve the consolidation of multiple workloads onto one computer, software or firmware barriers between the workloads might be used, or entire copies of different operating systems might be run on the same system. The barriers separate virtual environments, which behave like independent computers to various degrees, depending on the virtualization technology. Once virtualization is accomplished, several benefits can be achieved, which fall into two categories:

- Cost reductions
  - Reduced aggregate acquisition costs of computers
  - Reduced aggregate support costs of computer hardware
  - Reduced data center space for computers
  - Reduced need for electricity to power computers and cooling systems
  - In some cases, reduced support costs for operating systems
  - In some cases, reduced license and support costs for application software
- Nonfinancial benefits
  - Increased architectural flexibility
  - Increased business agility due to improved workload mobility

Of course, nothing in life is free: There is a price to pay for these benefits. Some of the drawbacks of consolidation and virtualization are summarized here:

- Perceived increase in complexity: One physical computer will have multiple VEs; this is balanced by having fewer computers.
- Changes to asset tracking and run books: For example, rebooting a physical computer might require rebooting all of its VEs.
- Additional care needed when assigning workloads to computers: The computer and the virtualization technology represent a single point of failure for almost all technologies. It is important to balance availability with consolidation density.
- Potential for increased or new costs:
  - Some virtualization technologies have an upfront cost or recurring charge associated with licensing or support of the software.
  - A computer that supports virtualization may be more expensive than a single-workload system.
  - The level of support needed for a computer using virtualization may cost more than the level of support for the least important of the workloads

being consolidated; if most of the workloads were running on unsupported systems, support costs might actually increase.

- Data center architects and system administrators will need training on the virtualization technologies to be used.

1.1.4 Other Reasons for Virtualization

After years of implementing VEs solely to isolate consolidated workloads, some users realized that certain benefits of virtualization can be worth the effort even if only one workload is present on a system. For example, the business agility gained from simple VE mobility can prove highly useful. The ability to move a workload (a process called migration) enables businesses to respond more quickly to changing business needs. For example, you might move a VE to a larger system during the day, instead of planning the acquisition of a new, larger system and the reimplementation of the workload on that system. The VE provides a convenient "basket" of jobs that can be moved from one system to another. Virtual machines are particularly effective at providing this benefit.

Some tools even enable regular migrations to respond to periodic fluctuations in demand. For example, a batch processing workload might have minimal processing needs during the day but perform significant work at night. This workload could be migrated to a small system with other light loads in the early morning and then migrated to a larger, more powerful system in the early evening. This might avoid a lengthy start-up time before each day's processing.

Because VEs are convenient, manageable objects, other business needs can also be addressed with virtualization. A snapshot (i.e., a complete copy of a VE) can be made before the VE boots, or after its workload is quiesced. If the VE becomes damaged while it runs, whether accidentally or maliciously, the workload can be quickly restored from the snapshot. The data in the damaged copy can then be methodically inspected, both for valid transactions that should be rerun against the workload and as part of a thorough security analysis. Many file systems and storage systems include the ability to copy a storage object very quickly, reducing the effects of this operation on the service being provided.

Another advantage of VEs, even in a nonconsolidated configuration, is realized more fully by some virtualization technologies than by others—namely, security. Some types of VEs can be hardened to prevent users of the VE (even privileged ones) from making changes to the system. Operating system virtualization provides the most opportunities for novel security enhancements.

Virtualization can also help prepare the organization to handle future workloads. If the needs of future workloads are not known, it may be easier to meet those needs on a per-VE basis. For example, hypervisors can host different types of operating systems. A subsequent workload might use software that is available on only one operating system, which is a different OS than the one used by the first workload.

In summary, consolidation is used to reduce the costs of acquisition and operation, and virtualization is needed to isolate one workload from another workload so that each can operate as if it is the only workload running on the computer. Further, virtualization can be used in some cases for the unique advantages it brings, even on unconsolidated systems.

1.1.5 Support of Cloud Computing

As computer architects and administrators gained experience with virtualization, they realized that a new model of workload architecture could be achieved. This model has been named cloud computing. As we mentioned earlier, this is a subset of workload consolidation.

According to the U.S. National Institute of Standards and Technology (NIST), cloud computing is a "model for enabling ubiquitous, convenient, on-demand network access to a shared pool of configurable computing resources." Virtualization addresses the needs of several "essential characteristics":

- On-demand self-service: Many types of VEs boot more quickly than an entire computer would, because hardware self-tests are not necessary.
- Resource pooling: Mature virtualization technologies must include the isolation features necessary to ensure orderly pooling of resources.
- Rapid elasticity: Many virtualization solutions permit dynamic addition or removal of hardware resources from individual VEs, and all of them simplify and accelerate on-demand start-up of VEs.

Further, NIST defines three service models: Infrastructure as a Service (IaaS), Platform as a Service (PaaS), and Software as a Service (SaaS). Virtualization tools can be leveraged to enable each of these models.

1.1.6 Common Concepts

Many of the capabilities of VEs can be put into context and further investigated with common use cases.

All consolidated systems require resource management features to prevent one VE from overwhelming a finite resource and thereby preventing other VEs from using it. This possibility is discussed in the use case "General Workload Consolidation" (discussed later in this chapter).

In addition, all consolidated systems need firm security boundaries between VEs to prevent one VE from interacting with another in an unintended fashion. This concept is discussed in Chapter 2, "Use Cases and Requirements."

Virtualization creates the sense—and sometimes the reality—that there is something extra between the VE and the hardware. In some virtualization technologies, the extra layer creates performance overhead, reducing workload performance. This overhead also reduces scalability—the ability to run many workloads on the system. Nevertheless, the separation provided by this layer can be very beneficial, as it provides a more well-defined boundary between workload and hardware. This arrangement makes it easier to move a VE from one computer to another than it is to move an OS instance from one computer to another.

Learning to manage virtualized environments requires modifying your thinking and changing some practices. Some tasks that were difficult or impossible become easier. Other tasks that were relatively simple become more complicated. The lack of a one-to-one relationship between workload and physical computer presents a new challenge for many people. Also, a new opportunity afforded by virtualization—moving a workload from one computer to another while the workload is active—brings its own challenges, including keeping track of the workloads that you are trying to manage.

Fortunately, you can choose from a set of tools that aim to simplify the task of virtualization management. These tools perform hardware discovery, OS provisioning, workload provisioning, configuration management, resource management, performance monitoring and tuning, security configuration and compliance reporting, network configuration, and updating of OS and application software. This topic is discussed in Chapter 7, "Automating Virtualization."

1.2 System Virtualization Models

Many different models for system virtualization have been developed. These models share many traits, but differences between them abound. Some virtualization features are appropriate for some models; others are not.

Each model can be described in terms of two characteristics: flexibility and isolation. Those two characteristics have an inverse relationship: Typically, the more isolation between VEs, the less flexibility in resource allocation. Conversely,

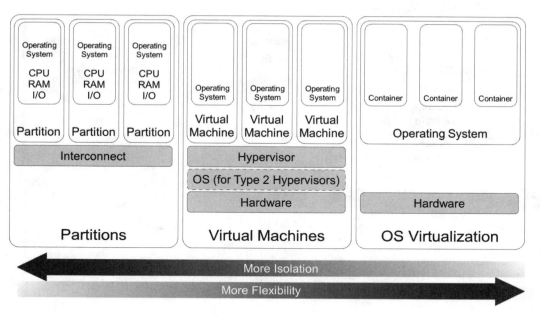

Figure 1.4 Virtualization Spectrum

flexibility requires sharing, which reduces isolation. Based on these characteristics, you can create a spectrum of resource flexibility versus workload isolation and place any particular virtualization model or implementation on that continuum, as shown in Figure 1.4.

As described in detail later in this chapter, hardware partitions offer the most isolation but the least flexibility. This arrangement is appropriate for business-critical workloads where service availability is the most important factor. Each partition has complete control over its hardware. At the other end of the spectrum, operating system virtualization (OSV) offers the most flexible configurations but the least isolation between the VEs, which are often called containers. Containers also provide the best scalability and have demonstrated the highest virtualization density. OSV is also discussed later in this chapter.

Between those two extremes, the virtual machines model creates the illusion that many computers are present, using one computer and a layer of firmware and/or software. That layer is the hypervisor, which provides multiplexed access from each operating system instance to the shared hardware. It also provides the ability to install, start, and stop each of those instances. Two types of VM implementations are possible: A Type 1 hypervisor runs directly on the hardware, while

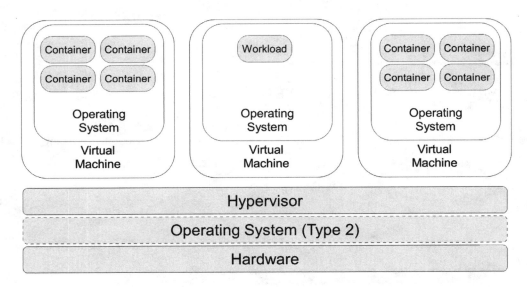

Figure 1.5   Multilayered Virtualization

a Type 2 hypervisor runs on an operating system. Both types of hypervisors are discussed later in more detail.

Some of these virtualization models can be combined in one system, as shown in Figure 1.5. For example, one virtual machine can run an OS that also supports OSV. You can use layered virtualization to take advantage of the strengths of each type. Note that this strategy does add complexity, which is most noticeable when troubleshooting problems.

The next few sections of this chapter describe each of the three virtualization categories shown in Figure 1.4: hardware partitions, virtual machines, and operating system virtualization. The descriptions provided here are generic, discussing factors common to related solutions in the industry. Implementations specific to the Oracle Solaris ecosystem are described in the next few chapters.

Each of the descriptions in this chapter mentions that model's traits and strengths. A detailed analysis of their relative strengths and weaknesses is provided in Chapter 8, "Choosing a Virtualization Technology." Also, the Appendix contains a detailed narrative of the history of virtualization.

1.2.1 Hardware Partitioning

Maximizing isolation within the same computer requires a complete separation of compute resources—software and hardware—that still achieves some level of savings or flexibility compared to separate systems. In the ideal case, an electrically isolated environment (a partition) is an independent system resource that runs its own copy of an operating system. The OS runs directly on the hardware, just as in a completely non-virtualized environment. With this approach, any single failure, either in hardware or software, in a component of one VE cannot affect another VE in the same physical computer. Hardware partitions are used, for example, to consolidate servers from different company departments when maximum isolation and technical support chargebacks are required.

In some implementations, the only shared component is the system cabinet, although such an approach yields flexibility but little cost savings. This is especially true if the resources in different partitions cannot be merged into larger VEs. Other implementations share interconnects, clock control, and, in some cases, multiple hardware partitions on a single system board. On a practical level, the minimum components held in common would consist of the system cabinet, redundant power supplies and power bus, and, to promote flexible configurations and minimally qualify as virtualization, a shared but redundant backplane or interconnect. The label "virtualization" can be applied to some of these systems because the CPUs, memory, and I/O components can be reconfigured on the fly to any partition while still maintaining fault isolation. This limited set of common components provides the best failure isolation possible without using separate computers.

Because of these characteristics, some people do not consider hardware partitioning to really be virtualization. Nevertheless, because of the role that hardware partitioning plays in consolidating and isolating workload environments, we will include this model in our discussions. The next few sections discuss some of the relevant factors related to hardware isolation.

1.2.1.1 Factors

Several factors should be considered when choosing the type of virtualization for a particular situation. We will describe the application of those factors to each of the virtualization types, in the following sections.

Failure Isolation

Limiting the set of components shared by two different partitions increases the failure isolation of those environments. With this approach, a failure of any hardware component in one partition will not affect another partition in the same system. Any component that can be shared, such as the backplane, must also be partitionable so that a failure there affects only the one partition using that component. This isolation scheme is shown in Figure 1.6.

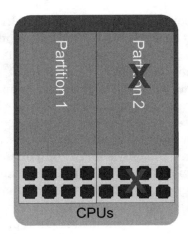

Figure 1.6   Failure Isolation of Hardware Partitions

Security Isolation

A complete implementation of partitions prevents the use of any type of covert communication channel. In essence, partitions are as secure as separate computers. The level of protection from security attacks relies solely on the applications, operating systems, and hardware. Denial-of-service attacks between partitions are not possible because nothing above the system's power grid is shared.

Operating System

Separate hardware requires a distinct copy of an operating system for each partition. This arrangement reinforces the separation of the partitions and maintains the benefits, and effort, of per-partition OS maintenance, such as OS installation and patching. To maximize partition independence, a failure in one OS instance must be prevented from affecting another partition.

Because each partition runs a separate operating system instance, it is possible to run different versions of an operating system, or different operating systems, in different partitions.

When using specialized software such as high-availability (HA) clustering, certain configurations may not achieve the desired availability goals. Proper configuration will prevent one failure from affecting both partitions. Some implementations used in the industry achieve this level of independence more effectively than others.

Flexibility and Granularity of Resource Configuration

Most hard-partitioning systems allow the partitions to be different sizes. A partition can usually be resized. With some types, this operation requires stopping

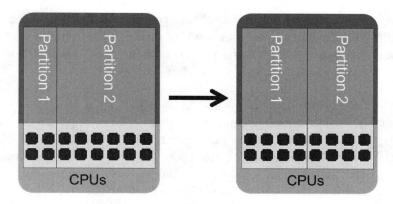

Figure 1.7 Dynamic Reallocation of Hardware Resources

all software, including the operating system, that was using the resources being reconfigured. The ability to reconfigure the quantity of resources contained in each partition without a service outage can be a powerful feature, enabling non-disruptive load-balancing. Changing the sizes of two partitions can be viewed as moving the barrier between them, as depicted in Figure 1.7.

Most of these systems are large-scale systems (more than four CPU sockets per system) and contain multiple CPU sockets on each circuit board. If such a system is configured with multiple partitions per CPU board, a hardware failure on that CPU board can cause multiple partitions to fail. CPU failures affect only the partition that was using that CPU. For that reason, where failure isolation is the most important consideration, only one partition should be configured per CPU board. In contrast, if partition density is the most important consideration, the ability to configure multiple partitions per CPU board will be an important feature.

Scalability

Two related types of scalability exist in the context of system virtualization: guest scalability and per-VE performance scalability. Guest scalability is the number of VEs that can run on the system without significantly interfering with one another. Hardware partitions are limited by the number of CPUs or CPU boards in the system, but can also be limited by other hardware factors. For some of these systems, only 2 partitions can be configured for each system; as many as 24 partitions can exist in others.

Because these systems are generally intended to perform well with dozens of CPUs in a single system image, they usually run large workloads on a small number of partitions. Their value derives from their combination of resource flexibility, failure isolation, and per-VE performance scalability.

Because hardware partitioning does not require an extra layer of software, there should be no performance overhead inherent in this type of virtualization. Applications will run with the same performance as in a nonpartitioned system with the same hardware.

Partition Management

Hardware isolation requires specialized hardware. This requirement usually includes components that aid in the management of the partitions, including the configuration of hardware resources into those partitions. These components may also assist in the installation, basic management, and health monitoring of the OS instances running on the partitions. Specialized ASICs control data paths and enforce partition isolation.

Relative Strengths of Hardware Partitions

Hardware partitions offer the best isolation in the virtualization spectrum. Whenever isolation is the most important factor, hardware partitions should be considered.

Partitions are the only virtualization method that achieves native performance and zero performance variability. Whether the workload is run on an eight-CPU partition or an eight-CPU nonpartitioned system, the performance will be exactly the same.

Compared to other virtualization methods, partitions offer some other advantages as well. Most notably, few changes to data center processes are required: Operating systems are installed and maintained in the same fashion as on non-virtualized systems.

1.2.1.2 Industry Examples

Several products offer excellent hardware isolation. This section provides a representative list of examples.

The first server to use SPARC processors and Solaris to implement hard partitioning was the Cray CS6400, in 1993. Sun Microsystems included Dynamic Domains on the Enterprise 10000 in 1997 and has continued this pattern in every subsequent SPARC generation, including the M6-32 and recently released M7 systems. The implementation of hardware isolation in the most recent generation of SPARC processors is described in Chapter 5, "Physical Domains."

On the CS6400, E10000, and the following generations of systems, this implementation provides complete electrical isolation between Dynamic Domains. There is no single point of failure in a domain that would affect all of the domains. However, a hardware failure of a component in the shared backplane can affect multiple domains. Starting in 1993, Dynamic Domains could be reconfigured without rebooting them.

Hewlett-Packard's (HP's) nPars feature was first made available on some members of the PA-RISC–based HP 9000 series. It is also a feature of some of HP's Integrity systems. In 2007, HP added the ability to reconfigure these partitions without rebooting them.

Amdahl's Multiple Domain Facility (MDF) and subsequently IBM's mainframe Logical Partitions (LPARs) were among the earliest implementations of hardware-based partitioning, available since the 1980s. MDF and LPARs use specialized hardware and firmware to create separate execution contexts with assigned CPUs, RAM, and I/O channels. A domain or partition may have dedicated physical CPUs or logical CPUs that are implemented on a physical CPU shared with other domains and shared according to a priority weighting factor. Physical RAM is assigned to one partition at a time, and can be added or removed from a partition without rebooting it.

1.2.2 Virtual Machines

The first type of virtualization to become possible, and still one of the most popular approaches, is virtual machines. This model provides the illusion that many independent computers are present in the system, each running a copy of an OS. Each of these VEs is called a virtual machine. Software or firmware, or a combination of both, manages the OS instances and provides multiplexed access to the hardware. This supporting layer, which acts as the hypervisor, gives this model its flexibility but adds a certain amount of performance overhead while it performs its tasks.

Failure isolation of hypervisors varies with the implementation. Each shared resource is a single point of failure, including the hypervisor itself.

Most hypervisors provide virtual machines that mimic the physical hardware. A few of them emulate a completely different hardware architecture. Some of these hypervisors are used to develop new hardware, simulating the hardware in software or testing software that will run on the hardware. Others are used to run software compiled for a CPU architecture that is not available or is not economical to continue operating.

1.2.2.1 Type 1 Hypervisors

A Type 1 hypervisor comprises software or firmware that runs directly on the computer's hardware. It typically has components found in a complete operating system, including device drivers. Some implementations offer the ability to assign a set or quantity of physical CPUs or CPU cores to a specific VE. Other implementations use a scheduler to give each operating system instance a time slice on the CPU(s). Some versions offer both choices. Each VE appears to be its own computer, and each appears to have complete access to the hardware resources assigned to it, including I/O devices. Although hypervisors also provide shared access to I/O devices, this capability inflicts a performance penalty.

Type 1 hypervisors implement a small feature set designed exclusively for hosting virtual machines. When the system starts, the hypervisor is placed into the main system RAM or specific area of reserved memory; in some architectures, additional elements reside in firmware, hardware, and BIOS. The hypervisor may make use of or require specialized hardware-assist technology to decrease its overhead and increase performance and reliability.

The Type 1 hypervisor is a small environment designed specifically for the task of hosting virtual machines. This model has several advantages over Type 2 hypervisors—namely, simplicity of design, a smaller attack surface, and less code to analyze for security validation. The primary disadvantages of Type 1 hypervisors are that they require more coding and they do not allow a base operating system to run any applications with native performance. Also, they cannot freely leverage services provided by a host OS. Even mundane features such as a management interface or a file system may need to be built "from scratch" for the hypervisor. Adding these features increases the complexity of the hypervisor, making it more like an OS.

In most cases, Type 1 hypervisors use one VE as a management environment. The administrator interacts with that VE via the system console or via the network. The VE contains tools to create and otherwise manage the hypervisor and the other VEs, usually called guests. Some Type 1 systems also allow for one or more specialized VEs that virtualize I/O devices for the other VEs. Figure 1.8 shows the overall structure of a Type 1 hypervisor implementation, including a virtual management environment (VME) and a virtual I/O (VIO) VE.

Hypervisors that offer VIO guests typically provide an alternative to their use—namely, direct, exclusive access to I/O devices for some VEs. Direct access offers better I/O performance but limits the number of VEs that can run on the system. If the system has only four network connectors, for example, then only three VEs can have direct network access, because the virtualization management console (VMC) needs at least one NIC for its own use. This limit can be relieved on some virtualization platforms by Single Root I/O Virtualization (SR-IOV), a hardware specification that lets a single PCIe device appear to be multiple devices, each of which can be assigned to different VEs.

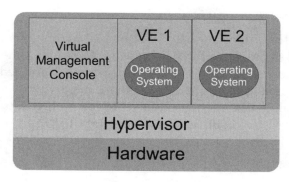

Figure 1.8   Virtual Machines and a Hypervisor

Failure Isolation

The VEs of Type 1 hypervisors offer good failure isolation. A software failure that occurs in one guest is not more likely to cause the failure of another guest, compared to two separate computers.

Failure of a shared hardware component, however, may cause a service disruption in multiple guests. Also, failure of the hypervisor will stop all of the guests. Because of the potential for failure of shared components, both software and hardware, multiple guests in one computer should not be used to achieve high availability.

Security Isolation

Type 1 hypervisors tend to be very secure, but the details of that security depend on the implementation. Access to the hypervisor must be strongly protected because a successful attack on the hypervisor will enable the attacker to control all of the virtual machines that the hypervisor manages, including their storage.

In most implementations, guests share hardware resources. When those implementations are used, denial-of-service attacks between guests will be possible unless suitable resource controls are used.

Operating Systems

Because each guest runs a separate copy of an operating system, Type 1 hypervisors have the potential to support heterogeneous operating systems, and many of them do. Even hypervisors that are able to run only one operating system type can use different versions of that operating system in different guests.

Resource Granularity and Flexibility

With hypervisors, the potential exists for one guest to consume a sufficient volume of resources to cause problems for other guests. Although some early hypervisors did not include resource controls, the potential for problems led to the implementation of fairly complete controls. Most Type 1 hypervisors implement controls on CPU usage, and dedicate a section of RAM for each guest. In addition, some of these hypervisors place controls on the amount of I/O throughput that may be consumed by each guest.

Scalability

The scalability of hypervisors is limited by the efficiency of the hypervisor and the available hardware. Software hypervisors run on the computer's CPU(s), reducing the effective CPU time available to guests, though this amount depends on the available features and the efficiency of resource usage. Each guest must be configured with its own RAM (usually at least a few gigabytes). Scalability of hypervisor guests is constrained more often by the amount of RAM than by any other resource.

Databases are particularly sensitive to resource availability. They require the ability to run certain software threads without delay, and they require large amounts of RAM. Further, they may not run well when virtual I/O is in use because they depend on low-latency I/O transactions.

Some workloads require only a small portion of the resource capacity available in modern systems. In this case, dozens of guests may run effectively with a Type 1 hypervisor.

Guest Management

Virtualization may reduce the quantity of computers needed, but hypervisors do not reduce the management burden. Each guest includes an operating system that must be managed.

Industry Examples

IBM developed the first hypervisors, and coined the term by which they became known, for its mainframes in the 1960s. VM/370, a popular hypervisor for IBM mainframes, was introduced in 1972. Its descendant on current mainframes is z/VM, which supports virtual machines running IBM operating systems such as z/OS and z/VM, and open operating systems including several distributions of Linux.

Dell's VMware ESXi is a Type 1 hypervisor for x86 systems. It supports common operating systems such as Microsoft Windows, Oracle Solaris, and OS X, and many releases of Linux distributions such as CentOS, Debian, Oracle Linux, Red

Hat Enterprise Linux, SUSE Linux, and Ubuntu. Its virtualization management console (VMC) is called the service console.

Oracle VM Server for x86 and Citrix XenServer are commercial implementations of the open-source Xen hypervisor for x86 systems. Xen supports a variety of guest operating systems, but differs in architecture from VMware ESX: Xen uses specialized guest domains for parts of the virtualization infrastructure. A specially privileged "dom0" guest, running a Linux or BSD distribution, provides a VMC and often provides virtual I/O to other guests.

Oracle VM Server for SPARC, which is discussed in detail later, is a SPARC hypervisor on chip multithreading (CMT) servers that is used to support guests running Solaris. The VMC is called the control domain. Virtual devices are implemented by the control domain or one or more specialized VEs called service domains and I/O domains. Service domains can be grouped into HA pairs to improve availability of I/O devices. System administrators can also assign devices directly to VEs.

IBM's PowerVM Hypervisor is a combination of firmware and software that creates and manages LPARs (logical partitions) on Power CPU cores. These systems also support a virtualization technology called Micro-Partitioning that can run multiple OS instances on a CPU core.

PowerVM LPARs may run AIX or Linux operating systems. PowerVM offers VIO partitions and direct device assignment.

1.2.2.2 Type 2 Hypervisors

Type 2 hypervisors run within a conventional operating system environment, enabling virtualization within an OS. The computer's OS (e.g., Oracle Solaris, Linux distributions, Microsoft Windows) boots first and manages access to physical resources such as CPUs, memory, and I/O devices. The Type 2 hypervisor operates as an application on that OS. Like the Type 1 hypervisor, the Type 2 hypervisor may make use of or require hardware-assist technology to decrease overhead attributable to the hypervisor.

Type 2 hypervisors do have some disadvantages. For example, they must depend on the services of a hosting operating system that has not been specifically designed for hosting virtual machines. Also, the larger memory footprint and CPU consumed by unrelated features of a conventional OS may reduce the amount of physical resources remaining for guests.

The primary advantage of Type 2 hypervisors for desktop systems is that the user can continue to run some applications—such as e-mail, word processing, and software development programs—with the user's favorite OS and its tools, without incurring a performance penalty. Other advantages include the ability to leverage features provided by the OS: process abstractions, file systems, device drivers, web servers, debuggers, error recovery, command-line interfaces, and a network stack. Similar advantages apply in server environments: Some applications on a server may run directly on the OS, whereas other applications are hosted in virtual machines, perhaps to provide increased isolation for security purposes, or to host a different OS version without the disruption of installing a Type 1 hypervisor on the bare metal. These advantages can be compelling enough to compensate for the memory footprint of the hosting OS and the performance penalty of the hypervisor.

It is sometimes assumed that a Type 2 hypervisor is inherently less efficient than a Type 1 hypervisor, but this need not be the case. Further, a Type 2 hypervisor may benefit from scalability and performance provided by the underlying OS that would be challenging to replicate in a Type 1 hypervisor.

Examples of Type 2 hypervisors include Oracle VM VirtualBox, VMware Server, VMware Fusion, Parallel Inc. Parallels Workstation, and Microsoft Windows Virtual PC.

Failure Isolation

The isolation of software and hardware failures with Type 2 hypervisors is similar to that provided by Type 1 hypervisors. Instead of relying on a Type 1 hypervisor to protect guests from hardware failures, a Type 2 guest relies on both the Type 2 hypervisor and the underlying operating system. The host operating system is more complex, however, and this complexity offers additional opportunities for failure.

Security Isolation

Because Type 2 hypervisors are typically a component of a desktop computer environment, rather than a server, workloads in Type 2 hypervisor guests are less valuable targets and are rarely attacked specifically. Generally, the responsibility for their protection falls on the operating system. The security characteristics of the operating system should be considered before implementing a Type 2 hypervisor, if sensitive data will reside on the guests. When security is a concern, users should prohibit remote access and use antivirus software.

Operating Systems

Many Type 2 hypervisors initially ran on only one type of host operating system, and supported only one type of guest operating system. Most of them now support multiple guest OS types, and many run on multiple types of hosts.

Resource Granularity and Flexibility

Resource management features vary greatly among the Type 2 hypervisors.

Scalability

The ability to run multiple guests efficiently depends on the implementations of both the hypervisor and the host operating system. Physical resource limitations restrict the absolute quantity of compute and memory capacity available to the guests. Insufficient RAM is more frequently a problem than insufficient CPU.

Guest Management

Each Type 2 hypervisor includes a user interface for management of guests. Because these are desktop environments, tools for centralized management of multiple systems running Type 2 hypervisors are difficult to find.

1.2.2.3 Full Virtualization and Paravirtualization

Another distinction between different forms of hypervisor-based virtualization is whether the hypervisor offers full virtualization, paravirtualization, or both. When full virtualization is used, the hypervisor creates virtual machines that are architecturally consistent with the "bare metal" physical machine. With paravirtualization, the hypervisor provides software interfaces that virtual machines can use to communicate with the hypervisor to efficiently request services and receive event notifications. Paravirtualization can greatly reduce performance overhead— a factor that plagues many hypervisor solutions.

The advantage of full virtualization is that unmodified operating systems can be run as guests, simplifying migration and technology adoption, albeit at the cost of requiring the hypervisor to implement all platform details. This approach can create substantial overhead depending on the platform, especially for I/O, timer, and memory management.

Paravirtualization offers the opportunity to optimize performance by providing more efficient software interfaces to these and other functions. It can include cooperative processing between guest and hypervisor for memory management (e.g., memory ballooning, shared pages for I/O buffers), shortened I/O path length (e.g., device drivers making direct calls to the hypervisor or combining multiple I/O requests into a single request), clock skew management, and other optimizations. The main disadvantage of paravirtualization is that it requires source code to port the guest OS onto the virtualized platform, or at least the ability to add optimized devices drivers.

Examples of paravirtualization include Xen implementations such as Oracle VM Server for x86 and Citrix XenServer, Oracle VM Server for SPARC, the guest/host additions in Oracle VM VirtualBox, the VMware Tools for VMware ESX, and the Conversational Monitor System (CMS) under VM/370.

1.2.2.4 Relative Strengths of Hypervisors

Hypervisors typically represent a "middle ground" between the isolation of hard partitions and the flexibility of OSV. The additional isolation of separate OS instances compared to that afforded by OSV allows for the consolidation of completely different operating systems. The hypervisor layer also provides a convenient point of separation for VEs, thereby facilitating and simplifying VE mobility.

Some hypervisors offer optional CPU and I/O partitioning, which can significantly reduce the overhead of the hypervisor. Of course, the scalability of this method is limited by the number of CPUs and I/O buses. Systems with few CPUs must share these resources among the VEs.

1.2.3 Operating System Virtualization

Hardware partitioning and virtual machine technologies share a common trait: Each virtual environment contains an instance of an operating system. Most of those technologies allow different operating systems to run concurrently.

In contrast, operating system virtualization (OSV) uses features of the operating system to create VEs that are not separate copies of an operating system. This approach provides the appearance of an individual operating system instance for each VE. Most OSV implementations provide the same OS type as the hosting OS. The two most commonly used terms used for guests of OSV implementations are "containers" and "zones."

Figure 1.9 shows the relationships among the hardware, OS, and VEs when using OSV.

We have already discussed the importance of isolation to virtualization. The isolation between OSV VEs is just as important as the isolation noted in other models. For OSV, this isolation is enforced by the OS kernel, rather than by a hypervisor or hardware.

In the OSV model, all processes share the same operating system kernel, which must provide a robust mechanism to prevent two different VEs from interacting directly. Without this isolation, one VE could potentially affect the operation of another VE. The kernel must be modified so that the typical interprocess communication (IPC) mechanisms do not work between processes in different VEs, at least in a default configuration. The network stack can be modified to block network traffic between VEs, if desired. Existing security features can be enhanced

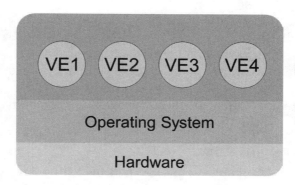

Figure 1.9   Operating System Virtualization

to provide this level of isolation. In some implementations, it is easier to achieve a security goal in a container than in a non-virtualized environment.

OSV implementations are usually very lightweight, taking up less disk space and consuming less RAM than virtual machines. They also add very little CPU overhead. Nevertheless, although they can easily mimic the same operating system, most of them do not support the ability to appear as either another operating system or an arbitrary version of the same OS.

Another strength of this model of virtualization relates to the possibility of hardware independence. Because a physical computer is not being simulated, an operating system that runs on multiple CPU architectures can potentially provide the same feature set, including OSV features, on different types of computers.

1.2.3.1 Factors

Later in this book we will discuss an approach that can be used to choose a virtualization technology based on prioritizing certain factors, including the ability to isolate software and hardware faults. This section describes these factors in the context of operating system virtualization.

Failure Isolation

With OSV, all isolation of software and hardware failures must be provided by the operating system, which may utilize hardware failure isolation features if they exist. For example, the operating system may be able to detect a hardware failure and limit the effects of that failure to one VE. Such detection may require hardware features to support this functionality.

The isolation between processes in different VEs can also be used to minimize propagation of software or hardware failures. A failure in one VE should not affect other VEs. This kind of isolation is easier to achieve if each VE has its own network services, such as sshd.

Further, the operating system must prevent any event that is occurring in one VE from affecting another VE. This includes unintentional events such as software failures as well as actions taken by a successful intruder.

To be both robust and efficient, these hardware and software features must be tightly integrated into the OS implementation.

Operating System Features

All of the necessary functionality of OSV is provided by the OS, rather than by hardware or an extra layer of software. Usually this functionality is provided via features integrated into the core of the OS. In some cases, however, the features are provided by a different organization or community and integrated on-site, with varying levels of application compatibility and processing efficiency.

The shared kernel offers a privileged user the ability to observe all processes running in all VEs, which simplifies the process of performance analysis and troubleshooting. You can use one tool to analyze resource consumption of all processes running on the system, even though many are running in different VEs. After the problem is understood, you can use the same centralized environment to control the VEs and their processes.

This type of global control and observability is nothing new for consolidated systems, but it provides a distinct advantage over other virtualization models, which lack a centralized environment that can inspect the internals of the guests. Indeed, analyzing an OSV system is no more complicated than analyzing a consolidated one.

After the resource usage characteristics of a particular workload are known, resource management tools should be used to ensure that each VE has sufficient access to the resources it needs. Notably, centralized control offers the potential for centrally managed, fine-grained, dynamic resource management. Many operating systems already have sophisticated tools to control the consumption of resources in one or more of these ways:

- Assigning CPU time, which is performed by a software scheduler. This control can be achieved through process prioritization or by capping the amount of CPU time that a process uses during an interval of real time.
- Providing exclusive assignment of a group of processes to a group of processors.
- Dedicating a portion of RAM to a group of processes, capping the amount of RAM that a group of processes can use, or guaranteeing that a VE will be able to use at least a specific amount of RAM.

- Dedicating a portion of the network bandwidth of a physical network port to an IP address or a group of processes.

Because most operating systems already have the ability to control these resources with fine granularity, if these controls are extended to the VEs, their resource consumption can be managed with the same granularity.

Some operating systems include automated features that detect and handle error problems. For example, system software might detect that a network service such as sshd has failed and attempt to restart that service. In the context of resource management, dynamic resource controls can be used to react to changing processing needs of different workloads by changing resource control values on the fly.

The basic model of OSV assumes that the VEs provide the same operating system interfaces to applications as a non-virtualized environment provided by the host operating system (e.g., system calls). If this similarity can be achieved, there is no need to modify applications.

Additionally, a particular implementation may mimic a different operating system if the two are sufficiently similar. In this case, the functionality of an OS kernel can be represented by its system calls. A thin layer of software can translate the system calls of the expected guest OS into the system calls of the hosting OS. This strategy can allow programs and libraries compiled for one OS to run—unmodified—in a VE that resides on a different OS, as long as they are all compiled for the same hardware architecture.

In such a multiple-OS configuration, the extra operations involved in translating one set of functionality to another will incur a certain amount of CPU overhead, decreasing system performance. Achieving identical functionality is usually challenging, but sufficient compatibility can be achieved to enable common applications to run well.

Access to Hardware

Operating system virtualization features must allow isolated access to hardware so that each VE can make appropriate use of hardware but cannot observe or affect another VE's hardware accesses. In such a system, each VE might be granted exclusive access to a hardware resource or, alternatively, such access might be shared. Existing implementations of OSV provide differing functionality for hardware access.

Figure 1.10 shows most VEs sharing most of the CPUs and a network port. In this system, one VE has exclusive access to another port and two dedicated CPUs.

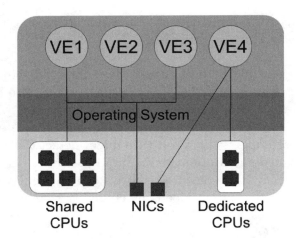

Figure 1.10   Shared or Exclusive Hardware Assignments

Software Infrastructure

As part of the OSV design, engineers choose the line of division between the base OS operations and the VEs. A VE may include only the application processes or, alternatively, each VE may include some of the services provided by the operating system, such as network services and naming services.

Flexibility and Granularity of Resource Configuration

Because one control point exists for all of the hardware and the VEs, all resource management decisions can be made from one central location. For example, the single process scheduler can be modified to provide new features for the system administrator. These features can be used to ensure that the desired amount of compute power is applied to each VE to meet its business needs. Because the scheduler can monitor each process in each VE, it can make well-informed scheduling decisions; it does not need to give control to a separate scheduler per VE.

An alternative method to moderate CPU power as a resource gives one VE exclusive access to a set of CPUs. This approach means that the VE's processes have access to the entire capacity of those CPUs and reduces cache contention. RAM can be treated similarly—that is, either as an assignment of a physical address range or as a simple quantity of memory.

Other resource constraints can include limits or guaranteed minimum amounts or portions.

Scalability

Operating system virtualization technologies tend to scale as well as the underlying operating system. From one perspective, all processes in all VEs can be seen as a set of processes managed by one kernel, including inter-VE isolation rules. If the kernel scales well to many processes, then the system should likewise scale well to many VEs of this type. At least one implementation of OS virtualization—Solaris Zones—has demonstrated excellent scalability, with more than 100 VEs running on one Solaris instance.

Platform Management

Operating system features must provide the ability to create, configure, manage, and destroy VEs. This capability can be extended to remote management.

1.2.3.2 Relative Strengths

Similar to other virtualization models, OSV has its particular strengths. Some of these benefits are specific goals of OSV implementations; others are side effects of the OSV model.

Many of the strengths of OSV implementations are derived from the tight integration between the OSV technology and the OS kernel. Most of these operating systems are mature and have well-developed facilities to install and maintain them and to manage multiple workloads. It is usually possible to extend those features to the environments created via OSV.

A significant strength of OSV is its efficient use of resources. This efficiency applies to the use of CPU time, RAM, and virtual memory.

When implemented correctly, OSV will not add any CPU overhead compared to a consolidated but non-virtualized system. The OS must still perform the same operations for that set of running applications. However, to perform well with more than three or four VEs, the OS must be scalable—that is, it must be able to switch the CPU(s) among the dozens or hundreds of processes in the VEs. It must also be able to efficiently manage the many gigabytes of RAM and swap space used by those processes.

Because OSV VEs do not have a separate OS instance, they do not consume hundreds of megabytes of RAM per VE for each OS kernel. Instead, the amount of RAM needed for multiple VEs typically is limited to the memory footprint of the underlying OS plus the amount of RAM used by each of the consolidated applications. In some implementations, operating systems that reuse a program's text (program) pages can reduce the memory footprint of a VE even further by sharing those text pages across VEs.

Because of the single OS instance found in OSV, a centralized point exists for security controls. This arrangement also creates the possibility of per-VE configurable security and centralized auditing.

The primary goal for OSV implementations is to minimize the effort needed to maintain many operating systems in a data center environment. Put simply, fewer OS instances means less activity installing, configuring, and updating operating systems. Because the OS is already installed before a VE is created, provisioning VEs is usually very rapid, taking anywhere from a few seconds to a few minutes. The minimalist nature of OSV also reduces the time to boot a VE—if that step is even needed—to a few seconds.

1.2.3.3 Industry Examples

Examples of OS virtualization include Oracle Solaris Zones (also called Solaris Containers from 2007 to 2010), HP-UX Secure Resource Partitions, Linux Containers, and AIX Workload Partitions. Each of these products follows the model described earlier, with their differences reflecting their specific use of network and storage I/O, security methods and granularity, and resource controls and their granularity.

1.3 Summary

Server consolidation improves data center operations by reducing the number of servers, which in turn reduces hardware acquisition costs, hardware and software support costs, power consumption, and cooling needs. Virtualization enables consolidation of workloads that might otherwise interfere with one another, and of workloads that should be isolated for other reasons, including business agility and enhanced security.

Three general virtualization models exist. Operating system virtualization creates virtual OS instances—that is, software environments in which applications run in isolation from one another but share one copy of an OS and one OS kernel. Virtual machines rely on a hypervisor to enable multiple operating system instances to share a computer. Hardware partitioning separates a computer into separate pools of hardware, each of which acts as its own computer, with its own operating system.

Each of these models has both strengths and weaknesses. Each has also been implemented on multiple hardware architectures, with each implementation being most appropriate in certain situations. The better you understand the models and implementations, the more benefit you can derive from virtualization.

2

Use Cases and Requirements

Consolidation via virtualization delivers more productivity than is possible with a smaller environment. This chapter explores the uses of virtualization and the requirements that must be fulfilled to achieve its goals.

2.1 Introduction

In this chapter, we visit the following cases, discussing the value and notable requirements of each:

- General workload consolidation: resource management and availability
- Asynchronous workloads: balancing resource utilization throughout the day
- Software development: consolidation of similar environments
- Test and staging: consolidation of similar environments
- Simplifying workload mobility
- Maintaining a legacy OS on new hardware
- Flexible, rapid provisioning
- Relieving scalability constraints of a given OS via multiple instances
- Fine-grained operating system modifications
- Configurable security characteristics

2.2 General Workload Consolidation

The most common use of virtualization is the consolidation of multiple, often unrelated, workloads from multiple computers into one computer. This approach
avoids potential problems caused by mixing applications in the same virtual environment (VE). Once it has been determined that it is safe to run a particular
application in a specific implementation of virtualization, there should be no need
to verify a particular instance of that application or a particular combination of
application instances for correct functionality.

Although the applications may function correctly, their performance characteristics will probably change when they are running in a consolidated environment.
Several different factors may cause this change:

- Shared I/O channels are typical in most virtualization implementations, and
  will reduce available bandwidth to networks and persistent storage.
- Disks may be shared, increasing read and write transaction latency.
- If there are more workloads than CPUs, workloads may wait longer before
  getting a time slice on a CPU, thereby increasing response time.
- If multiple workloads share a set of physical CPUs and there are more workloads than CPUs, there is a greater chance of a process being assigned to a
  different CPU than the previous time slice, negating the benefits of a CPU's
  caches.

In addition to the potential for decreased performance, workload performance
may be less consistent in a consolidated environment unless resource controls are
used. On any one day, two workloads might experience their daily peaks in CPU
utilization at different times, and response times may be similar to those observed
on unconsolidated systems. The next day, the peaks for those two workloads might
coincide, leading to competition for physical resources such as CPUs and RAM.
Response times for each workload may then suffer.

In other words, aggregate CPU usage of one workload should not change because of consolidation, but the deviation from average response time may increase.
However, a complete understanding of the performance demands of the workloads
should allow you to minimize this problem, because you will be able to place VEs
on different systems to minimize this kind of performance deviation.

Resource partitioning technologies, including some virtual machine implementations, dedicate hardware resources to each resource partition. This practice

insulates each partition from the CPU consumption of other domains. You can use this feature to improve performance consistency.

Besides the effects of workload consolidation, virtualization can cause changes in workload performance. Many virtualization technologies require use of the system CPUs to perform virtualization activities. The result is performance overhead, in the form of CPU cycles that are not performing work directly related to the applications. The amount of overhead depends on several factors, including the following:

- The method of virtualization (e.g., partitioning, virtual machines, or operating system virtualization):
  - A partitioned system does not run virtualization software and has no overhead.
  - A hypervisor runs on the system CPUs and creates overhead, but this is generally limited to I/O activities if the CPU has virtualization-assist features.
  - Paravirtualization can significantly decrease performance overhead caused by a hypervisor.
  - Operating system virtualization results in more processes in the single OS instance. This can be challenging for some operating systems, but the overhead directly associated with virtualization activities is negligible.
- The mix of computing activity versus I/O activity:
  - Computing activity does not increase overhead because the process runs directly on the CPU.
  - Memory-intensive applications can increase overhead unless the CPU has features to minimize this possibility.
  - For hypervisors, I/O activity must be controlled to prevent one VE from accessing information owned by another VE: This activity increases overhead.
  - Hardware features may simplify some virtualization tasks, reducing overhead.

The combination of unpredictable patterns of effective performance and the potential for denial-of-service attacks makes resource management an essential component of any virtualization solution. Resource controls ensure that the consolidated systems can meet their service level objectives and be protected from resource starvation. Six resource categories are commonly managed:

- CPU capacity: Controls are used to ensure that each VE gets enough CPU time to provide appropriate responsiveness and to prevent denial-of-service attacks, either from compromised VEs on the same system or from traditional network attacks.

- Amount of RAM used: Controls should be used to ensure that each VE has enough RAM to perform well.

- Amount of virtual memory or swap space used: Unless each VE has its own private swap device or partition, this type of control can be used to ensure that each VE has enough swap space to work correctly and to prevent denial-of-service attacks.

- Network bandwidth consumed: Controls can be used to provide an appropriate quality of service for each workload and to prevent denial-of-service attacks.

- Persistent storage bandwidth consumed: Some technologies offer the ability to limit the amount of storage bandwidth consumed by one VE.

- Use of kernel data structures: Examples include shared memory identifiers, including structures of finite size and structures that use another finite resource such as RAM.

2.2.1 Types of Resource Controls

Several methods to control sharing of resources exist. One method is to divide a resource into chunks and assign each chunk to one workload. Resources with a finite size, such as RAM or CPUs, can be divided using that method. However, this approach wastes a portion of the resource because the portion that is currently assigned to one VE is not in use but could be used by another VE. Some implementations of this method reduce the amount of waste by dynamically resizing the reserved resource based on resource usage.

A second method to control resource allocation is a software-regulated limit, also called a resource cap. The controlling mechanism—a hypervisor or the operating system—prevents VEs from using more than a specified amount of the resource. The remaining, unused portions of the resource can be used by other VEs.

A third method to apportion CPU cycles—and the least wasteful of the three methods—is the fair share scheduler (FSS). If there is sufficient capacity for every VE to get the amount of CPU cycles it wants, each VE can use that amount. Conversely, if there is contention for the resource, instead of enforcing a maximum amount of consumption, this method guarantees availability of a minimum portion of a resource. An FSS allocates the resource in portions controlled by the administrator—a strategy akin to that underlying the concept of a service level agreement (SLA), which corporate customers often require.

Allocation of network bandwidth is similar to allocation of CPU cycles. If you are patient, you can always get more of a resource—for example, a time slice for CPUs, or a time slot for network access. For this type of resource, it may not make sense to reserve a quantity, but it does make sense to cap the rate at which one VE consumes the resource over a brief sampling period.[1]

The following resource controls are available in virtualization implementations. They can be used to manage the resource categories listed earlier.

- CPU partitioning is the ability to assign a particular CPU or set of CPUs to a VE. It reserves all of the compute power of a set of CPUs, but any unused CPU cycles cannot be used by another VE and are wasted unless the reservation can be changed dynamically and automatically. However, this method provides predictable performance and avoids performance overhead. A workload assigned to a set of CPUs will always have access to its assigned CPUs, and will never be required to wait until another VE completes its time slice. A resource manager can reduce wasted capacity by reassigning idle CPUs.

  The amount of waste will be determined by two factors: (1) reconfiguration latency—the time it takes to shift a CPU from one partition to another and (2) resource granularity—the unconsumed partition of, at most, a single CPU. This model of CPU control is shown in Figure 2.1.

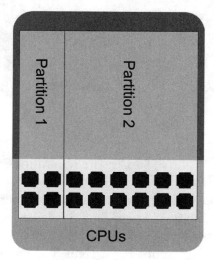

Figure 2.1 CPU Partitioning

---

1. There are exceptions—for example, very-low-latency applications such as video and financial transactions that require reserved bandwidth to function correctly.

- A software scheduler such as FSS may allow the administrator to enforce minimum response times either directly or via VE prioritization. Early implementations included software schedulers for VM/XA on mainframes and BSD UNIX on VAX 11/780s in the 1980s. This approach is often the best general-purpose solution. It is very flexible, in that the minimum amount of processing power assigned to each VE can be changed while the VE is running. Moreover, a software scheduler does not force workloads to wait while unused CPU cycles are wasted.

System administrators can use an FSS to enforce the assignment of a particular minimum portion of compute capacity to a specific workload. A quantity of shares—a unitless value—is assigned to each workload, as depicted in Figure 2.2. The scheduler sums the shares assigned to all of the current workloads, and divides each workload's share quantity by the sum to obtain the intended minimum portion.

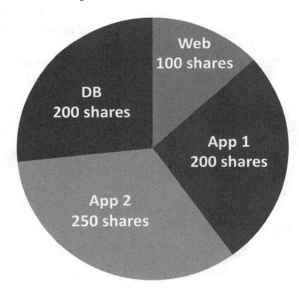

Figure 2.2   Using FSS to Ensure Minimum CPU Portions

Insufficient memory can cause more significant performance problems than insufficient CPU capacity. If a workload needs 10% more CPU time than it is currently getting, it will run 10% more slowly than expected. By comparison, if a program needs 10% more RAM than it is currently getting, the result will be excessive paging. Such paging to the swap disk can decrease workload performance by an order of magnitude or more.

Excessive memory use by one VE may starve other VEs of memory. If multiple VEs begin paging, the detrimental effects on performance can be further exacerbated by various factors:

- A shared I/O channel can be a bottleneck.

- If VEs share swap space, fragmentation of the swap space can cause excessive head-seeking within the swap area.

- If each VE has a separate swap area but all of these areas are present on one disk drive, the drive head will continuously seek between the two swap areas.

If paging cannot be avoided, swap areas should be spread across multiple drives or, if possible, placed on low-latency devices such as solid-state drives (SSDs). In most cases, it is difficult to justify the extra cost of those devices. Instead, you should try to avoid paging by configuring sufficient RAM for each VE.

Memory controls can be used to prevent one VE from using so much RAM that another VE does not have sufficient memory for its work. Indeed, the appropriate use of memory controls should be a general practice for consolidated systems. Inappropriate use of memory controls can cause poor performance if applications are granted use of less RAM than the "working set" they need to operate efficiently. Memory controls should be used carefully and with knowledge of actual RAM requirements.

Per-VE memory partitioning (RAM reservation or swap reservation) is available for some virtualization implementations. This type of control provides each VE with immediate access to all of its memory, but any reserved-but-unused memory is wasted because no other VE can use it. Also, modifying the reservation after the VE is running is not possible in some implementations.

Recently, virtual machine implementations have begun to include methods that enable the hypervisor to reduce a guest's RAM consumption when the system is under memory pressure. This feature causes the VE to begin paging, but allows the guest to decide which memory pages it should page out to the swap device.

- A per-VE limit, also called a *memory cap*, is more flexible and less wasteful than a memory partition or reservation. The virtualization software tracks the amount of memory in use by each VE. When a VE reaches its cap, infrequently used pages of memory are copied to swap space for later access, using the normal demand paging virtual memory system. There is a potential drawback, however: As with dedicated memory partitions, overly aggressive memory caps can cause unnecessary paging and decrease workload performance.

- Other controls have been implemented on miscellaneous resources offered by the hypervisor or OS. One such resource is locked memory. Some operating systems allow applications to lock data regions into memory so that they cannot be paged out. This practice is widely used by database software, which works best when it can lock a database's index into memory. As a consequence, frequently used data is found in memory, rather than on relatively slow disk drives. If the database is the only workload on the system, it can choose an appropriate portion of memory to lock down, based on its needs; there is no need to be concerned about unintended consequences.

  On a consolidated system, the database software must still be able to lock down that same amount of memory. At the same time, it must be prevented from locking down so much more RAM than it needs that other workloads suffer from insufficient memory.

  Well-behaved applications will not cause problems with locked memory, but an upper bound should be set on most VEs.

- Per-VE limits on network bandwidth usage can be used to ensure that every VE gets access to a reasonable portion of this resource.

- Per-VE network bandwidth reservations can be used to ensure that a particular workload always has the bandwidth it needs, even if that means wasting some bandwidth.

2.2.2 Need for Availability

With one workload per system, a hardware failure in a computer can affect only that workload and, potentially, any workloads on other systems on which it depends. In contrast, consolidating multiple unrelated workloads onto one system requires different planning, because a hardware failure can then bring down multiple services. High-availability (HA) solutions are justified by the greater total value of workloads in the computer.

Fortunately, VEs can be configured as nodes in HA clusters using products such as Oracle Solaris Cluster or Veritas Cluster Server. If you want to minimize just downtime due to application failure or OS failure, the primary and secondary VEs can be configured on one computer.

More commonly, the two nodes are configured on different computers to minimize downtime due to hardware failure. Multiple HA pairs can be configured in the same cluster. Often, primary nodes are spread around the computers in the cluster

HA Cluster

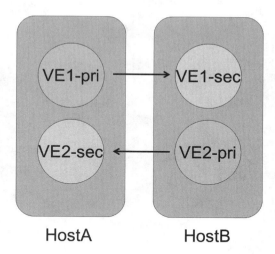

Figure 2.3 Load-Balanced Cluster Pairs

to balance the load under normal operating conditions, as shown in Figure 2.3. This configuration requires sufficient resources on each node to run both workloads simultaneously if one computer fails, albeit perhaps with degraded performance.

A slight twist on the HA concept uses several computers or VEs to simultaneously provide the same service to its consumers. With this model, the failure of any one computer or VE will not cause a service outage. The remaining entities continue providing the service, but the load-balancing mechanism no longer sends transactions to the failed unit.

Because no service outage occurs, this model is often preferred to the simpler failover model. Nevertheless, it can be used only with certain types of applications. Applications that provide a read-only service, such as DNS lookups, scale well with this model. In contrast, applications that modify data, such as databases, must be modified to synchronize the modification activities across the cluster nodes.

Oracle Solaris Cluster implements this model via its Scalable Services functionality for web server software and some other applications. Oracle also provides this capability for a database service with the Oracle RAC product.

Figure 2.4 shows two VEs in each of two computers that are part of a scalable cluster. Each computer has two VEs that are providing the same service. This model is often used when the application does not scale well. After a failure, only one fourth of the processing power of the cluster is lost.

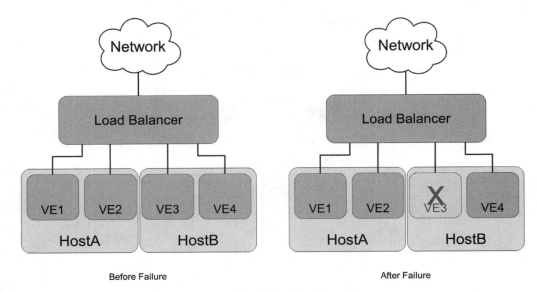

Figure 2.4   Scalable Services Cluster

2.2.3 Summary

In summary, consolidated systems offer clear benefits, but they also require a return to some of the mainframe practices of the past, including more assertive efforts to manage the resources and availability of the system. Using VEs as cluster nodes improves isolation between workloads, making it easier to run more applications in the cluster.

2.3 Asynchronous Workloads

Many workloads are active for a certain period of time each workday but otherwise use few system resources. For example, employees of a small business might all work in one time zone, and their online transaction processing (OLTP) environment might have few transactions running at night. In contrast, a batch job for the same business might run for 6 hours each night. Although the business may use two separate systems for these workloads, the average utilization for each system will be less than 40%.

You can combine those two workloads on one system in several ways. For example, you can take advantage of the differences in their schedules by running both workloads on the same system, hoping that there will not be any adverse interactions between them. Alternatively, you can prevent adverse interactions by isolating the workloads with virtualization. If the two workloads need roughly equivalent resources to provide the desired response time and completion time, the graph of utilization versus time might look like Figure 2.5.

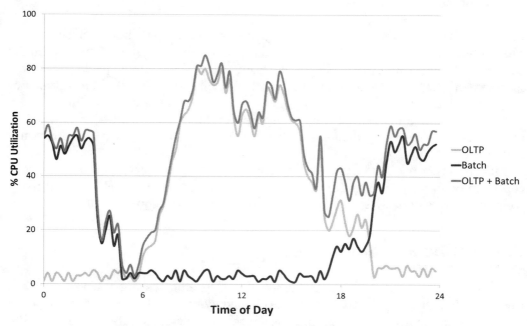

Figure 2.5   CPU Utilization of Asynchronous Workloads

2.4 Software Development and Other Bursty Workloads

A software developer typically generates intense system activity during short periods of time when compiling software, followed by periods of little activity. This uneven workload results in computers that are under-utilized most of the time, wasting most of the investment in those systems.

If a programmer's computer is occupied by compiling only 5% of the time, 20 programmers could share one computer if they took turns compiling their own jobs. Of course, that is not an ideal situation, and would likely reduce productivity while each programmer waited for a turn to compile his or her programs. Several optimizations can be made to that model, but the following problems must still be solved:

- Programmers must not be able to harm another programmer's activities.
- Some programmers will need specific versions of the operating system and its components, including development tools and test environments.
- Software development that modifies the operating system must be tested on a non-shared operating system.

In other words, the activities of each programmer must be isolated from the activities of the others. Each programmer needs an instance of an operating system for each target operating system. In many cases, each programmer needs an operating system instance for code development as well. However, for many types of programming, multiple developers can share an operating system instance.

Consolidation allows multiple programmers to use the same hardware resources. Virtualization provides the necessary isolation if application separation is needed.

Although this use case has been described as "software development," the concepts apply equally well to any large set of workloads that are characterized by frequent bursts of activity and have loose response time requirements.

2.5 Testing and Staging

Many test environments are configured for a specific testing purpose but are under-utilized because testing is not performed every day. It may not make sense to reinstall an operating system and configure it each time a different test is to be run, as that practice would lead to a proliferation of test servers—which is a waste of capital investment.

Most functional testing can be performed in a virtualized environment without affecting the outcome of the tests. This setup allows consolidation of many testing environments, with one test per VE. The VE runs only while its test is being performed. Normally, only one of the VEs is running.

Other factors must be considered as well. In particular, this model is best applied to functional testing rather than performance or scalability tests. For example, one test might require exclusive access to all of the storage bandwidth of the system's I/O bus to produce meaningful results. It may not be possible to provide sufficient isolation of this test, so tests must be scheduled at different times. Fortunately, most virtualization technologies allow VEs to be turned off individually, leaving just a single test environment running. With this approach, many teams can share one system, utilizing a small number of test systems with little unscheduled time.

Performance testing in virtualized environments is appropriate only if the workload will be deployed in a VE. Similar resource controls should be applied to the test and production environments.

Another advantage of testing with VEs is the ability to take a snapshot (a point-in-time image) of a VE and save it to disk. This snapshot can be copied, and the copy may then be used to ensure that each successive iteration starts from exactly the same state, with the same system configuration and test data.

2.6 Simplifying Workload Mobility

Systems should originally be configured with sufficient excess resource capacity to accommodate expected growth in workload needs. Even when systems are initially set up with extra capacity, workloads may occasionally outgrow the physical capacity of the system. If the computer was purchased with empty slots (e.g., for CPU or memory), additional resources can be added to the system to expand it and accommodate this growth.

Figure 2.6 shows a system at three points in time. In the first instance, the system is partially filled with a type of component, such as CPUs; the workload uses only a portion of the available resource. In the middle snapshot, the workload has grown to the point where it is consuming almost all of the physical resource. However, the system was purchased without a full complement of that resource. After filling the available physical slots, as shown in the last snapshot, the workload can grow even further without suffering performance problems.

At some point, however, further system enhancements are neither possible nor desirable. Although in some cases the workload can be broken down into multiple

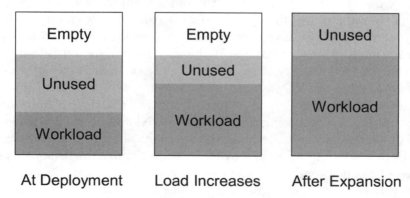

Figure 2.6 Accommodating a Growing Workload with Additional Resources

components and run on multiple small systems, this solution is rarely appropriate. Instead, the workload must be moved to a new, larger system. Without virtualization, that process can be time-consuming and involve many manual, error-prone steps. In addition, the new system may need to be certified for proper installation and operation—another significant investment.

Virtualization provides useful separation between the VE and the hardware. This containment simplifies the process of extracting a VE from the original system and moving it to a new system. This operation, which is often called migration, is depicted in Figure 2.7.

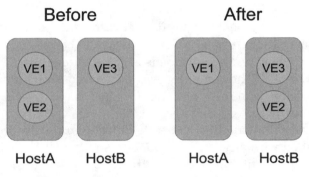

Figure 2.7   Migrating a VE

Three types of migration are possible, each of which is characterized by the amount of time during which the workload is not providing service, and by the amount of workload state that is lost during the migration.

"Cold" migration is simply the orderly halting of the original environment and its workload, the transfer of files from the old system to new storage or reconfiguration of shared storage, followed by start-up on the new computer. If shared storage is used to house the environment, this process is straightforward and does not require a lengthy service outage. If the application should retain its state, however, it might be necessary to save that state to persistent storage and reload the information when the VE restarts.

The other two types of migration—"warm" migration and "live" migration—do not require halting and rebooting the VE. Unlike cold migration, processes are not shut down during use of these methods, so they maintain the state of their current activities. Both warm migration and live migration require the use of shared storage for the OS, applications, data, and swap space.

Warm migration, shown in Figure 2.8, implies a noticeable service outage, usually on the order of tens of seconds. During that period, the system effectively pauses the VE in its original system, creates a new VE in the destination system, and copies a memory image of the related processes to the target system. The processes then continue their execution on the target system and the memory image for those processes on the original system is destroyed.

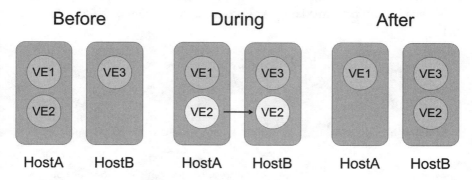

Figure 2.8 Migrating a VE: Warm Migration

Figure 2.9 depicts live migration, which differs from warm migration in terms of the length of service outage. This outage is short enough that users do not notice it. Further, applications running on other systems are not affected by the outage. Unlike warm migration, which briefly pauses the VE while its memory pages are copied to the destination, live migration methods copy the VE while it is running. After the memory pages have been copied, the VE is paused and a final set of data is transferred. Control of the VE then passes to the target system. This transfer of control often takes less than one second.

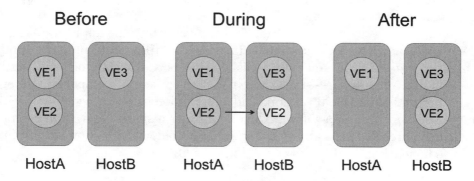

Figure 2.9 Migrating a VE: Live Migration

Another form of migration is the conversion from a physical environment to a virtual environment, and from one virtualization technology to another. When discussing these activities, we use the letters "P" and "V" as a shorthand notation for "physical" and "virtual," respectively. For instance, moving an existing OS instance from a physical computer to a virtual machine provided by a hypervisor is called P2V. All four permutations are possible, and are shown at a high level in Table 2.1.

Table 2.1 Virtualization Conversions

	P	V
P	P2P Move a system (Tools predate virtualization)	P2V Virtualize a system, sometimes as part of consolidation
V	V2P Un-virtualize Uncommon, rarely used	V2V Migrate a VE to another system, or convert to another VE technology via a standard image format

2.7 Maintaining a Legacy Operating System on New Hardware

Across the world, many older computers are running operating systems that are a version or more behind the current version. The difficulty of upgrading these computers to use new hardware or a new version of the OS varies. In some cases, software tools can be used to upgrade the operating system while the application is still running. Other systems are simply impossible to upgrade. Many systems fall between those two extremes.

For many of those systems, the best choice is rehosting the application on new hardware with new operating system features, while still maintaining the application and its configuration. Achieving this "best of both worlds" solution requires a low-level layer of software—for example, a new version of an operating system that can pretend to be an old version. The new version provides a virtual instance of an old version through a software layer, which translates old system calls into new ones. The result is the ability to maintain an older application environment while also benefiting from a new OS and new hardware.

2.8 Flexible, Rapid Provisioning

The computer industry has developed many solutions to address the challenge of deploying an operating system on a computer. Many of these software solutions rely on the use of low-level tools embedded in the hardware of the target system. Because they are simple tools, their flexibility is limited, and the provisioning software must take on almost all of the burden of OS deployment. For example, hardware features rarely include a simple command to install an OS image from a repository to local disk and boot from it. Also, because provisioning systems rely on hardware from different manufacturers, many methods must be maintained in an up-to-date state.

Virtualization can provide a rich set of tools as a foundation on which virtual environments are deployed. Its use simplifies the software that deploys virtual environments. An industry standard, Open Virtualization Archive (OVA) has been developed for VM images, enabling the deployment of an image created with one vendor's hypervisor onto that of another vendor simply by copying the image. Those technological advancements enable the storage of preconfigured operating system images that can be copied easily to create a new VE and accessed via a shared storage framework such as SAN or NAS.

Because of the small disk footprint of OS virtualization environments, provisioning from a preconfigured master image may take less than 1 second. This speed is causing people to see system provisioning and updating in a whole new light. One example of newfound flexibility is described next.

Figure 2.10 depicts a VE provisioning system. In this diagram, the provisioning system owns the master images for the various applications used by the data center, with one image per application. Each image has been tailored for the use of that particular application, including remote file system mount points for the application, an appropriate level of security hardening, user accounts, and other factors. When a new instance of a particular application is needed, a management tool is used to perform the following tasks:

1. Clone the image.

2. Fine-tune the image—for example, with a link to the data to be used.

3. Complete the process of making the image ready for use, including steps necessary for use on a particular server.

4. Detach the image from the provisioning system and boot it on the deployment server.

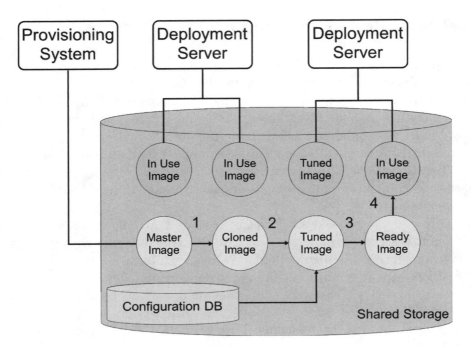

Figure 2.10   Provisioning System for VEs

2.9 Relieving Scalability Constraints

When you purchase a computer, especially a server, you must determine the maximum resource capacity that will be needed over the life of the system, including the quantity of CPUs, the amount of RAM, and other resources. If the workload grows to consume the maximum quantity of a particular resource, you must purchase a larger system and move the workload to it. Without virtualization, this type of upgrade typically means installing the operating system and applications on the new computer, which is a time-consuming and error-prone process.

With virtualization, fewer larger systems can be deployed, reducing the complexity associated with managing many systems. When a workload outgrows its system, an existing system with sufficient unused capacity can usually be found. By taking advantage of the various tools available to migrate a VE from one system to another, this process can be as simple as clicking and dragging an icon in a management application. Figure 2.11 shows a migration to a larger system, where the application will rarely be constrained by the quantity of resources in the computer.

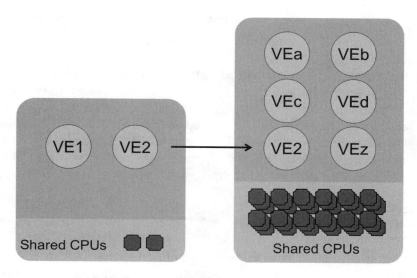

Figure 2.11   Providing More Room for a VE

2.10 Fine-Grained Operating System Modification

A challenge of consolidated but non-virtualized workloads is the decreased flexibility of the system. One workload may need a particular version of an operating system or a specific set of tuning parameters for the operating system. One application may be tested and supported only with a specific set of operating system components installed. Without virtualization, it is sometimes difficult to meet the needs of every workload on a consolidated system.

System virtualization technologies virtualize an instance of an operating system or of a computer. In each case, one VE can be tailored to meet the needs of its workload, while another VE is customized to meet the needs of another workload.

2.11 Configurable Security Characteristics

Single-user systems have clear security needs, such as firewalls to keep out intruders. Multiuser systems share all of these needs but also have some unique security requirements of their own—for example, mechanisms to protect one user from another. Systems with VEs also have their own specific security considerations.

Some virtualization technologies offer the ability to modify the security environment of VEs. Configurable security enables you to selectively harden different aspects of a VE by allowing a VE to perform only those actions needed for its workload. An example is immutable zones, which are described in Chapter 3, "Oracle Solaris Zones."

Any software component has the potential to create a security weakness, and virtualization software is no different. In turn, virtualization software must be subjected to the same stringent security analysis that other infrastructure software undergoes. For more on this topic, see the book *Solaris Security Essentials*.

If the hypervisor can limit inter-VE interactions to those already possible between separate computers, the hypervisor cannot be used as a covert channel, and the shared system's security is not compromised compared to separate systems.

2.12 Summary

Virtualization can be applied to a diverse set of situations. The specific technologies that you choose must include features and characteristics that support your environment and intended uses.

3

Oracle Solaris Zones

Operating system virtualization (OSV) was virtually unknown in 2005, when Solaris 10 was released. That release of Solaris introduced Solaris Zones—also called Solaris Containers, and now called Oracle Solaris Zones—making it the first fully integrated, production-ready implementation of OSV. In response, several other implementations have been developed or are planned for other operating systems (OS). Zones use a basic model similar to an earlier technology called jails. Chapter 1, "Introduction to Virtualization," provided a complete description of OSV. To summarize the key points here, OSV creates virtual OS instances, which are software environments in which applications run; these instances are isolated from each other but share one copy of an OS, or part of an OS and one OS kernel.

Oracle Solaris Zones provide a software environment that appears to be a complete OS instance from within the zone. To a process running in a zone, the primary differences are effects of the robust yet configurable security boundary around each zone. Zones offer a very rich set of features, most of which were originally features of Solaris, but then were applied to zones. The tight level of integration between zones and the rest of Solaris minimizes software incompatibility and improves the overall "feel" of zones. Zones provide the following capabilities:

- Configurable isolation and security boundaries
- Multiple namespaces—one per zone
- Flexible software packaging, deployment, and flexible file system assignments
- Resource management controls

- Resource usage reporting
- Network access
- Optional direct access to devices
- Centralized or localized patch management
- Management of zones (e.g., configure, boot, halt, migrate)

This chapter describes the most useful features that can be used with zones, and offers reasons to use them. Although a complete description of each of these features is beyond the scope of this book, more details can be found at `docs. oracle.com`. The next few sections describe these features and provide simple command-line examples of their usage.

This chapter assumes that you have experience with a UNIX/Linux operating system and are familiar with other Solaris features, including the Solaris 11 packaging system (IPS) and ZFS.

The command examples in this chapter use the prompt `GZ#` to indicate that a privileged user has assumed the root role so as to execute commands in the computer's global zone. The prompt `zone1#` indicates that a command is entered as a privileged user who has assumed the root role in the zone named `zone1`.

3.1 Introduction

Since their release at the beginning of 2005 as a new feature set of Solaris 10, Oracle Solaris Zones have become a standard environment in many data centers. Further, Solaris Zones are a key architectural element in many Oracle Optimized Solutions. This widespread adoption has been driven by many factors, including zones' isolation, resource efficiency, observability, configurable security, flexibility, ease of management, and no-cost inclusion in Solaris.

As a form of operating system virtualization, Solaris Zones provide software isolation between workloads. A workload in one zone cannot interact with a workload in another zone. This isolation provides a high level of security between workloads.

Zones are also among the most resource-efficient server virtualization technologies. Their implementation does not insert additional instructions into the code path followed by an application, unlike most hypervisors. For this reason, applications running in zones rarely suffer from excess performance overhead, unlike many other types of virtualization.

Chapter 1 discussed another advantage of OSV over virtual machines: observability. From the management area, called the global zone, a system administrator with appropriate privileges can observe the actions occurring inside zones. This insight improves the system's manageability, making it easier to develop a holistic, yet detailed view of the consolidated environment.

Combining multiple workloads into one larger system can enable one workload to temporarily run faster because more resources are available to it. In contrast, a prolonged state of overutilization can prevent another workload from meeting its desired response time. Solaris includes a comprehensive set of resource management features that may be used to limit resource consumption in such situations.

To tailor your implementation of zones, you can choose from among a variety of Solaris Zone structures and characteristics. You can also choose the best model for your environment based on the characteristics and features it offers.

The original model, often called "native zones," reduces the labor involved in managing many virtual environments (VEs). Most software packaging operations are executed in the global zone and applied to all of these zones automatically. Management is easiest from the global zone, but all of these zones are tied to the global zone, and are updated together as a unit.

Immutable Zones are a variant of the previous model, and offer the most robust security. The Solaris file systems in an Immutable Zone cannot be changed from within the zone, even by a privileged user. This model is the ideal choice for web-facing workloads, which are always the most accessible to malicious users.

New to Solaris 11.2, Kernel Zones offer more independence between a zone and the system's global zone. This model is appropriate when a zone will be managed as a separate entity. One feature that sets kernel zones apart from other types of zones is the ability to move them to a different computer while they are running—that is, live migration.

Solaris 10 Zones are a Solaris 10 software environment in a Solaris 11 system. Software that will not run in a Solaris 11 environment may run in a Solaris 10 Zone instead. These zones are not affected by the package management operations that modify native zones.

Other types also exist, such as cluster zones and labeled zones. This book does not describe them in detail.

The rest of this chapter describes the features that can be modified to tailor the characteristics of Oracle Solaris Zones.

3.2 What's New in Oracle Solaris 11 Zones

Solaris 10 users may benefit from a concise list of the new features and significant changes in Solaris 11 Zones:

- Kernel Zones offer increased isolation and flexibility, and enable live migration.
- Immutable Zones enhance security and manageability by preventing changes to the operating environment.
- IPS simplifies Solaris software packaging and ensures consistent and supportable configurations.
- Integration with the Solaris 11 Automated Installer enables automated provisioning of systems with Solaris Zones.
- Solaris Unified Archives dramatically increase the flexibility of deployment and recovery, including any-to-any transformation.
- Multiple per-zone boot environments improve the system's availability and flexibility.
- Solaris 10 Zones deliver an operating environment that is compatible with Solaris 10.
- Zones may be NFS servers.
- Integration with network virtualization features improves the network isolation of high-scale environments, and enables the creation of arbitrary network architectures within one Solaris instance.
- Live zone reconfiguration improves the availability of Solaris Zones.
- Zone monitoring is greatly simplified with a new command, `zonestat(1M)`.

These new features and changes are described in this chapter.

3.3 Feature Overview

The Solaris Zones feature set was introduced in the initial release of Solaris 10 in 2005, and later extended in Solaris 11. The Solaris Zones implementation of OSV includes a rich set of capabilities. This section describes the features of zones and provides brief command-line examples illustrating the use of those features.

Solaris Zones are characterized by a high degree of isolation, with the separation between them being enforced by a robust security boundary. They serve as the underlying framework for the Solaris Trusted Extensions feature set. Trusted Extensions has achieved the highest commonly recognized global security certification, which is a tribute to the robustness of the security boundary around each zone.

The Oracle Solaris 10 documentation used two different terms to refer to combinations of its OSV feature set: containers and zones. Solaris 11 no longer distinguishes between those terms, and this book uses the term *zones* exclusively. However, Solaris Zones are similar in many ways to other OSV implementations that have been added to other operating systems since the release of Solaris Zones. Many of those implementations are also called "containers."

This chapter describes the features of a Solaris 11.3 system, providing brief examples of their use. Some of the features described in this section did not exist in early updates to Solaris 11. To determine the availability of a particular feature, see the "What's New" documents for Solaris 11 at `docs.oracle.com`.

3.3.1 Basic Model

When you install Oracle Solaris 11 on a system, the original operating environment—a traditional UNIX-like system—is also called the *global zone*. A sufficiently privileged user running in the global zone can create "non-global zones," which are usually called "zones" for simplicity. Several types of zones exist. We will call the default "native zones" or simply "zones" when there is no ambiguity.

Most types of zones cannot contain other zones, as shown in Figure 3.1. The exception is kernel zones, which may contain their own non-global zones. If a kernel

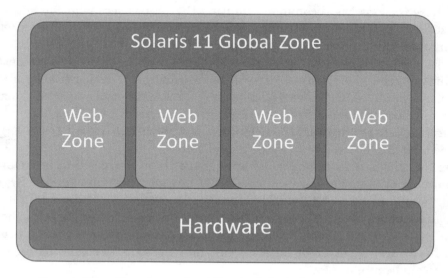

Figure 3.1   Structure of an Oracle Solaris System with Zones
(Block Diagram of Layers)

zone does have its own zones, we will call its global zone the kernel global zone; its non-global zones are called "hosted zones." However, we discourage nesting zones in this manner, due to the additional complexity and lack of compelling use cases for this practice.

In a system with Solaris Zones, the global zone is the platform management area with the sole purpose of managing zones and the system's hardware and software resources. It is similar to the control domain (or "dom0") of a hypervisor-based system in two ways:

- The global zone requires resources to operate, such as CPU cycles and RAM. If an application running in the global zone consumes too much of a resource needed by the global zone's management tools, it may become difficult or even impossible to manage the system.

- Users and processes in the global zone are not subject to all of the rules of zones. In terms of process observability, for example, a process in one zone cannot detect processes in other zones. As with a one-way mirror, processes in the global zone—even non-privileged ones—can detect processes in the zones, but users in the zones cannot see processes in the global zone. There is one exception to this observability rule: Processes in a kernel zone are invisible to processes in the global zone.

For these reasons, we recommend limiting the set of users who can access the global zone to system administrators, and limiting their activities to tasks related to the management of hardware and system software.

The system administrator uses Solaris commands in the global zone to perform tasks directly related to hardware, including installation of device driver software. The Solaris Fault Management Architecture (FMA) is also managed from the global zone, because its tools require direct access to hardware. Most zones do not have direct access to hardware. Zone management tools such as `zonecfg(1M)` and `zoneadm(1M)` can be used only in the global zone.

A kernel zone is a special case. It can manage the resources that are available to it, but cannot manage those resources that have not been assigned to it. As an example, suppose you assign two CPU cores to a kernel zone. The kernel zone can then manage those two CPU cores, but it cannot use other cores at all. In general, we will use the phrase "global zone" to mean the base instance of Solaris running on the hardware, with direct access to all hardware, rather than to mean the operating environment of a kernel zone.

Zones have their own life cycle, which remains somewhat separate from the life cycle of the global zone. After Solaris has been installed and booted, zones can be configured, installed, booted, and used as if they were discrete systems. They can easily and quickly be booted, halted, and rebooted. In fact, booting or halting a zone takes less than 5 seconds, plus any time needed to start or halt applications running in the zone. When you no longer need a zone, you can easily destroy it.

One difference between Solaris Zones and virtual machines is the relationship between the VE and the underlying infrastructure. Zones do not use processes in the global zone to perform any tasks, except the occasional use of management features. The processes associated with a zone access the Solaris kernel directly, using exactly the same methods—system calls—as they use when they are not running in a zone. When a zone's process accesses an I/O device, or a kernel resource, it uses the same methods and the same code. This consistency explains the lack of performance overhead incurred by an application running in a native zone.

Kernel zones use a different method, because they run their own copies of the Solaris kernel. A kernel zone's kernel makes efficient, customized calls into the global zone's kernel so as to access devices. This method is similar in some ways to the paravirtualization used by some virtual machines.

Zones are very lightweight entities, because they are not an entire operating system instance. They do not need to test the hardware or load a kernel or device drivers. Instead, the base OS instance does all that work once—and each zone then benefits from this work when it boots and then accesses the hardware, if permitted by the list of privileges configured for the zone (see Section 3.3.2.1 for a discussion of privileges). Given these characteristics, zones, by default, use very few resources.

A default configuration uses approximately 3 GB of disk space, and approximately 90MB of RAM when running; other types of zones may use more space. When it is not running, a zone does not use any RAM at all. Further, because there is no virtualization layer that runs on a CPU, zones have negligible performance overhead. (All OSV technologies should have this trait.) In other words, a process in a zone follows the same code path that it would outside of a zone unless it attempts to perform an operation that is not allowed in a zone. Because it follows the same code path, it has the same performance.

Solaris Zones were originally designed to support VEs that use the same version of Solaris. To enable the use of other versions (called "brands"), a framework was created to perform translations of low-level computer operations.

One of these brands is Solaris 10. A Solaris 10 Zone behaves just as a Solaris 10 system does, with a few exceptions. Another brand implements low-level high-availability (HA) functionality for Solaris Cluster. The newest brand is kernel zones, which are described later in this chapter.

Although a zone is a slightly different environment from a normal Oracle Solaris system, a basic design principle underlying all zones is software compatibility. A good rule of thumb is this: "If an application runs properly as a non-privileged user in a Solaris 11 system that does not have zones, it will run properly in a native zone." Nevertheless, some applications must run with extra privileges—traditionally, applications that must run as a privileged user. These applications may not be able to gain the privileges they need and, therefore, may not run correctly in a zone. In some cases, it is possible to enable such applications to run in a zone by adding more privileges to that zone, a topic discussed later in this chapter. Kernel zones do not have this limitation, as we shall see later.

3.3.2 Isolation

The primary purpose of zones is to isolate workloads that are running on one Oracle Solaris instance. Although this functionality is typically used when consolidating workloads onto one system, placing a single workload in a single zone on a system has a number of benefits. By design, the isolation provided by zones includes the following factors:

- Each zone has its own objects: processes, file system mounts, network interfaces, and System V IPC objects.
- Processes in one zone are prevented from accessing objects in another zone.
- Processes in different zones are prevented from directly communicating with each other, except for typical intersystem network communication.
- A process in one zone cannot obtain any information about a process running in a different zone—even confirmation of the existence of such a process.
- Each zone has its own namespace and can choose its own naming services, which are mostly configured in /etc. For example, each zone has its own set of users (via LDAP, /etc/passwd, and other means).
- Architecturally, the model of one application per OS instance maps directly to the model of one application per zone while reducing the number of OS instances to manage.

In addition to the functional or security isolation constraints listed here, zones provide for resource isolation, as discussed in the next section.

3.3.2.1 Oracle Solaris Privileges

The basis for a zone's security boundary is Solaris privileges. Thus, understanding the robust security boundary around zones starts with an understanding of Solaris privileges.

Oracle Solaris implements two sorts of rights management. User rights management determines which privileged commands a non-privileged user might execute. Consider the popular `sudo` program as an example of this kind of rights management. Process rights management determines which low-level, fine-grained, system-call–level actions a process can carry out.

Oracle Solaris privileges implement process-rights management. Privileges are associated with specific actions—usually actions that are not typically permitted for non-privileged users. For example, there is a Solaris privilege associated with modifying the system's clock. Normally, only privileged users are permitted to change the clock. Solaris privileges reduce security risks: Instead of giving a person the root password just so that person can modify the system clock, the person's user account is given the appropriate privilege. The user is not permitted to perform any other actions typically reserved for the root role. Instead, the Solaris privileges allow the system administrator to grant a process just enough privilege to carry out its function but no more, thereby reducing the system's exposure to security breaches or accidents.

For that reason, in contrast to the situation noted with earlier versions of Solaris and with many other UNIX-like operating systems, the root role in Oracle Solaris is able to perform any operation not because its UID number is zero, but rather because it has the required privileges. However, a privileged user can grant privileges to another user, enabling specific users to perform specific tasks or sets of tasks. When a process attempts to perform a privileged operation, the kernel determines whether the owner of the process has the privilege(s) required to perform the operation. If the user—and therefore the user's process—has that privilege, the kernel permits that user to perform the associated operation.

3.3.2.2 Zones Security Boundary

A zone has a specific configurable subset of all privileges. The default subset provides normal operations for the zone, and prevents the zone's processes from learning about or interacting with other zones' users, processes, and devices. The root role in the zone inherits all of the privileges that the zone has. Non-privileged users in a zone have, by default, the same set of privileges that non-privileged users in the global zone have.

The platform administrator can configure zones as necessary, including increasing or decreasing the maximum set of privileges that a zone has. No user in that zone can exceed that maximum set—not even privileged users. Those privileged users can modify the set of privileges assigned to the various users in that zone, but cannot modify the set of privileges that the overall zone can have. In other words, the maximum set of privileges that a zone has cannot be escalated from within the zone. At the same time, processes with sufficient privileges, running within the global zone, can interact with processes and other types of objects in zones. This type of interaction is necessary for the global zone to manage zones. For example, the privileged users in the global zone must be able to diagnose a performance issue caused by a process in one zone. They can use DTrace to accomplish this task because privileged processes in the global zone can interact with processes in zones in certain ways.

Also, unprivileged users in the global zone can perform some operations that are commonplace on UNIX systems, but that are unavailable to non-privileged users in a zone. A simple example is the ability to list all processes running on the system, whether they are running in zones or not. For some systems, this capability is another reason to prevent user access to the global zone.

The isolation of zones is very thorough in Oracle Solaris. The Solaris Zones feature set is the basis for the Solaris Trusted Extensions feature set, and the capabilities of Solaris Trusted Extensions are appropriate for systems that must compartmentalize data. Solaris 11 with Solaris Trusted Extensions achieved Common Criteria Certification at Evaluation Assurance Level (EAL) 4+, the highest commonly recognized global security certification. This certification allows Solaris 11 to be deployed when multilevel security (MLS) protection and independent validation of an OS security model is required. Solaris 11 achieved this certification for SPARC and x86-based systems, for both desktop and server functionality.

The isolation of zones is implemented in the Oracle Solaris kernel. As described earlier, this isolation is somewhat configurable, enabling the global zone administrator to customize the security of a zone. By default, the security boundary around a zone is very robust. This boundary can be further hardened by removing privileges from the zone, which effectively prevents the zone from using specific features of Solaris. The boundary can be selectively enlarged by enabling the zone to perform specific operations such as setting the system clock.

The entire list of privileges can be found on the `privileges(5)` man page. Table 3.1 lists the privileges that are most commonly used to customize a zone's security boundary. The third column in Table 3.1 indicates whether the privilege is part of the default privilege set for zones. Note that some nondefault settings described elsewhere, such as `ip-type=shared`, change the list of privileges automatically.

Table 3.1 Privileges for Zones

This privilege . . .	Gives a process the ability to . . .	Default?
dtrace_proc	Use DTrace process-level tracing	No
dtrace_user	Use DTrace user-level tracing	No
file_flag_set	Set file attributes	No
net_icmpaccess	Send and receive ICMP packets	Yes
net_privaddr	Bind to privileged ports	Yes
net_rawaccess	Have raw network access, which is necessary to use snoop	No
proc_clock_highres	Allow the use of high-resolution timers	No
proc_info	Examine /proc for other processes in the same zone	Yes
proc_lock_memory	Lock pages in physical memory	Yes
proc_owner	See and modify other process states	Yes
proc_priocntl	Increase your priority or modify your scheduling class	No
proc_session	Send signals or trace processes outside your session	Yes
sys_acct	Enable, disable, and manage accounting via acct(2)	Yes
sys_admin	Set nodename, domainname, and nscd settings; use coreadm(1M)	Yes
sys_audit	Start the audit daemon	Yes
sys_ipc_config	Increase the size of the System V IPC message queue buffer	No
sys_ip_config	Configure a system's NICs, routes, and other network features (a privilege automatically given to exclusive-IP zones)	No
sys_resource	Exceed the resource limits of setrlimit(2) and setctl(2)	Yes
sys_time	Change the system clock via stime(2), adjtime(2), and ntp_adjtime(2)	No

Some privileges can never be added to a zone. These privileges control hardware components directly (e.g., turning a CPU off) or control access to kernel data. The prohibition against accessing the kernel data is intended to prevent one zone from examining or modifying data about another zone. Table 3.2 lists these privileges.

The configurable security of zones is very powerful and flexible. In addition to the privileges listed in Table 3.1, each zone has additional properties that you can use to tailor the security boundary and capabilities of Solaris Zones. Table 3.3 lists these resources and properties and indicates the section in this book that describes them.

Table 3.2   Privileges Not Allowed in Zones

This privilege . . .	Gives a process the ability to . . .
`dtrace_kernel`	Use DTrace kernel-level tracing
`proc_zone`	Signal or trace processes in other zones
`sys_config`	Perform file system–specific operations, quota calls, and creation and deletion of snapshots
`sys_devices`	Create device special files; override device restrictions
`sys_linkdir`	Link and unlink directories
`sys_mount`	Mount and unmount file systems; add and remove swap devices
`sys_res_config`	Administer CPUs, processor sets, and resource pools
`sys_suser_compat`	Manage third-party modules' use of the kernel `suser()` function

Table 3.3   Security-Related Zone Resources and Properties

Resource or Property	Description
`anet:mac-*`	Multiple MAC-related fields
`file-mac-profile`	Limits the ability of a zone to modify its own files
`net:allowed-address`	Limits the set of IP addresses that a zone can configure for itself
`net:configure-allowed-address`	Automatically configures the `allowed-address`
`anet:allowed-address`	Similar to `net:allowed-address`
`anet:auto-mac-address`	If `mac-address` is set to `random`, Solaris will store randomly chosen addresses in this field so they are persistent across reboots
`anet:configure-allowed-address`	Similar to `net:configure-allowed-address`
`anet:allowed-dhcp-cids`	Sets the `dhcp-nospoof` flag on the VNIC
`anet:link-protection`	Can be used to prevent MAC, IP, or DHCP address spoofing; also limits the network protocols that can be sent on this VNIC

3.3.3 Namespaces

Each zone has its own namespace. In UNIX systems, a namespace is the complete set of recognized names for entities such as users, hosts, printers, and others. In other words, a namespace represents a mapping of human-readable names to names or numbers that are more appropriate to computers. The user namespace maps user names to user identification numbers (UIDs). The host name namespace maps host names to IP addresses. As in any Oracle Solaris system, namespaces in zones can be managed using the `/etc/nsswitch.conf` file.

One simple outcome of having an individual namespace per zone is separate mappings of user names to UIDs. When managing zones, remember that a user in one zone with UID 238 is different from a user in another zone with UID 238. This concept should be familiar to people who have managed NFS clients. Also, each zone has its own Service Management Facility (SMF). SMF starts, monitors, and maintains network services such as SSH. As a consequence, each zone appears on the network just like any other Solaris system, using the same well-known port numbers for common network services.

3.3.4 Brands

Each zone includes a property called its *brand*. A zone's brand determines how it interacts with the Oracle Solaris kernel. Most of this interaction occurs via Solaris system calls. A native zone uses the global zone's system calls directly, whereas other types add a layer of software that translates the zone's system call definitions into the system calls provided by the kernel for that Solaris distribution. A kernel zone has its own kernel, which uses a special mechanism to communicate with the system's global zone.

Each Solaris distribution—for example, Solaris 11—has a default brand for its zones. The default brand for Solaris 11 is called `solaris`, but other brands exist for Solaris 11. Table 3.4 lists the current set of brands.

Table 3.4   Brands

Purpose	Brand Name	Description
Solaris 11 Zones	`solaris`	Native Solaris 11 environment
Solaris 10 Zones	`solaris10`	Host Solaris 10 environments on Solaris 11 computers
Solaris Cluster Zone	`cluster`	Solaris cluster zones
Separate Solaris kernel	`solaris-kz`	A kernel zone can be a different Solaris update or version
Compartmented data	`labeled`	Implement Solaris Trusted Extensions

3.3.5 Packaging and File Systems

Solaris engineers tightly integrated the different feature sets of Solaris so that each benefits from the capabilities of the others. This section describes the integration of zones, IPS, and ZFS.

3.3.5.1 File System Location

A zone's Solaris content exists in ZFS file systems. By default, the file systems are part of the global zone's root pool. You can choose to implement a zone in its own pool, which enables zone mobility. Non-Solaris content, such as application data, may be stored in ZFS or non-ZFS file systems.

A set of ZFS file systems is created for each native zone. This step is necessary so that the Solaris 11 packaging system and boot environments will work correctly. In turn, the zone benefits from all of the advantages of ZFS.

Most zones use ZFS storage that is managed in the global zone. Such an approach to storage uses ZFS mirroring or RAIDZ to protect against data losses due to disk drive failure, and automatically benefits from ZFS checksums, which protect against myriad forms of data corruption.

When you create a zone, Oracle Solaris creates the necessary file systems, in which all of the zone's directories and files reside. The highest level of those file systems is mounted on the zone's `zonepath`, one of the many properties of a zone. The default `zonepath` is `/system/zones/<zonename>`, but you can also change it to a valid file system name in a ZFS pool.

3.3.5.2 Packaging

Solaris 11 uses IPS for operating system and application software package management. IPS and related features enable you to manage the entire life cycle of software in a Solaris environment, including package creation, manual and automated deployment of Solaris and applications, and updating of those software packages. This section assumes that you are already familiar with IPS, so it does not describe this system's features except in terms of their application to Solaris Zones. For more information on IPS and related features such as the Automated Installer and Distribution Constructor, see the Oracle Solaris Information Library at `www.oracle.com`.

With IPS and its related features, you can perform the following functions:

- Understand the set of packages and their contents that are installed in a native zone or that are available to a native zone
- Add optional software to a zone, and update or remove that software
- Create and destroy boot environments in a native zone
- Create repositories in a zone, including Solaris repositories and repositories of other software

In the context of IPS, an "image" is an installed set of packages. An image that can be booted is called a boot environment (BE). An instance of Solaris can have one or more BEs. Each BE consists of several ZFS file systems, but in general you do not manage the file systems individually. You use the command `beadm(1M)` to manage BEs, including creating and destroying them, activating the BE to be booted next, and mounting a BE temporarily to view or modify it, among other tasks.

A native zone in a S11 instance is called a "linked image." Each linked image has its own copy of most of the Solaris package's content, but not all of it. Its Solaris content has hard-coded dependencies on some global zone packages; that is, these dependencies cannot be modified by the user. In the documentation, this type of linking is occasionally called a "parent–child" relationship, where the global zone is the parent and the native zone's linked image is the child.

Every native zone has a BE that matches a BE in the global zone. However, global zone BEs that predate the installation of a native zone will not have a matching BE in the native zone.

3.3.5.3 Updating Packages

Solaris IPS greatly simplifies the process of updating Solaris on a computer. When used in a system without zones, the following command will update all of the packages maintained by IPS to the newest versions available:

```
GZ# pkg update
```

If certain core packages will be updated, Solaris automatically creates a new BE, using ZFS snapshots, and prepares the system to use that BE when Solaris is next rebooted. If a new BE is not needed, the software updates may be available immediately.[1]

When you update Solaris in the global zone using that method, all of the native zones are automatically updated. This operation will also update all of the packages installed in the global zone. If you have installed additional packages in native zones, they will be updated as well.

By default, native zones are updated serially. If desired, you can use the `-C` option to indicate that a certain number of zones should be updated simultaneously.

In addition, you can choose to update any packages that you installed separately into a zone. However, as with all updates, IPS will update these packages according to the dependency rules that are configured into each package. For example,

---

1.   We advise the frequent use of ZFS snapshots as an "undo" feature.

you might find that you must update the global zone first, before updating a specific package in a zone.

3.3.6 Boot Environments

Solaris 11 automatically uses multiple boot environments, which are related bootable Solaris environments of one Solaris instance. The name and the purpose of this feature are similar to those of the corresponding features in Solaris 10 boot environments, but the implementation in Solaris 11 is new, and much more tightly integrated with other Solaris 11 features such as ZFS and zones. This level of integration leverages the combined strengths of the BEs and the other Solaris 11 features.

When you update Solaris 11, it automatically creates a new boot environment that will be used the next time that Solaris boots. When it creates that boot environment, it also creates a new boot environment for each native zone that is currently installed. Moreover, rebooting into a different boot environment configures the associated BEs configured for those zones. When any one of them boots, it will boot into the BE associated with the global zone's currently running BE.

You should be aware of some subtle side effects of this implementation. If you install Solaris, and then update it, create a zone, and reboot into the original BE, it will seem as if the zone has disappeared. That is an illusion, however: The zone is still available in the updated BE. However, because it did not exist when the original BE was running, booting back into that BE returns the system to its state at the time when the original BE was running—a state that did not include the zone.

A zone can only boot into a BE associated with the BE currently running in the global zone. The output from the command `beadm list` marks unbootable BEs with the flag "!". However, a privileged user in a native zone can create a new BE that will be associated with the currently running BE in the global zone. At that point, the zone will have two BEs from which it can choose. Either BE may be modified, and a privileged user in that zone may activate either BE and reboot the zone.

3.3.7 Deployment

You can use a few different methods to deploy native zones. The most basic method requires the use of two Solaris commands, `zonecfg(1M)` and `zoneadm(1M)`. The Solaris Automated Installer can install zones into a system while it is also installing Solaris. Solaris Unified Archives can store a zone or a Solaris instance that contains one or more zones. The rest of this section will describe the two zone administrative commands, as well as zone-specific information for Unified Archives.

Using the command `zonecfg`, you can specify a zone's configuration or modify the configuration, potentially while the zone is running. The `zoneadm` command controls the state of a zone. For example, you would use `zoneadm` to install Solaris into a zone, or to boot a zone.

Solaris Unified Archives enable you to manage archives of Solaris environments, both physical and virtual. The Unified Archives tools also perform transformations during deployment, which means converting an archive of a physical system into a virtual environment, or vice versa. Further, an archive of a physical system can include its Solaris Zones, and they can be deployed individually or together.

The Unified Archives command can create two types of archives: system recovery archives and clone archives. System recovery archives are useful for restoring a system during a disaster recovery event. In contrast, clone archives allow you to easily provision a large number of almost identical systems or zones. Unified Archives are described in detail later in this chapter.

3.3.8 Management

As the global zone administrator, you can configure one or more other global zone users as administrator(s) of a zone. The following abilities can be delegated to a zone administrator, as described later in this chapter:

- Use `zlogin(1)` from the global zone, to access the zone as a privileged user
- Perform management activities such as installing, booting, and migrating the zone
- Clone the zone to create a new one
- Modify the zone's configuration for the next boot or reboot
- Temporarily modify the zone's configuration while it runs

3.4 Feature Details

Features that can be applied to zones include all of the configuration and control functionality you would expect from an operating system *and* from a virtualization solution. Fortunately, almost all of the features specific to zones are optional. Thus, you can investigate and use each set of features separately from the others.

The zone-related features can be classified into the following categories:

- Creation and basic management, such as booting
- Packaging
- File systems
- Security
- Resource controls
- Networking
- Device access
- Advanced management features, such as live migration

Many of the configuration features may be modified while the zone runs. For example, you can add a new network interface to a running zone. This ability is described in a later section, "3.4.7.2 Live Zone Reconfiguration."

The following sections describe and demonstrate the use of these features.

3.4.1 Basic Operations

The Solaris Zones feature set includes both configuration tools and management tools. In the typical case, you will begin the configuration of a zone using one command. After you have configured the zone, Solaris stores the configuration information. Management operations, such as installing and booting the zone, are performed with another command; this section describes those commands.

3.4.1.1 Configuring an Oracle Solaris Zone

The first step in creating a zone is to configure it with at least the minimum information.

All initial zone configuration is performed with the `zonecfg(1M)` command, as illustrated in the following example. The first command merely shows that there are no non-global zones on the system yet.

```
GZ# zoneadm list -cv
ID NAME    STATUS   PATH BRAND    IP
0  global running /     solaris shared
GZ# zonecfg -z myzone
myzone: No such zone configured
Use 'create' to begin configuring a new zone.
zonecfg:myzone> create
create: Using system default template 'SYSdefault'
zonecfg:myzone> exit
GZ# zoneadm list -cv
```

```
ID NAME    STATUS     PATH                  BRAND    IP
0  global  running    /                     solaris  shared
-  myzone  configured /zones/roots/myzone   solaris  excl
GZ# zonecfg -z myzone info
zonename: myzone
zonepath: /system/zones/myzone
brand: solaris
autoboot: false
autoshutdown: shutdown
bootargs:
file-mac-profile:
pool:
limitpriv:
scheduling-class:
ip-type: exclusive
hostid:
tenant:
fs-allowed:
anet:
   linkname: net0
   lower-link: auto
...
```

The output from the `info` subcommand of `zonecfg` shows all of the global properties of the zone as well as some default settings. Table 3.5 lists most of the global properties and their meanings. Other properties are discussed in the subsections that follow.

Table 3.5 Global Properties of Zones

Property	Meaning
zonename	Name of the zone. It cannot be changed by `zonecfg` after the zone has been installed; use "`zoneadm ... rename`" instead.
zonepath	Directory name that contains all of the zone's files. This is always the root of a file system.
brand	Type of zone: `solaris`, `solaris10`, `solaris-kz`.
autoboot	Determines whether the zone will be booted when the system boots.
autoshutdown	Specifies the action to be taken when the global zone shuts down cleanly. It can be shutdown, halt, or, for kernel zones, suspend.
bootargs	Arguments to be used with `zoneadm(1M)` when the zone boots.
file-mac-profile	Defines the Mandatory Access Control profile for Solaris content. This can be used to make portions of Solaris read-only ("immutable") and immune from certain types of security attacks.

(continued)

Table 3.5 Global Properties of Zones (continued)

Property	Meaning
pool	Resource pool of CPUs that this zone will use for its processes.
admin	Enables a user or role to perform specific administration functions for this zone.
zpool	A zpool configured exclusively for this zone.
rootzpool	A list of storage devices to be used as the zone's root pool.
limitpriv	The set of privileges(5) that this zone can have; if this field is empty, the zone has the default set of privileges.
scheduling-class	The default scheduling class for this zone: either TS (the default), IA, FSS, FX, or RT.
ip-type	Type of IP networking which this zone will use: either "shared" or "exclusive." Shared-IP zones can share one or more NICs with other shared-IP zones. Exclusive-IP zones have exclusive access to their NICs.
Tenant	A property used for Elastic Virtual Switches.
fs-allowed	List of additional file system types that this zone can use. Use of this property has security implications. This is not a list of file systems.

A zone can be reconfigured after it has been configured, and even after it has been booted. However, any change in its configuration will not take effect until the next time that the zone boots unless you use the −r option with zoneadm, as described in the section "3.4.7.2 Live Zone Reconfiguration." The next example changes the zone so that the next time the system boots, the zone boots automatically.

```
GZ# zonecfg −z myzone
zonecfg:myzone> set autoboot=true
zonecfg:myzone> exit
```

3.4.1.2 Installing and Booting the Zone
After you have configured the zone, you can install it, making it ready to run.

```
GZ# zoneadm −z myzone install
Preparing to install zone <myzone>.
Creating list of files to copy from the global zone.
Copying <7503> files to the zone.
Initializing zone product registry.
Determining zone package initialization order.
Preparing to initialize <1098> packages on the zone.
Initialized <1098> packages on zone.
Zone <myzone> is initialized.
```

```
The file </zones/roots/myzone/root/var/sadm/system/logs/install_log> contains a log of
the zone installation.
GZ# zoneadm list -cv
ID NAME STATUS PATH BRAND IP
0 global running / native shared
- myzone installed /zones/roots/myzone native shared
```

During the installation process, zoneadm creates the file systems and directories required by the zone. Directories that contain system configuration information, such as /etc, are created in the zone's file structure and populated with the default configuration files.

Zones boot much faster than virtual machines, mostly because there is so little to do. The global zone creates a zinit process that starts the zone's Services Management Facility (SMF) and creates a few other processes. Those processes then spawn other processes that initialize the system's services within the zone. At that point, the zone is ready for use.

```
GZ# zoneadm -z myzone boot
GZ# zoneadm list -cv
ID NAME STATUS PATH BRAND IP
0 global running / native shared
1 myzone running /zones/roots/myzone native shared
```

When first booting after installation, the zone needs system configuration information to complete this step; this information is usually collected by Solaris systems when you are installing Solaris. You can provide this information via the zlogin(1) command, which enables privileged global zone users to access a zone. With just one argument—the zone's name—zlogin enters a shell in the zone as the root role. Arguments after the zone's name are passed as a command line to a shell in the zone, and the output is displayed to the user of zlogin. One important option is -C, which provides access to the zone's virtual console. A privileged user in the global zone can use that console whenever it is not already in use. The privilege to use zlogin can be granted either through Solaris RBAC, with the solaris.zone.login authorization, or with the delegated administration feature. For more information on the latter, see the section "3.4.7.1 Delegated Administration" later in this chapter.

The first time that the zone boots, it immediately issues its first prompt to the zone's virtual console. After connecting to the virtual console, you might need to press Enter once to get a new terminal type prompt. After you respond to a short series of questions, the zone will reboot and is then ready for use.

Alternatively, instead of providing the system configuration information manually as just described, you could automate the configuration process. The first step in this process is to create a system configuration file; this file should then immediately be renamed so that you do not overwrite it the next time this automated process runs.

```
goldGZ# sysconfig create-profile -o /opt/zones
<questions and responses omitted>
goldGZ# mv /opt/zones/sc_profile.xml /opt/zones/web_profile.xml
```

The other commands are similar to the previous examples, but use the configuration profile that you just created. These two commands configure and install a new zone:

```
voyGZ# zonecfg -z web20 create
voyGZ# zoneadm -z web20 install -c /opt/zones/web_profile.xml
```

3.4.1.3 Halting a Zone

Not only does the `zoneadm` command install and boot zones, but it also stops them. Two methods exist to terminate these zones; one is graceful, and the other is not.

The `shutdown` subcommand gracefully stops the zone. Using it is the same as executing the following command:

```
GZ# zlogin myzone /usr/bin/init 0
```

The `halt` subcommand to `zoneadm` simply kills the processes in the zone. It does not run scripts that gracefully shut down the zone but, as you might suspect, it is faster than the `shutdown` command.

Figure 3.2 shows the entire life cycle of a zone, along with the commands you can use to manage one.

3.4.1.4 Modifying a Zone

Before installation of a zone, all of its parameters may be modified—both resources and properties. A zone may subsequently be modified after its installation is complete, and even later, after it has been running. Nevertheless, a few parameters, such as the brand, may not be modified after the zone has been installed. The rest of the parameters may be modified so that the changes to them will take effect the next time that the zone boots. To cause changes to parameters to

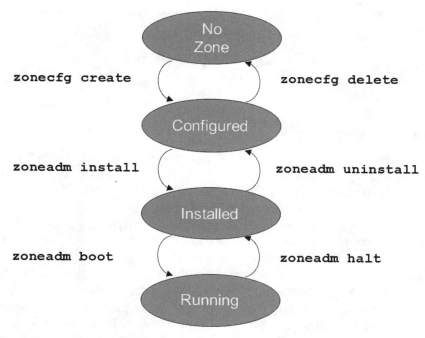

Figure 3.2 Zone States

take effect immediately, you must specifically indicate this preference by including the appropriate option to the `zonecfg` command. The section "3.4.7.2 Live Zone Reconfiguration" describes this type of modification.

Although the `zonepath` and `rootzpool` parameters may not be modified after the zone's installation, a zone may be moved by using the `zoneadm` command. Moving a zone that uses a `rootzpool` will not move the contents of the zone, but rather will merely modify the `zonepath`.

The list of resources and properties that can be changed, for each type of zone, is listed on the brand-specific `man` page: `solaris(5)`, `solaris10(5)`, and `solaris-kz(5)`.

3.4.1.5 Modifying Zone Privileges

Earlier in this chapter, we discussed Oracle Solaris privileges, including the fact that you can modify the set of privileges that a zone can have. If you change the privileges that a zone can have, you must reboot the zone before the changes will take effect. The following example depicts the steps to add the `sys_time` privilege to an existing zone:

```
GZ# zonecfg -z web
zonecfg:web> set limitpriv="default,sys_time"
zonecfg:web> exit
GZ# zoneadm -z web boot
```

3.4.2 Packaging

Solaris systems retrieve packages from a package repository. Native zones use the global zone's "system repository" to access repositories. In essence, the global zone acts as a proxy, retrieving information and package content on behalf of the native zone. In addition, a zone can configure other publishers and obtain content from them. The system repository can proxy http, https, file-based repositories available to the global zone, and repository archives (.p5p files). The last option is the most convenient method to move and install a single custom package.

You can configure a global zone with a publisher that the global zone does not use, but that is used by its zones. For this scheme to work correctly, the global zone must be able to access the publisher. Such an approach may be very useful when multiple zones will install packages that the global zone should not install. If only one zone needs access to a publisher, it may be simpler to configure that access within the zone itself.

A native zone can see the global zone's publisher configuration and, therefore, the configurations of the publishers it automatically accesses via the global zone. For example, in the global zone, the following output lists two publishers, neither of which is proxied:

```
jvictor@tesla:~$ pkg publisher -F tsv
PUBLISHER STICKY SYSPUB ENABLED TYPE    STATUS URI             PROXY
solaris   true   false  true    origin  online http://pkg.oracle.com/solaris/release/ -
```

However, in a native zone, the same command distinguishes between publishers that use the global zone as a proxy ("solaris") and publishers configured in the zone itself ("localrepo"). The latter might be an NFS mount, as shown in the second command here:

```
testzone:~# mount -F nfs repo1:/export/myrepo /mnt/localrepo
testzone:~# pkg set-publisher -g file:///mnt/repo localrepo
testzone:~# pkg publisher -F tsv
PUBLISHER  STICKY  SYSPUB  ENABLED  TYPE    STATUS   URI              PROXY
localrepo  true    true    true     origin  online   file:///mnt/repo/ -
solaris    true    true    true     origin  online
↳http://pkg.oracle.com/solaris/release/ http://localhost:1008
```

A native zone accesses a system repository via two required services. One service, the zone's proxy client, runs in the zone; its complete name is `application/pkg/zones-proxy-client:default`. The other service runs in the global zone: `application/pkg/zones-proxyd:default`. Both services are enabled automatically, but examination of their states may simplify the process of troubleshooting packaging problems in zones. A native zone cannot change the configuration of publishers that it accesses via the global zone.

Changing a global zone's publishers also changes the repositories from which its zones get packages. For that reason, before you remove a publisher from the global zone's list, you should confirm that its zones have not installed any packages from the soon-to-be-removed publisher. If the zone can no longer access that publisher, it will not be able to update the software, and it may not be able to uninstall that package.

3.4.3 Storage Options

Several options exist that specify the location of storage for the zone itself and the locations of additional storage beyond the root pool. Also, some options related to storage enable you to further restrict the abilities of a zone, thereby enhancing its security. These options are discussed in this section.

3.4.3.1 Alternative Root Storage

Instead of storing a zone in the global zone's ZFS root pool, you can store it in its own zpool. Although that pool can reside on local storage, an even better option is to use remote storage that can be accessed by another Solaris computer. Ultimately, remote shared storage simplifies migration of zones.

The configuration of a zone onto shared storage requires only one additional configuration step: specifying the location of the storage. To configure the root pool storage for a zone, use `zonecfg(1M)` and its `rootzpool` resource. The storage can be any of these types, and different storage types can be mixed within one pool. Note, however, that mixing storage types can lead to adverse performance and has security implications. Currently, the following types of storage are supported:

- Direct device (e.g., `dev:dsk/c0t0d0s0`)
- Logical unit (FC or SAS) (e.g., `lu.name.naa.5000c5000288fa25`)
- iSCSI (e.g., `iscsi:///luname.naa.600144f03d70c80000004ea57da10001` or `iscsi:///target.iqn.com.sun:02:d0f2d311-f703,lun.6`)

For more details on those storage types and their specification, see the `suri(5)` `man` page.

Solaris will automatically create a ZFS pool in the storage area.

3.4.3.2 Adding File Systems

Access to several types of file systems may be added to a zone. Some of these types allow multiple zones to share a file system. This ability can be useful, but is vulnerable to two pitfalls: synchronization of file modifications and security concerns.

Storage managed by ZFS can be added in two different ways. The first approach is to mount a ZFS file system that exists in the global zone into a non-global zone. In the zone, this file system is simply a directory. The second method is to make a global zone file system appear to be a pool in a non-global zone.

The first method assumes that the ZFS file system `rpool/myzone1` exists in the global zone. When the zone boots, its users will be able to access that file system at the directory `/mnt/myzfs1`. Processes running in the zone can access the storage available to the ZFS file system `rpool/myzone`.

```
GZ# zonecfg -z myzfszone
zonecfg:myzone> add fs
zonecfg:myzone:fs> set dir=/mnt/myzfs1
zonecfg:myzone:fs> set special=rpool/myzone1
zonecfg:myzone:fs> set type=zfs
zonecfg:myzone:fs> end
```

This method cannot be used to share files between zones. When this approach is used, if two zones are configured with the same ZFS file system, the first to boot will run correctly. An attempt to boot the second zone, however, will fail. Further, the file system will not be available to users in the global zone.

We recommend setting a quota on all file systems assigned to zones so that one zone does not fill up the pool and prevent other workloads from using the pool.

The second method assigns a ZFS data set to the zone. This method delegates administration of the data set to the zone. A privileged user in the zone can control attributes of the data set and create new ZFS file systems in it. That user also controls attributes of those file systems, such as quotas and access control lists (ACLs).

You can add a ZFS file system or volume to a zone as a ZFS pool. To the global zone, this resource appears to be a file system. Inside the zone, it appears to be a ZFS pool. Administration of the data set is delegated to the zone, so that a privileged user in the zone can control attributes of the data set and create new ZFS file systems in it. That user also controls attributes of those file systems, such as quotas and ACLs.

Although a privileged user in the zone can manage the data set from within, a global zone administrative user can manage the top-level data set, including setting a quota on it.

When using the `zonecfg` command, you supply the name of the data set as it is known in the global zone, along with an "alias"—the name of the zpool as seen in the zone. If you omit the alias, Solaris uses the final component of the file system name as the name of the pool.

```
GZ# zonecfg -z myzone
zonecfg:myzone> add dataset
zonecfg:myzone:dataset> set name=mypool/myfs
zonecfg:myzone:dataset> set alias=zonepool
zonecfg:myzone:dataset> end
zonecfg:myzone> exit
```

Regardless of the type of file system being used, any arbitrary directory that exists in the global zone can be mounted into a zone, with either read-only or read-write status. This step requires the use of a loopback mount, as shown in the next example for a different zone:

```
GZ# zonecfg -z myufszone
zonecfg:myzone> add fs
zonecfg:myzone:fs> set dir=/shared
zonecfg:myzone:fs> special=/zones/shared/myzone
zonecfg:myzone:fs> set type=lofs
zonecfg:myzone:fs> end
zonecfg:myzone> exit
```

In this example, the `dir` parameter specifies the global zone's name for that directory. The `special` parameter specifies the directory name in the zone on which to mount the global zone's directory.

A brief digression is warranted here: When managing zones, keep in mind the two different perspectives that are possible for all objects such as files, processes, and users. In the last example, a process in the global zone would normally use the path name `/zones/shared/myzone` to refer to that directory. A process in the zone, however, must use the path `/shared`.

Alternatively, a non-ZFS file system can be mounted into a zone so that only the zone can access it. Processes in other zones then cannot use that file system, and only privileged users in the global zone can access the file system. In the next example, `dir` has the same meaning as in the previous example, but *special* indicates the name of the block device that contains the file system. The *raw* property specifies the name of the raw device.

```
GZ# zonecfg -z myufszone
zonecfg:myzone> add fs
zonecfg:myzone:fs> set dir=/mnt/myfs
zonecfg:myzone:fs> set special=/dev/dsk/c1t0d0s5
zonecfg:myzone:fs> set raw=/dev/rdsk/c1t0d0s5
zonecfg:myzone:fs> set type=ufs
zonecfg:myzone:fs> end
zonecfg:myzone> exit
```

All of these mounts—ZFS, UFS, lofs, and others—are created when the zone is booted. For more information on the various types of file systems that can be used within a zone, see the Oracle Solaris 11 documentation.

3.4.3.3 Read-Only Zones

It seems that every month brings a news story describing the latest theft of personal or corporate data from supposedly secure computers. Solaris offers a diverse set of security features intended to prevent various types of attacks. One of these features is read-only, or "immutable," zones.

Some attacks rely on the perpetrator's ability to change the configuration of a system, or modify some of its system software. To thwart this type of attack, Solaris 11 Zones can be configured in such a way that the configuration, or the programs that make up Solaris, cannot be modified from within the zone, even by someone who was able to gain some or all of the privileges available within that zone.

Three choices are available for this kind of configuration, each of which specifies the Solaris files that are writable:

1. Only configuration files can be modified, including everything in /etc/*, /var/*, and root's home directory /root/*. With this method, packages cannot be installed, and the configuration of syslog and the audit subsystem can be changed. This choice of configuration, which is intended to prevent an attacker from modifying commands and leaving Trojan horses, is named flexible-configuration.

2. Only content in /var/* may be modified, except for some directories that contain configuration information. This method prevents attacks that require changing passwords, adding users, changing network information, and more. It is named fixed-configuration.

3. No content in the root pool can be changed. This method prevents attacks that require modifying any parts of Solaris. Unfortunately, it may also prevent some software from functioning correctly, such as software that temporarily stores files in /var/tmp. This choice is named strict.

You can achieve this level of protection by adding just one line to the configuration:

```
GZ# zonecfg -z troy
zonecfg:troy> create
zonecfg:troy> set file-mac-profile=strict
zonecfg:troy> exit
```

These strategies raise a key question: If even a privileged user in a zone cannot change its configuration files, how can those files be changed when necessary? The Trusted Path feature enables a privileged user in the global zone to use the -T option to the zlogin command. With this feature, the user can modify files that cannot be modified from within the zone. To use this feature, a user either will need the Solaris RBAC authorization solaris.zone.manage/<zonename> or must be delegated the authorization named manage.

For more details on the latter strategy, see the section entitled "Delegated Administration" later in this chapter.

3.4.4 Resource Management

Resource management includes monitoring resource usage for the purpose of setting initial control levels, and modifying controls in the future to accommodate normal growth. The Solaris Zones feature set includes comprehensive resource management features, also called resource controls. These controls allow the platform administrator to manage those resources that are typically controlled in VEs. Use of these controls is optional, and most are disabled by default. We strongly recommend that you take advantage of these features, as they can prevent many problems caused by over-consumption of a resource by a workload. The following resources were mentioned in previous chapters:

- CPU capacity—that is, the portion of a CPU's clock cycles that a VE can use
- Amount of RAM used
- Amount of virtual memory or swap space used
- Network bandwidth consumed

- Use of kernel data structures—both structures of finite size and ones that use another finite resource such as RAM

This section describes the resource controls available for zones. It also demonstrates the use of Solaris tools to monitor resource consumption by zones. You should apply these monitoring tools before attempting to configure the resource controls, so that you will clearly understand the baseline resource needs of each workload.

The `zonecfg` command is the most useful tool for setting resource controls on zones. By default, its settings do not take effect until the next time the zone boots, but a command-line option may be used to specify immediate reconfiguration of a running zone.

The `zonestat(1M)` command is a very powerful monitoring tool. It reports on both resource caps and resource usage. Examples are provided in the sections that follow.

Other useful commands that apply resource controls include `prctl(1)` and `rcapadm(1M)`, both of which have an immediate effect on a zone. Resource control settings can also be viewed with the commands `prctl`, `rcapstat(1)`, and `poolstat(1M)`, in addition to `zonestat`.

Oracle Solaris 11 includes a wide variety of tools that report on consumption of specific resources, including `prstat`, `poolstat(1M)`, `mpstat(1M)`, `rcapstat(1M)`, and `kstat(1M)`. Many of these features can be applied to zones using command-line options or other methods. In addition, Oracle Enterprise Manager Ops Center was designed as a means to perform complete life-cycle management of both virtual and physical systems, including monitoring of resource consumption by the global zone and by individual zones. This section discusses only those tools that are included with Oracle Solaris 11. Chapter 7, "Automating Virtualization," discusses OEM Ops Center and OpenStack, another virtualization life-cycle system.

One of the greatest strengths of Solaris Zones is common to most OSV implementations but absent from other forms of virtualization—namely, the ability of tools running in the management area to provide a holistic view of system activity, by aggregating all VEs, as well as a detailed view of the activity in each VE. The monitoring tools described in this section are widely used Solaris tools that provide either a holistic view, a detailed view, or options to obtain both views.

Oracle Solaris includes a text-based "dashboard" for Solaris Zones: `zonestat(1)`. Similar to other "stat" monitoring commands, `zonestat` takes an argument that sets the length of the interval(s) during which it collects data, reporting averages at the end of each interval. Without any other arguments, the output shows basic information.

```
GZ$ zonestat 3
Collecting data for first interval...
Interval: 1, Duration: 0:00:03
SUMMARY          Cpus/Online: 4/4   PhysMem: 31.8G  VirtMem: 33.8G
              ----------CPU---------- --PhysMem-- --VirtMem-- --PhysNet-
     ZONE  USED %PART  STLN %STLN  USED %USED  USED %USED PBYTE %PUSE
   [total]  0.06 1.53%  0.00 0.00%  9200M 28.2% 6652M 19.2%   459 0.00%
  [system]  0.00 0.00%     -     - 7710M 23.6% 4606M 13.3%     -     -
    global  0.06 1.52%     -     - 1398M 4.29% 1972M 5.69%   459 0.00%
     zone1  0.00 0.00%     -     - 91.0M 0.27% 73.6M 0.21%     0 0.00%
```

The output shown here has several components:

- An announcement that data is being collected
- An announcement of the first interval report
- The interval report itself, which includes:
  - Data aggregated across the global zone and all zones
  - Data limited to processes running in the global zone
  - Data aggregated across each zone during the interval

The section labeled "CPU" shows the amount of CPU time used for each entry, normalized to one CPU thread, as well as the portion of CPU time used compared to that available to the zone during that interval. The "PhysMem" and "VirtMem" sections provide data about RAM and virtual memory. The latter considers both RAM and swap space used, and compares them to the total amount configured. The final section, "PhysNet," displays network data.

The `zonestat` monitoring command can be used with a plethora of options to produce final aggregated reports, details of individual groups of CPUs and network ports, both physical and virtual, and much more. Some of these options will be illustrated later in this chapter.

3.4.4.1 CPU Controls

Oracle Solaris offers multiple methods for controlling a zone's use of CPU time. The simplest is Dynamic Resource Pools, which enable you to exclusively assign CPUs to a zone; the resulting set of CPUs is called a pool. Perhaps the most flexible means of CPU control is the Fair Share Scheduler (FSS). FSS allows multiple zones to share the system's CPUs, or a subset of them, while ensuring that each zone receives sufficient CPU time to meet its service level agreement (SLA). Lastly, CPU caps enforce a maximum amount of computational ability on a zone. Although you can use a zone without any CPU controls, we recommend applying these controls to achieve consistent performance.

Dynamic Resource Pools

By default, all processes in all zones share the system's processors. An alternative—Solaris Dynamic Resource Pools—ensures that a workload has exclusive access to a set of CPUs. When this feature is used, a zone is configured to have its own pool of CPUs for its exclusive use. Processes in the global zone and in other zones never run on that set of CPUs. This type of resource pool is called a temporary pool, because it exists only when the zone is running. Alternatively, it may be called a private pool, reflecting that those CPUs are dedicated (private) to just one zone and its processes.

A resource pool can be of fixed size, or it can be configured to vary in size within a range that you choose. In the latter situation, the OS will shift CPUs between pools as their needs change, as shown in Figure 3.3. Each CPU is assigned to either a (non-default) resource pool or the default pool. The default pool, which always exists, holds all CPUs that have not been assigned to other pools. CPUs in the default pool are used by global zone processes and processes in zones that are not configured to use a pool.

A private pool is not created until its zone boots. If sufficient CPUs are not available to fulfill the needs of the configuration, the zone will not boot, and a diagnostic message will be displayed instead. In that case, you must take one of the following steps to enable the zone to boot:

- Reconfigure the zone with fewer CPUs.
- Reconfigure the zone to share CPUs with other zones.
- Shift CPUs out of the private pools of other zones and into the default pool.
- Move the zone to a system with sufficient CPUs.

The simplest approach is to configure pools to have fixed size (e.g., 4 CPUs). A zone that uses a private, fixed-size pool will always be able to use all of the compute capacity of those CPUs. If you choose to use fixed-size pools, you can ignore the ability to dynamically adjust the sizes of the resource pools.

Other situations call for flexibility—specifically, the ability to automatically react to a change in processing needs. For example, consider Figure 3.3, which shows a 32-CPU system with a default pool of 4–32 CPUs and with zones named Web, App, and DB, which are configured with pools of 2–6 CPUs, 8–16 CPUs, and

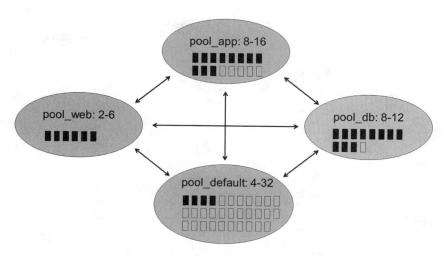

Figure 3.3 Dynamic Resource Pools

8–12 CPUs, respectively. Solaris will attempt to assign the maximum quantity of CPUs to each pool, while leaving the default pool with its minimum quantity of CPUs. By default, the quantity of CPUs assigned to each pool is balanced within the configuration constraints.

In the example shown in Figure 3.3, the Web zone will get 6 CPUs, and the App and DB zones will each get 11 CPUs, leaving 4 CPUs for the default pool. After the zones have been running for a while, if the CPU utilization of a pool exceeds a configurable threshold, Solaris will automatically shift 1 CPU into it from an under-utilized pool.

Figure 3.4 shows graphs of CPU allocation and utilization for three different zones and the system's default pool. As the workloads become more active, they need more processing capacity, and Solaris dynamically provides this resource as necessary.

For example, "Web CPUs" in Figure 3.4 is the number of CPUs configured in the Web zone's pool as time passes. As the utilization of one pool grows so that it exceeds a configurable threshold, Solaris shifts a CPU into the pool. As the workload increases, Solaris shifts more CPUs until it has reached the maximum quantity configured for that pool, or until there are no more CPUs that can be shifted to the pool. After the utilization of a pool has decreased below the threshold for a suitably long period, Solaris shifts a CPU out of the zone's pool and back into the default pool.

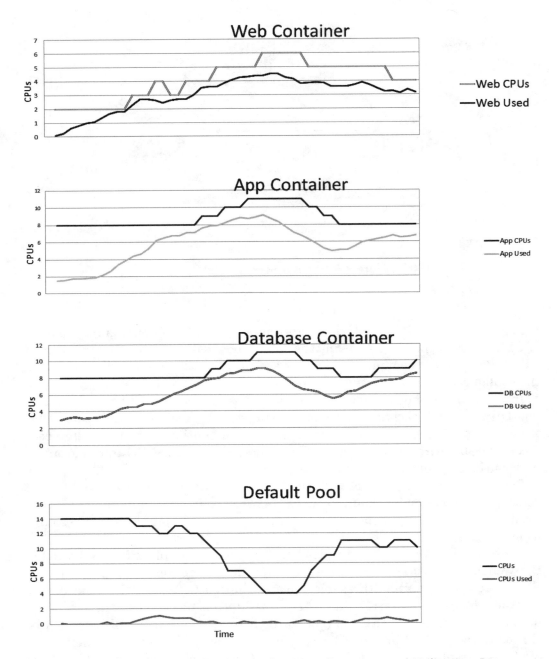

Figure 3.4   Dynamic Resource Pools: CPU Allocation and Utilization Rates

Note that the App zone's pool and the DB zone's pool have a minimum of 8 CPUs each. During at least some periods of time, these pools have excess capacity that other zones cannot use. Maintaining that excess capacity offers a notable benefit: Those zones can use that capacity instantly when they need it, without waiting for Solaris to shift a CPU to their own pools. In other words, they can react more quickly to changing needs for processor time.

Configuring Resource Pools

Configuring a zone to use a private pool is very easy, with a variety of options being available to increase the flexibility of this process. To dedicate two CPUs to a zone named `web`, run the following commands:

```
GZ# zonecfg -z web
zonecfg:web> add dedicated-cpu
zonecfg:web:dedicated-cpu> set ncpus=2
zonecfg:web:dedicated-cpu> end
zonecfg:web> exit
GZ# zoneadm -z web boot
```

The set of CPUs assigned to a zone using this method can be changed while the zone runs, using the live zone reconfiguration feature described later in this chapter.

Global zone administrators can view the current configuration of pools, and CPU usage relative those pools, with the `zonestat` command.

```
GZ# zonestat -r psets 3
Collecting data for first interval...
Interval: 1, Duration: 0:00:03
PROCESSOR_SET                   TYPE ONLINE/CPUS    MIN/MAX
pset_default        default-pset          2/2         1/-
           ZONE  USED %USED  STLN %STLN   CAP  %CAP   SHRS  %SHR %SHRU
        [total]  0.48 16.2%  0.00 0.00%     -     -      -     -     -
       [system]  0.03 1.26%     -     -     -     -      -     -     -
         global  0.44 14.9%     -     -     -     -      -     -     -

PROCESSOR_SET                   TYPE ONLINE/CPUS    MIN/MAX
web                 dedicated-cpu         2/2         2/2
           ZONE  USED %USED  STLN %STLN   CAP  %CAP   SHRS  %SHR %SHRU
        [total]  0.00 0.09%  0.00 0.00%     -     -      -     -     -
       [system]  0.00 0.05%     -     -     -     -      -     -     -
            web  0.00 0.04%     -     -     -     -      -     -     -
```

Note that the zone is associated with a processor set that contains the CPUs. It is possible to manually create a resource pool and assign one or more zones to that pool. The `zonestat` output would then show multiple zones in the listing for one processor set. This technique will not be explored in detail, as it is beyond the scope of this book.

To change the pool size so that it will be a dynamic quantity the next time the zone boots, you can run the following commands to allocate between two and four processors to the zone. The first command enables the service `poold`, which dynamically adjusts the pool size but is not needed for static pools. This service monitors resource pools that have been configured with a variable quantity of CPUs. It tracks CPU utilization of those pools and, if one is over-utilized, shifts a CPU to it from an under-utilized pool. If multiple pools are over-utilized, the `importance` parameter informs the OS of the relative importance of this pool compared to other pools.

```
GZ# svcadm enable pools/dynamic
GZ# zonecfg -z web
zonecfg:web> add dedicated-cpu
zonecfg:web:dedicated-cpu> set ncpus=2-4
zonecfg:web:dedicated-cpu> set importance=5
zonecfg:web:dedicated-cpu> end
zonecfg:web> exit
GZ# zoneadm -z web boot
```

The size of a pool can be changed while the zone runs by manually shifting CPUs from one pool to another. This step is performed by using the live zone reconfiguration feature described later in this chapter.

Until now we have ignored the meaning of the acronym "CPU" while describing features that address it, the CPU's use, and the Solaris kernel's interpretation of it. For decades, "CPU" meant the chip that ran machine instructions, one at a time. The operating system created a process, branched execution to it, and cleaned up when it was done. A multiprogramming OS ran one process for a small period of time, then switched the CPU to another process if one was ready to run.

Today, however, both multicore processors and multithreaded cores are available. Multicore processors are simply multiple CPUs implemented on a single piece of silicon, although some models provide some shared resources for those cores, such as shared cache. Multithreaded cores improve throughput performance by duplicating some—but not all—of a core's circuitry within the core. To make the most of those hardware threads, the operating system must be able to efficiently schedule processes onto the threads, preferably with some knowledge of the CPU's internal workings and memory architecture.

Oracle Solaris has a long history of efficiently scheduling hundreds of processes on dozens of processors, going back to the E10000 with its 64 single-core CPUs. Because of its scalability, Solaris was modified to schedule processes on any hardware thread in the system, maximizing the total throughput of the platform.

Unfortunately, this scheme can be a bit confusing when you are configuring resource pools, because each type of CPU has its own type and amount of hardware threading. Each CPU also has its own per-thread performance characteristics. Table 3.6 lists various CPUs that will run Oracle Solaris 11 and core and thread data. It also shows some sample systems.

Table 3.6 Multithreaded CPUs

CPU Name	Cores per Chip	Sample System Model	Max CPU Chips	Max Cores	Max CPUs (Threads)
E5-2600 v3	18	Oracle X5-2	2	36	72
E7-8800 v3	18	Oracle X5-4	4	72	144
SPARC T5	16	T5-8	8	128	1024
SPARC M6	12	M6-32	32	384	3072
SPARC M7	32	M7-16	16	512	4096

Because Solaris identifies each hardware thread as a CPU, you can create very flexible resource pools. For example, on an Oracle T7-2, a SPARC-based computer with 2 CPU chips, you can create twelve 32-CPU pools and still have 128 CPUs left for the global zone! Most multithreaded CPUs have some shared cache, so if you want to optimize performance you should configure CPU quantities in multiples of 4 or 8, depending on the architecture of that CPU.

Certainly, all of that flexibility is very useful—but in many situations, other factors are even more important. Some workloads will run best if you configure the zone with one or more entire cores. Similar features enable you to choose specific cores by identification number. The `psrinfo -t` command displays the ID number of CPU threads, CPU cores, and CPU sockets. The following example shows the difference in syntax, and configures four cores for use by a zone:

```
GZ# zonecfg -z dbzone
zonecfg:dbzone> add dedicated-cpu
zonecfg:dbzone:dedicated-cpu> set cores=4-7
zonecfg:dbzone:dedicated-cpu> end
zonecfg:dbzone> exit
```

Variations of that feature allow you to choose specific hardware threads or entire CPU chips, which are called "sockets."

Finally, the kernel does not enforce a limit on the total number of CPUs configured in different pools or zones until they are actually running. Thus you could configure and install ten 120-core zones on a T5-8 as long as you run only one zone at a time. Alternatively, you could configure and run 10 zones, each with 100 CPUs (threads). In other words, you can over-subscribe CPUs.

Fair Share Scheduler

The Fair Share Scheduler was discussed in Chapter 2, "Use Cases and Requirements." FSS can control the allocation of available CPU resources among workloads based on the level of importance that you assign to them. This importance is expressed by the number of CPU shares that you assign to each workload. FSS compares the number of shares assigned to a particular workload to the aggregate number of shares assigned to all workloads. For example, if one workload has 100 shares and the total number of shares assigned to all workloads is 500, the scheduler will ensure that the workload receives at least one-fifth of the compute capacity of the available CPUs.

The last point is very important, as a key advantage of this CPU control mechanism over the other options is that it does not waste idle CPU cycles. With FSS, any workload can use idle CPU cycles as long as each workload receives its guaranteed minimum compute time. The FSS method does not force any process to wait if a CPU is available somewhere within the system, unlike the other methods of CPU control.

To use FSS with zones, you must first enable it for use across the Solaris instance. As is often the case, one command is needed to tell Solaris to change a specific setting the next time Solaris boots, and a different command is needed to tell Solaris to change its behavior immediately. The `dispadmin(1M)` command shown here changes the default scheduler to be used the next time that Solaris boots. The `priocntl(1)` command changes the default scheduler that Solaris is using now for all existing processes.

```
GZ# dispadmin -d FSS
GZ# priocntl -s -c FSS -i all
```

Once FSS has become the default scheduler, you must assign sufficient shares to the global zone to ensure that its processes get sufficient CPU time. Choose a value that is of the same magnitude as the values used for the other zones. Set a value with `zonecfg` for the next time the system boots. Also, use `prctl` to set a value for right now. The order of execution does not matter.

```
GZ# zonecfg -z global
zonecfg:web> set cpu-shares=100
zonecfg:web> exit
GZ# prctl -t privileged -n zone.cpu-shares -v 100 -i zone global
```

The next step is to allocate 100 `cpu-shares` to a zone, using the following command:

```
GZ# zonecfg -z web
zonecfg:web> set cpu-shares=100
zonecfg:web> exit
GZ# zoneadm -z web boot
```

After the zone is rebooted, this value can be queried with the following command:

```
GZ$ zonestat -r psets 3
Collecting data for first interval...
Interval: 1, Duration: 0:00:03
PROCESSOR_SET          TYPE  ONLINE/CPUS     MIN/MAX
pset_default      default-pset          4/4         1/-
           ZONE  USED %USED STLN %STLN   CAP %CAP   SHRS %SHR %SHRU
        [total]  1.15 38.6% 0.00 0.00%     -    -      2    -     -
       [system]  0.01 0.49%    -    -      -    -      -    -     -
            web  0.99 33.1%    -    -      -    -    100  50% 33.1%
         global  0.14 4.92%    -    -      -    -    100  50%  5.2%
```

This resource constraint can also be changed dynamically for a running zone, using the live zone reconfiguration feature described later in this chapter.

Whenever share assignments are changed or zones using FSS are added or removed, the proportion of CPU time allowed for each zone changes to reflect the new total number of shares. The new proportions will be shown by `zonestat`.

A final note on efficiency and FSS: Although this method does not leave idle CPU cycles if a workload needs to use them, the presence of a large number of zones on a busy system will tax the scheduler. In this scenario, the scheduling algorithm will use a measurable amount of CPU cycles. On medium and large systems, dozens of running zones would be needed for this effect to be noticeable.

Oracle Solaris CPU Caps

The final CPU resource control available for zones is the CPU cap. You can use such a cap to tell Solaris that the processes of a specific zone should not be allowed to use more than a certain amount of CPU time, measured in terms of a CPU, over a small sampling period. This cap allows granularity to be specified in hundredths of a CPU—for example, 5.12 CPUs.

For example, to assign a CPU cap equivalent to 1.5 CPUs, use the following command:

```
GZ# zonecfg -z web
zonecfg:web> add capped-cpu
zonecfg:web:capped-cpu> set ncpus=1.5
zonecfg:web:capped-cpu> end
zonecfg:web> exit
GZ# zoneadm -z web boot
```

This value can be queried with the following command:

```
# zonestat -r psets 3
Collecting data for first interval...
Interval: 1, Duration: 0:00:03
PROCESSOR_SET                   TYPE  ONLINE/CPUS      MIN/MAX
pset_default            default-pset         4/4          1/-
            ZONE   USED %USED  STLN %STLN   CAP  %CAP   SHRS  %SHR %SHRU
         [total]   1.12 37.6%  0.00 0.00%     -     -      0     -     -
        [system]  0.01 0.51%     -     -      -     -      -     -     -
             web   0.99 33.1%     -     -  1.50 66.2%      -     -     -
          global  0.11 3.93%     -     -      -     - no-fss     -     -
```

Similarly, this resource constraint can be changed dynamically for a running zone, using the live zone reconfiguration feature described later in this chapter.

Unlike when dedicated CPUs are assigned to a zone, you can run several zones with CPU caps even if the sum of their caps exceeds the quantity of CPUs in the system. In other words, you can over-subscribe CPUs with this resource control.

You can combine a CPU cap with FSS to ensure that a zone receives a specific minimum amount of compute time, but no more than another specified amount. It does not make sense to apply both a CPU cap and a pool to a zone, and the kernel does not allow this kind of dual control.

CPU controls should be used to prevent one workload from using more CPU time than it should, either accidentally or intentionally as a result of a denial-of-service attack.

Choosing a CPU Control

Each of those CPU controls affects processing in different ways. Which one should you use? Every situation is different, but some general statements can be made about the conditions in which their use is optimal.

- Dedicated CPUs allow you to minimize software licensing costs for some software. Instead of licensing the software for all 384 CPU cores in a SPARC M6-32, for example, you may be able to assign a much smaller quantity (e.g., 16) to a zone and pay for only a 16-core software license. When configured correctly, dedicated CPUs also maximize the performance of the associated zone because its processes are more likely to return to the same CPU every time that CPU gets a time slice, thereby reducing the effects of cache eviction and maintaining data in memory attached to that CPU.

- FSS is a good all-around CPU control, but has its limitations. All zones can access all of the CPUs, so there are never idle CPU cycles that cannot be used by a zone that is trying to use more—which is sometimes a problem with dedicated CPUs or a CPU cap. A new zone can be added without reassigning CPUs—a step that may be required when using dedicated CPUs. However, the FSS scheduling algorithm can consume an unacceptable amount of CPU time if dozens of zones' processes must be scheduled.

- A workload can achieve optimal performance if it can monopolize a CPU's internal resources. This outcome can be achieved with dedicated CPUs, but not with FSS or a CPU cap.

- A CPU cap can be used to limit the amount of CPU time consumed by a zone, perhaps to enforce a contractual limit. It can also be applied to set reasonable user expectations among a small set of early users of a system. Otherwise, users may become accustomed to the response time they observe when they can use all of the CPUs in the system, only to be disappointed later by the system's response time when they are sharing the CPUs with users added later.

CPU Usage Monitoring Tools

In addition to `zonestat`, Oracle Solaris 11 includes some CPU monitoring tools that are available on most UNIX-like operating systems as well as some that are unique to Solaris. These tools include `ps`, `prstat`, `poolstat`, and `mpstat`. Some of these tools also include command-line options that are specific to zones.

For example, the `ps` command has two new options to help observe zones:

- **-Z**: Adds a new column of output labeled ZONE (the name of the zone in which the process is running)
- **-z** *<name>*: Limits the output to processes in the zone specified by *<name>*

The following example shows output from the ps command, limited to the processes in one zone. Notice that zsched has a parent PID of 1, which is the global zone's init process. Also, note that zsched is the parent of the zone's init process, and that the zone's svc.startd and svc.configd services have been inherited by the global zone's init process.

```
GZ# ps -fz myzone
UID PID PPID C STIME TTY TIME CMD
root 1076 1 0 18:15:15 ? 0:00 zsched
root 1089 1076 0 18:15:16 ? 0:00 /sbin/init
root 1091 1 0 18:15:16 ? 0:06 /lib/svc/bin/svc.startd
root 1093 1 0 18:15:16 ? 0:08 /lib/svc/bin/svc.configd
...
```

Of course, users of the zone can use the ps command. As mentioned earlier, the zlogin command can be issued from the global zone to run a program in the zone—in this case, ps -ef.

```
GZ# zlogin myzone ps -ef
UID PID PPID C STIME TTY TIME CMD
root 1335 1331 0 15:22:51 ? 0:00 ps -fz myzone
root 1076 1076 0 18:15:15 ? 0:00 zsched
root 1089 1076 0 18:15:16 ? 0:00 /sbin/init
root 1091 1076 0 18:15:16 ? 0:06 /lib/svc/bin/svc.startd
root 1093 1076 0 18:15:16 ? 0:08 /lib/svc/bin/svc.configd
...
```

In the previous output, note that from within the zone, we are not allowed to know anything about the outside world. Even the PID number of the global zone's init process remains hidden from us. The kernel replaces that forbidden information with safe information—in this case, the PID of the zone's zsched process. Any process that would normally be inherited by init is, seemingly, inherited by zsched. Note also that the parent PID of zsched is hidden—through the display of a PPID equal to its PID!

The -Z option adds the ZONE column to the ps output. This column is very helpful when you are trying to understand the relationship between processes and the zone with which they are associated.

```
GZ# ps -efZ
ZONE UID PID PPID C STIME TTY TIME CMD
global root 0 0 0 15:24:18 ? 0:25 sched
global root 1 0 0 15:24:20 ? 0:00 /sbin/init
...
myzone root 1076 1 0 18:15:15 ? 0:00 zsched
global root 1075 1 0 18:15:15 ? 0:00 zoneadmd -z myzone
global root 1500 1042 0 21:46:19 pts/3 0:00 ps -efZ
```

3.4.4.2 Memory Controls

Zones also offer several memory controls. Each control can be configured separately, or various controls can be used in combination. Some memory controls constrain the use of a physical resource, such as the RAM cap or the virtual memory cap. The latter is actually a physical resource despite its name—it is the sum of RAM and swap space.

Other memory controls limit the use of special types of memory resources that the kernel allocates, including locked memory and shared memory. The virtual memory system does not page those memory pages out to the swap device. If one zone allocates a large amount of locked memory or shared memory, it can prevent other zones from allocating sufficient memory to run well. The ability to lock down pages must be limited to prevent one zone from locking down all of its memory pages, thereby potentially starving other zones and preventing them from using RAM. This feat can be accomplished through the proper use of resource controls.

Virtual Memory Tools

A virtual memory cap prevents one zone from using more swap space than it should. Over-utilization of this resource can happen when a workload grows too quickly or when an application "leaks" memory. It can also result from a denial-of-service attack that tries to starve the system of swap space. A system that runs out of swap space has few options for recovering from this state: It will either crash, stop itself gracefully, or forcefully halt processes in an attempt to free up swap space.

The virtual memory cap that can be assigned to each zone is called a "swap cap." That name is a bit misleading, because it really limits the amount of virtual memory—that is, the allocated physical RAM plus swap disk. The following command can be used to limit a zone to 4 GB of virtual memory:

```
GZ# zonecfg -z web
zonecfg:web> add capped-memory
zonecfg:web:capped-memory> set swap=4g
zonecfg:web:capped-memory> end
zonecfg:web> exit
GZ# zoneadm -z web boot
```

After the zone has been rebooted, the processes running in that zone will be able to use only 4 GB of virtual memory, in aggregate. The first attempt by one of those processes to use more virtual memory will fail with the same error code that appears when all virtual memory has been exhausted on a system:

```
web# ls
bash: fork: Not enough space
```

In essence, an application in that zone will behave as if it is running on a non-virtualized system that has exhausted its virtual memory by filling up the swap partitions. Unfortunately, some applications do not handle this condition gracefully. For this and other reasons, caution should be used to avoid this situation in normal operating situations. Choosing a reasonable quantity for this cap is similar to sizing swap space for a non-virtualized system.

Because this kind of cap on virtual memory is an administrative constraint, you can configure zones to have an aggregate cap larger than the amount of VM configured in the system. In other words, you can over-subscribe the swap cap.

This limit can also be changed while the zone is running. For more information, see the section "Live Zone Reconfiguration" later in this chapter.

Virtual Memory Usage Monitoring Tools

You can monitor the amount of virtual memory used by each zone with the `zonestat` command.

```
$ zonestat -r memory 3
Collecting data for first interval...
Interval: 1, Duration: 0:00:03
...
VIRTUAL-MEMORY              SYSTEM MEMORY
vm_default                         33.8G
                       ZONE   USED %USED   CAP  %CAP
                    [total] 6917M 19.9%     -     -
```

```
     [system] 4671M 13.4%     -     -
       global 2099M 6.06%     -     -
        zone1 73.6M 0.21%     -     -
          web 73.4M 0.21% 16.0G 0.44%
```

The amount of virtual memory used by a zone is shown in the "CAP" column. In the same output, the "USED" column shows the amount of RAM used by the zone's processes. Notice how little RAM and virtual memory zones need.

Physical Memory Tools

Other zones, including the global zone, will not be directly affected if one zone has reached its virtual memory cap. Nevertheless, they might be affected if most or all of the RAM is consumed as a side effect. Whether there is a shortage of virtual memory or not, the over-consumption of RAM will cause excessive paging, which might affect all zones on the system.

To protect against over-consumption of RAM by one zone, you can establish a memory cap for physical memory. To add a memory cap to the zone configured earlier, enter the following command:

```
GZ# zonecfg -z web
zonecfg:web> select capped-memory
zonecfg:web:capped-memory> set physical=2g
zonecfg:web:capped-memory> end
zonecfg:web> exit
GZ# zoneadm -z web reboot
```

We used `select` in that example instead of `add` because a capped-memory entry was added in the previous example.

Physical Memory Usage Monitoring Tools

You can monitor the amount of virtual memory used by each zone with the `zonestat` command.

```
$ zonestat -r memory 3
Collecting data for first interval...
Interval: 1, Duration: 0:00:03
PHYSICAL-MEMORY         SYSTEM MEMORY
mem_default                     31.8G
                       ZONE  USED %USED   CAP  %CAP
```

```
   [total] 9345M 28.6%     -      -
  [system] 7648M 23.4%     -      -
   global 1513M 4.64%     -      -
      web 92.6M 0.28% 2048M 4.52%
```

Alternatively, you can modify this physical memory cap while the zone is running. For more information, see the section "3.4.7.2 Live Zone Reconfiguration" later in this chapter.

How should the OS enforce a RAM cap? If a process running in a memory-capped zone attempts to exceed its memory usage limit, the application behavior should be consistent with the application behavior in a non-virtualized system with insufficient RAM. In other words, the OS should begin forcing memory pages out to swap disk. Other than the performance penalty of paging, this action should be transparent to the application. However, performance would become inconsistent if the application was temporarily suspended while memory pages were paged out. Because paging takes time, it should be possible for the application to continue to allocate RAM while the pager tries to catch up. The operation of enforcing the cap must be asynchronous.

An optional feature of Oracle Solaris is the resource capping daemon, a program called `rcapd(1M)`. One of its objectives is to limit the amount of RAM that a zone's processes can use at one time. If a zone's processes begin to use more memory than the physical memory cap that has been specified for that zone, `rcapd` will begin to force memory pages associated with that zone out to swap disk. To maintain consistency with non-capped behavior, the application is allowed to continue running while paging occurs. As a result, a zone's processes may temporarily exceed its physical memory cap.

As with the virtual memory cap, this memory cap does not reserve space for a zone. Because no RAM is wasted waiting for a zone to use it, you can over-subscribe this cap.

Care should be taken when setting this cap. Caps that are set too low will cause excessive paging, which can drag down overall system performance. This outcome is especially likely if other zones are also causing paging or are using the same disk or storage I/O connection.

Also, the program that enforces the RAM cap, `rcapd`, uses some CPU cycles to track the amount of memory used by the various processes. This overhead will become noticeable on larger systems with hundreds of processes or millions of memory pages in use.

If you use the resource capping feature, you should monitor the amount of work that the kernel performs to manage these caps. You can use the `rcapstat` command with its `-z` option to accomplish this goal:

```
GZ# rcapstat -z 5
id zone    nproc vm  rss  cap at avgat pg avgpg
1 ProdWeb1 30    0K  0K   8G 0K 0K    0K 0K
1 ProdWeb1 -     644M 454M 8G 0K 0K   0K 0K
1 ProdWeb1 -     966M 908M 8G 0K 0K   0K 0K
1 ProdWeb1 -     1610M 1362M 8G 0K 0K 0K 0K
1 ProdWeb1 -     2568M 1702M 8G 0K 0K 0K 0K
```

This output shows that the zone never uses more than roughly 2.5 GB of RAM, an amount well under the cap of 8 GB. If any paging activity (values greater than zero) appears in the four columns on the right, their presence indicates that the zone's processes are paging. A small amount of infrequent paging is normal for operating systems that manage virtual memory, but frequent paging, or infrequent paging of large amounts of memory, is a sign of a problem. In those situations, the zone is using more RAM than you expected, either because there is a problem with the workload or because you chose a value that is too low for normal operations.

Another Solaris command that can report information on a per-processor-set basis is `vmstat`. The default output reports basic paging activity, which is collected separately for each processor set. If you run `vmstat` in a zone, the paging activity reported is that of the processors in the zone's processor set.

The `-p` option to `vmstat` reports details of paging activity. When that option is used with `vmstat` in a zone that is running in a processor set, the paging activity information reported is that of the zone's processors.

Another tool for providing visibility into per-zone paging is `zvmstat`, a tool found in the DTrace Toolkit.[2] Its output provides similar information to the `vmstat` command, but the data is aggregated per zone. This tool also displays the amount of paging for each type of page:

- Executable: program binary
- Anonymous: memory allocated by the program
- File: memory pages that represent portions of a file

2. The DTrace Toolkit can be found in `/usr/dtrace/DTT`.

```
GZ# zvmstat 3
ZONE    re   mf    fr     sr  epi epo epf api apo apf fpi fpo fpf
global  43  431  1766  16760  65   0 678   0 378 378   1   4 710
myzone   0    1     0      0   0   0   0   1   0   0   0   0   0
myzone2  0    0     0      0   0   0   0   0   0   0   0   0   0
ZONE    re   mf    fr     sr  epi epo epf api apo apf fpi fpo fpf
global   0    0     4      0   0   0   0   0   0   0   0   4   4
myzone  25  276     0      0   5   0   0  45   0   0  57   0   0
myzone2  0    0     0      0   0   0   0   0   0   0   0   0   0
ZONE    re   mf    fr     sr  epi epo epf api apo apf fpi fpo fpf
global   0    1    12      0   0   0   0   1   0   0   0  12  12
myzone   1   17     0      0   0   0   0  10   0   0   0   0   0
myzone2  0    0     0      0   0   0   0   0   0   0   0   0   0
```

Shared Memory and Locked Memory Tools

Some applications use shared memory so that multiple processes can access one set of data. For example, database software uses shared memory to store table indexes. If that data is paged out to disk, database performance will be severely affected. When applications use shared memory pages via Solaris OSM (Optimized Shared Memory), ISM (Intimate Shared Memory), or DISM (Dynamic ISM), those memory pages are locked into memory and cannot be paged out by the operating system.

In some cases, overly aggressive software might use more shared memory than is appropriate. Also, this functionality might be used to craft a denial-of-service attack. Although a RAM cap will prevent some of these problems, the design of virtual memory systems is based on the assumption that most of a workload's memory pages can be paged out.

Under normal operations, a workload that needs 30 GB of RAM in a 32 GB system may need to lock down only 2 GB. Allowing its processes to lock all 30 GB may reduce the RAM available to other zones to the point that they cannot function normally. To prevent a zone from hoarding so much shared memory that other workloads begin to suffer from deprivation, a resource cap for shared memory can be established. Enter the following command to set a shared memory cap of 2 GB for the zone:

```
GZ# zonecfg -z web
zonecfg:web> set max-shm-memory=2g
zonecfg:web> exit
GZ# zoneadm -z web reboot
```

Just as with the other examples, this resource constraint can be changed dynamically for a running zone, using the live zone reconfiguration feature described later in this chapter.

In addition to shared memory, a program can lock down other memory pages. Oracle Solaris provides this functionality for well-behaved applications so as to improve their performance. Of course, this ability can be abused—just as shared memory can be. To limit the amount of memory that a zone can lock down, enter the following command:

```
GZ# zonecfg -z web
zonecfg:web> select capped-memory
zonecfg:web:capped-memory> set locked=2g
zonecfg:web:capped-memory> end
zonecfg:web> exit
GZ# zoneadm -z web boot
```

This resource constraint can also be changed dynamically for a running zone, using the live zone reconfiguration feature.

Because the `proc_lock_memory` privilege is included in a zone's default privilege set, we strongly encourage the use of this memory cap.

Monitoring Shared Memory and Locked Memory

The `zonestat` commands makes it easy to monitor the use of shared and locked memory:

```
$ zonestat -r shm-memory 3
Collecting data for first interval...
Interval: 1, Duration: 0:00:03
SHM_MEMORY                 SYSTEM LIMIT
system-limit                    -

                       ZONE  USED %USED  CAP  %CAP
                    [total] 9984K 0.00%    -     -
                   [system]     0 0.00%    -     -
                     global 9984K 0.00%    -     -
                        web     0 0.00% 2048M 0.00%
```

To monitor locked memory:

```
$ zonestat -r memory 3
Collecting data for first interval...
Interval: 1, Duration: 0:00:03
...
```

```
LOCKED-MEMORY                    SYSTEM MEMORY
mem_default                           31.8G
                            ZONE    USED  %USED    CAP   %CAP
                         [total]   4635M  14.2%      -      -
                        [system]   4431M  13.6%      -      -
                          global   204M   0.62%      -      -
                             web       0  0.00%  2048M  0.00%
```

3.4.4.3 Miscellaneous Controls

One method that is notorious for over-consuming system resources is a fork bomb. This method does not necessarily consume a great deal of memory or CPU resources, but rather seeks to use up all of the process slots in the kernel's process table. Software bugs can wreak similar havoc. Because non-global zones share the Solaris kernel, processes in one zone can fill the process table and affect other zones. Two related resource controls exist to forestall these situations.

The first cap is named `max-processes`. By default, a zone may create an unlimited number of processes. If you wish to prevent this kind of behavior, you can set this cap to a value that is higher than the number of processes that would normally be used.

A simple zone may have only approximately 25 processes. One or two users, or a simple application, may use only a few more processes. Thus, a cap of 100 processes may be reasonable, as shown in the following example:

```
GZ# zonecfg -z web
zonecfg:web> set max-processes=100
zonecfg:web> exit
GZ# zoneadm -z web reboot
```

In Oracle Solaris, a running process starts with just one thread of execution, also called a lightweight process (LWP). Many programs generate new software threads, becoming multithreaded processes. By default, Solaris systems can run more than 85,000 LWPs simultaneously. By comparison, a zone that has booted but is not yet running any applications may have as few as 75 LWPs. To prevent a zone from creating too many LWPs, a limit can be set on their use. The following command sets a limit of 300 LWPs for the zone:

```
GZ# zonecfg -z web
zonecfg:web> set max-lwps=300
zonecfg:web> exit
GZ# zoneadm -z web reboot
```

This parameter should not be set so low that the limit interferes with normal operation of the application. Instead, you should identify an accurate baseline for the number of processes and LWPs for a given zone, and then set this variable at an appropriate level. These resource constraints can also be changed dynamically for a running zone.

Unless you trust the users of the zone and their applications, we encourage the use of these caps to minimize the impact of fork bombs.

The number of processes and LWPs can be monitored with `zonestat`:

```
$ zonestat -r processes,lwps 3
Collecting data for first interval...
Interval: 1, Duration: 0:00:03
PROCESSES            SYSTEM LIMIT
system-limit              29.2K
                     ZONE  USED %USED   CAP  %CAP
                  [total]   166 0.54%     -     -
                 [system]     0 0.00%     -     -
                   global   147 0.49%     -     -
                      web    19 0.06%   200 9.50%


LWPS                SYSTEM LIMIT
system-limit              2047M
                     ZONE  USED %USED   CAP  %CAP
                  [total]  1022 0.00%     -     -
                 [system]     0 0.00%     -     -
                   global   956 0.00%     -     -
                    zone1    66 0.00%   400 16.5%
```

In this example, the Web zone currently has 19 processes and 66 LWPs. These values will change as processes are created or exit. They should be inspected over a period of time to establish a more reliable baseline and updated when the software, requirements, or workload changes.

To maximize the benefits obtained by applying these controls, you should pair them with a CPU control—for example, FSS or resource pools. Implementation of such a control will slow the rate of process and LWP creation. Sufficient CPU power must be available to global zone processes so that the platform administrator can fix the problem.

3.4.4.4 DTrace and Holistic Observability

DTrace is a feature set of Oracle Solaris that enables you to gather specific or aggregated data that is available to the kernel. Short DTrace commands or scripts specify the individual pieces of data or aggregations of data that you wish to see.

DTrace collects only the requested data, and then presents it to you. This parsimonious behavior minimizes the amount of CPU time that the kernel spends gathering the data you want. The design of DTrace makes it inherently safe to use: It is impossible to create an infinite loop in DTrace, and it is impossible to dereference an invalid pointer. For these and other reasons, it is safe to use DTrace on production systems. In contrast, you should not use the typical kernel debugger on live kernels.

OSV implementations include just one OS kernel, which is shared by all of the VEs. This facet of the OSV model enables you to use OS tools such as DTrace to look at all of the VEs as entities, or to peer into each VE and view its constituent parts.

Earlier, we saw how we could use DTrace to examine aggregate memory usage, with the `zvmstat` script. You can also use DTrace to gather and report data for a single zone. For example, if the output of the `vmstat` command revealed an unusually high system call rate, you could use these DTrace commands to determine which zone is causing these calls, which system call is being made the most often, and which program is issuing these calls.

```
GZ# dtrace -n 'syscall:::entry { @num[zonename] = count(); }'
dtrace: description 'syscall:::entry' matched 234 probes
^C
appzone 301
global 11900
webzone 91002
GZ# dtrace -n 'syscall:::entry/zonename=="webzone"/ \
{ @num[probefunc] = count(); }'
dtrace: description 'syscall:::entry' matched 234 probes
^C
exece 1
fork1 1
...
fstat6 9181
getdents64 9391
lstat64 92482
GZ# dtrace -n 'syscall::lstat64:entry/zonename=="webzone"/ \
{ @num[execname] = count(); }'
dtrace: description 'syscall::lstat64:entry' matched 1 probe
^C
find 107277
GZ# dtrace -n 'syscall::lstat64:entry/zonename=="webzone" && \
execname=="find"/ { @num[uid] = count(); }'
dtrace: description 'syscall::lstat64:entry' matched 1 probe
^C
1012 16439
```

Based on the preceding output, we know that the user with UID 1012 was running the find program in zone webzone, which was causing most of those system calls.

When used in combination, DTrace and Solaris Zones can solve problems that are otherwise difficult or impossible to solve. For example, when troubleshooting a three-tier architecture, you might want to create a chronological log of events on the three different systems. Each system has its own clock, making this feat impossible to accomplish. To gather the needed data, you could re-create the three tiers as three zones on the same system. Because the three zones would then share the kernel's clock, a DTrace script could collect data on the processes in the three different tiers, using a single time reference.

3.4.4.5 Resource Management Summary

Oracle Solaris offers an extensive set of resource management controls and tools to monitor resource consumption, enabling you to manage workload performance in high-density consolidated environments.

3.4.5 Networking

Almost all zones need access to a network to be useful. A zone can have network access via one or more of the computer's physical network ports (NICs). Usually, multiple zones share that access by using virtual NICs (VNICs)—a new feature in Solaris 11.

By default, a non-global zone is given exclusive access to networking, an approach called "exclusive IP." Exclusive IP not only maximizes network isolation between zones, but also limits the control that the global zone can exert over a zone's networking. Further, the default configuration is one VNIC per zone, which enables many zones to share a physical NIC, while still controlling their own network stack. With this configuration, after a zone boots, it can implement its own network configuration, including IP address, default router, and more.

Instead of accepting this default, you can configure a zone to have exclusive access to one or more physical NICs, or shared access to one or more NICs or VNICs. An administrator in the global zone controls the network configuration for a zone that uses the "shared IP" model.

3.4.5.1 Introduction to Virtual Networks

In 2011, Solaris introduced an extensive set of virtual networking features, including VNICs and IPoIB datalinks, virtual switches (vSwitches), and the ability to create virtual routers. These features may be combined in arbitrary architectures,

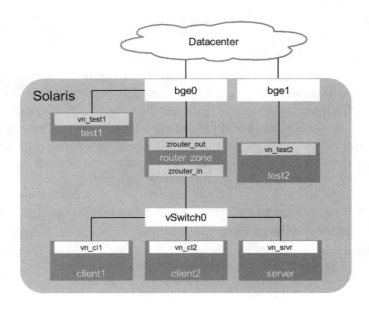

Figure 3.5   A Solaris System with a Virtual Network

such as the one shown in Figure 3.5. (A complete description of the virtual net-working features can be found in the Oracle Solaris documentation.)

Solaris Zones were modified to use these features. An "automatic network" (anet) resource specifies properties for a VNIC or IPoIB data link that will be created automatically by Solaris when the zone boots; this link is also automatically destroyed when the zone stops. The anet resource includes a comprehensive set of properties that give you the ability to configure the following items:

- A name for the VNIC; net0 is the default
- A physical NIC; by default, Solaris chooses an appropriate one at boot time
- A list of IP addresses that the zone can use; limited to shared-IP zones
- A default router
- Whether MAC address spoofing or IP address spoofing should be prevented
- The method that Solaris should use to choose a MAC address for this link
- A VLAN address
- Numerous quality of service (QoS, or COS) properties, including a cap on bandwidth that this link can consume

- MTU size
- Properties to control software-defined networking
- InfiniBand properties

By using these properties, a privileged user in the global zone can control the amount of freedom that a zone has to choose its network configuration.

3.4.5.2 Exclusive-IP Zones

Because exclusive-IP zones manage their own networking configuration, few parameters are needed to configure them. Specifically, the zone configures the IP parameters. For many situations, there is no need to specify networking properties within zonecfg. The following list shows a subset of the default settings:

```
linkname: net0
lower-link: auto
defrouter not specified
link-protection: mac-nospoof
mac-address: random
auto-mac-address: 2:8:20:bd:af:42
```

A default configuration includes one VNIC, named net0, which will be connected to an appropriate global zone NIC when the zone boots. The zone must configure its own IP address and default router, or retrieve that information from a DHCP server. A random MAC address was chosen for this zone by Solaris, and that address will be used each time the zone boots.

You can manage networking in an exclusive-IP zone with the same methods and commands as you would use in a non-virtualized system. To perform those steps, you must first log in to the zone as a privileged user.

The following example adds a second VNIC that uses a specific NIC.

```
GZ# zonecfg -z zone1
zonecfg:zone1> add anet
zonecfg:zone1:anet> set linkname=net1
zonecfg:zone1:anet> set lower-link=net3
zonecfg:zone1:anet> set maxbw=100m
zonecfg:zone1:anet> info
anet 1:
        linkname: net1
        lower-link: e1000g0
        defrouter not specified
```

```
      maxbw: 100m
      allowed-dhcp-cids not specified
      link-protection: mac-nospoof
      mac-address: auto
      ...
zonecfg:zone1:anet> end
zonecfg:zone1> exit
```

As you might expect, you can monitor network usage of individual NICs with the `zonestat` command.

```
GZ$ zonestat -r network -n net3 3
Collecting data for first interval...
Interval: 1, Duration: 0:00:03
NETWORK-DEVICE                SPEED        STATE       TYPE
net3                          1000mbps       up        phys
            ZONE TOBYTE  MAXBW %MAXBW PRBYTE %PRBYTE POBYTE %POBYTE
         [total]  44.6K      -      - 28.4K   0.00%  13.5K   0.00%
           zone1  42.5K   100m   0.3% 28.4K   0.00%  13.5K   0.00%
          global   1168      -      -     0   0.00%      0   0.00%
```

The non-obvious columns in this output are described here:

- TOBYTE: the number of bytes sent or received by that zone
- PRBYTE: the number of bytes received that used physical bandwidth
- %PRBYTE: PRBYTE, as a percentage of the available bandwidth
- POBYTE: the number of bytes sent that used physical bandwidth
- %POBYTE: POBYTE, as a percentage of the available bandwidth

3.4.5.3 Shared-IP Zones

Many situations call for network configuration within a zone. Centralized network management is appropriate for other zones, such as a group of horizontally scaled web servers with identical configurations. Centralized management calls for shared-IP zones.

All network controls, including routing, for shared-IP zones are managed from the global zone. Exclusive-IP zones manage their own networking configuration, including the assignment of IP addresses, routing table management, and bringing their network interfaces up and down.

Configuring network access for a shared-IP zone begins with removal of the anet resource, because such resources are not allowed in a shared-IP zone:

```
GZ# zonecfg -z myzone
zonecfg:myzone> remove anet 0
zonecfg:myzone> set ip-type=shared
zonecfg:myzone> add net
zonecfg:myzone:net> set physical=e1000g0
zonecfg:myzone:net> set address=192.168.4.4
zonecfg:myzone:net> set defrouter=192.168.1.1
zonecfg:myzone:net> end
zonecfg:myzone> exit
```

You can use the same syntax to add access to additional NICs.

3.4.5.4 Highly Available Networking

Oracle Solaris 11 offers several methods to combine multiple network ports so as to achieve continued network access in the face of port failure (high availability), increased network bandwidth, or both. This section discusses the newest option, Data Link Multipathing (DLMP). DLMP is simpler than IP Multipathing (IPMP), and offers more flexibility than trunking.

DLMP combines two or more physical NICs into one "aggregation." VNICs can be created on top of the aggregation. Each VNIC uses one NIC, but if a failure occurs, any VNIC assigned to it is automatically assigned to a different NIC.

The following commands create a DLMP aggregation and modify a zone so that its network port, net0, uses the aggregation instead of using a NIC that is chosen when the zone boots:

```
GZ# dladm create-aggr -m dlmp -l net0 -l net1 -l net2 aggr0
GZ# zonecfg -z web01
zonecfg:web01> select anet 0
zonecfg:web01:anet> set lower-link=aggr0
zonecfg:web01:anet> end
zonecfg:web01> exit
```

3.4.5.5 Networking Summary

The default network type (exclusive IP) is appropriate unless network management of multiple zones should be centralized in the global zone. The addition of virtual network features to Solaris 11 greatly expands the most desirable network configurations.

3.4.6 Direct Device Access

The security boundary around a zone prevents direct access to devices, because many types of direct device access allow one zone to affect other zones. One means of enforcing these boundaries is to establish a minimal list of device entries available to the zone. By default, a zone has very few entries in its /dev directory, and it does not have a /devices directory at all. The entries in /dev are limited to pseudo-devices that are considered safe and necessary, such as /dev/null.

Sometimes, however, you might want to give a zone direct access to a device. For example, you might want to test some software in a zone in a lab environment, but the test might require creating and destroying a UFS file system from within the zone. To do this, the zone needs device entries for the disk device that will contain the file system. You can accomplish this task with the add device subcommand, as shown in the following example:

```
GZ# zonecfg -z zone1
zonecfg:zone1> add device
zonecfg:zone1:device> set match=/dev/rdsk/c1t0d0s6
zonecfg:zone1:device> end
zonecfg:zone1> add device
zonecfg:zone1:device> set match=/dev/dsk/c1t0d0s6
zonecfg:zone1> end
GZ# zlogin zone1
zone1# newfs /dev/rdsk/c1t0d0s6
zone1# mount /dev/dsk/c1t0d0s6 /opt/local
```

The direct device method gives a zone's privileged users direct control over a file system's devices, thereby facilitating direct management of the file system. At the same time, these users gain greater control over the system's components, which may enable them to affect other zones. For example, just as the root user in a non-virtualized system can use device access to panic a UNIX system, so assigning direct device access to a zone may give users the ability to panic the system, stopping all of the zones. Also, enabling two zones to access one device may cause data corruption, and may have the unintended effect of creating a covert communication channel. Be very cautious when adding devices to a zone.

Because of the potentially negative implications of direct device access, you should use a different method, when possible, to achieve a similar goal. For example, instead of implementing direct access to storage devices, you might provide access to a ZFS pool with the zpool or rootzpool storage resources.

Finally, many third-party devices require device drivers that are not delivered with Solaris. The installation of these drivers must be performed in the global zone.

3.4.7 Virtualization Management Features

Life-cycle management of zones involves very few commands. You have already seen the two commands used to create, boot, and halt a zone. One of them, `zoneadm`, is also used to move a zone's root directory within the same system, and to move the zone to a different system.

In addition to the `zoneadm` subcommands discussed earlier, other features provide additional flexibility and abilities when working with zones. Some of these features are discussed in this section. The first, delegated administration, gives otherwise unprivileged users the ability to manage one or more zones. The second, live zone reconfiguration, enables privileged users to modify a zone while it runs. Following that, we describe other features that can be used to simplify and accelerate the provisioning of zones.

3.4.7.1 Delegated Administration

Many situations call for one or more of a system's zones to be managed by someone who does not manage the system as a whole. For these situations, Solaris offers the ability to delegate administration of those zones to an otherwise unprivileged Solaris user of the global zone. That user becomes a "zone administrator," who is able to interact with a zone directly from the global zone. There are no limits on the quantity of zones that one user can manage, and no limit on the number of users who can manage a zone.

Several distinct types of operations can be delegated to a zone administrator (ZA). These responsibilities can be combined so that all of the operations are delegated to the ZA.

The simplest type of delegation enables a ZA to log into the zone by using the `zlogin(1)` command. This command creates a shell process running in the zone as the root user, or as the zone's user when specified with the `-l` option.

A privileged global zone user can configure this delegation for the ZA with `zonecfg`:

```
GZ# zonecfg -z myzone
zonecfg:myzone> add admin
zonecfg: myzone:admin> set user=jeff
zonecfg: myzone:admin> set auths=login
zonecfg: myzone:admin> end
zonecfg: myzone > exit
```

The ZA can then use `zlogin`:

```
jeff$ pfexec zlogin -l zoneuser myzone
```

Another authorization option is "manage," which enables the ZA to use the management features of the `zoneadm(1M)` command, including booting and halting the zone, and many others.

```
GZ# zonecfg -z myzone
zonecfg:myzone> add admin
zonecfg: myzone:admin> set user=jeff
zonecfg: myzone:admin> set auths=manage
zonecfg: myzone:admin> end
zonecfg: myzone > exit
```

The ZA can then use `zoneadm`:

```
jeff$ pfexec zoneadm -z myzone reboot
```

Table 3.7 lists all of the possible authorizations and the abilities that they give to a ZA:

Table 3.7   Zone-Related Authorizations

Authorization	Ability	Command
login	Access the zone directly from the global zone.	`zlogin`
manage	Perform operations on a zone, such as boot, halt, and move; also, modify an immutable zone.	`zoneadm`
config	Configure a new zone, or modify the persistent configuration of an existing zone.	`zonecfg`
liveconfig	Modify the nonpersistent configuration of a running zone.	`zonecfg`
migrate	Use live migration to move a kernel zone to a different global zone.	`zoneadm`
clonefrom	Use the zone as a source for cloning. This also requires the "manage" authorization for the new zone.	`zoneadm`

3.4.7.2 Live Zone Reconfiguration

One advantage of virtual environments relative to physical systems is the ease of modifying the configuration. Entering commands to change the configuration of a virtual network is much easier than recabling a physical network. Not only does this ability reduce complexity, but it also opens up the possibility of modifying a configuration while the workload runs.

Solaris offers you the ability to make a temporary configuration change to a running zone, or to make a persistent change that will take effect only after the zone boots again. If you want the change to take effect immediately and then also during the next boot, you must perform both steps. With this feature, called live zone reconfiguration, you can modify many of the characteristics while the zone's workload runs.

The next example demonstrates the use of live configuration:

```
GZ# zlogin myzone dladm
LINK        CLASS   MTU      STATE   OVER
net0        vnic    1500     up      ?
GZ# zonecfg -rz myzone
zonecfg:myzone> add anet
zonecfg:myzone:anet> set linkname=net9
zonecfg:myzone:anet> end
zonecfg:myzone> commit
zone 'myzone': Checking: Adding anet linkname=net9
zone 'myzone': Applying the changes
zonecfg:myzone> exit
GZ# zlogin myzone dladm
LINK        CLASS   MTU      STATE   OVER
net0        vnic    1500     up      ?
net9        vnic    1500     up      ?
```

To maintain a proper security boundary, some zone properties, such as `limit-priv`, cannot be changed using live reconfiguration. Table 3.8 lists the properties and resource types that may be changed while the zone runs. (A dash indicates a feature that is never allowed with that brand. The letter "P" indicates a feature that is only partially supported.) An updated list is maintained in the per-brand man **pages** `solaris(5)`, `solaris-kz(5)`, `solaris10(5)`, and `labeled(5)`.

Table 3.8　Dynamic Resource Types and Properties

	solaris	solaris-kz	solaris10
anet	P	P	P
anet:defrouter	N	N	N
anet:*allowed-address	N	N	N
cpu-shares	Y	N	Y
capped-memory	Y	N	Y
dedicated-cpu	Y	N	Y
Device	Y	Y	Y
file-mac-profile	N	—	N
Fs	Y	—	Y

(continued)

Table 3.8 Dynamic Resource Types and Properties (continued)

	solaris	solaris-kz	solaris10
`fs-allowed`	N	—	N
`Hostid`	N	N	N
`Net`	P	P	P
`  net:defrouter`	N	N	N
`  net:*allowed-address`	N	N	N
`Pool`	Y	N	Y
`scheduling-class`	Y	N	Y
`Rctls`	Y	N	Y
`Tenant`	N	N	N
`virtual-cpu`	—	N	—
`Zpool`	N	—	N

3.4.7.3 Deploying Zones with Unified Archives

Solaris 11 introduced Unified Archives to achieve highly flexible and scalable platform recovery and cloning. Recovery archives are intended to re-deploy a computer with the same Solaris configuration, including the same host name, IP addresses, and more. Clone archives are intended for deployment of many similar workloads, and do not include per-system configuration information.

An archive can consist of a global zone, with or without some or all of its zones, or you can create an archive of one or more zones without a global zone. In all of those cases, from an archive you can deploy a zone as a new zone, a new global zone, or a new kernel zone. Further, you can deploy a global zone as a non-global zone. Archives may be deployed with Solaris Automated Installer, with the `zoneadm` command, or as Unified Archives bootable media.

As an example, you might create a clone archive that includes three zones: a standard web server zone, an application server zone, and a database zone. If you store this archive on a central file server, you can then use provisioning tools to deploy the desired type of environment on an as-needed basis, then provide more specific, per-instance configuration information.

Although you can create an archive of a zone from within the zone itself, the archive will be more useful if you create the archive from the global zone. An archive of a zone created from its global zone will include configuration information for the zone.

To illustrate this approach, we will add the use of Unified Archives to an earlier example of zone creation. The first command creates an archive that includes all zones on the system. The other commands deploy one zone from that archive.

```
goldGZ# archiveadm create /server1/prod.uar
voyGZ# zonecfg -z web20 create -a /server1/prod.uar -z web
voyGZ# zoneadm -z web20 install -c /opt/zones/web_profile.xml \
-a /server1/prod.uar -z web
```

3.4.7.4 Migrating Zones

Zones offer the ability to migrate a zone from one instance of Oracle Solaris to another. In this context, an instance can be a computer running a copy of Solaris, or it can be a VE running Solaris in a Dynamic Domain, in an Oracle VM Logical Domain, or on another hypervisor.

The types of migration permitted depend on the type of zone, and on the type of storage that is used for the zone. All types of zones may be migrated when they are not running. Doing so requires a service outage, but is the most flexible method. In addition, kernel zones may be migrated while they run, or they may be suspended briefly or indefinitely, and then restarted in a different Solaris instance. The rest of this section describes "cold" migration, which is the migration of a zone that has been stopped. A later section on kernel zones describes "warm" and "live" migration.

Two `zoneadm` subcommands are used to implement "cold" migration. The `detach` subcommand prepares a zone for migration and removes it from the list of zones that can be booted on the current system. The contents of the zone, underneath its `zonepath`, can then be transferred to the destination system using common file transfer methods, if necessary.

Migrating a zone is usually a straightforward process. The following example assumes that the zone was installed into shared storage by configuring a `rootzpool`:

```
hostA-GZ# zoneadm -z twilight shutdown
hostA-GZ# zonecfg -z twilight export -f /net/zones/twilight.cfg
hostA-GZ# zoneadm -z twilight detach
hostB-GZ# zonecfg -z twilight -f /net/zones/twilight.cfg
hostB-GZ# zoneadm -z twilight attach
hostB-GZ# zoneadm -z twilight boot
```

The destination system must be configured to have the same update of Oracle Solaris, or a newer update, than the original system. If the destination is newer, you should use the `-u` option to the `attach` subcommand.

You can also use the -u option when you are updating a system that includes zones to minimize the downtime of certain zones. The first step is to detach all of the zones; this step is followed by updating the system. When those steps are complete, certain zones may be quickly reattached to the system with the `attach` -u subcommand to `zoneadm`, followed by attachment of the remaining zones.

If the zone's root directory resides on storage space that is not shared with the destination system, the zone's contents must be archived with ZFS or by creating a Unified Archive. The archive must then be moved to the destination system, where `zoneadm` can be used to install it without unpackaging the archive. Obviously, shared storage for the zone or the data of its workload smooths zone migration considerably.

3.5 Oracle Solaris Kernel Zones

Solaris Kernel Zones are a new feature of Solaris 11, first introduced in Solaris 11.2. Kernel zones offer increased isolation between the zone and the global zone, and between kernel zones and other non-global zones.

This section discusses the differences between kernel zones and native zones that have been previously mentioned. They include many additional features as well as some brand-specific limitations. Because kernel zones may have their own zones, it is occasionally necessary to differentiate between the computer's global zone and the kernel zone's global zone. In such situations, we use the term "system global zone" for the former and "kernel global zone" for the latter.

The primary reasons to use a kernel zone instead of a native zone include package independence, greater software isolation, greater security isolation, independent allocations of RAM and swap disk space, and reduced observability (e.g.. the need to use `zlogin myzone ps` instead of `ps`). Reduced observability, for example, can be used to prevent users in the global zone from learning anything about the workload.

Kernel zones represent a hybrid of OSV and virtual machines. On the one hand, the CLI uses the same commands, and both require a running global zone. On the other hand, the border between a system global zone and its kernel zones is much clearer. The border also enables live migration, described later in this section.

3.5.1 Support

Kernel zones rely on hardware support for both SPARC and x86 systems. Most modern computers that use one of those CPU types provide the necessary support, including laptop computers. The `virtinfo(1M)` command displays information about the types of zones supported on that computer.

```
GZ# virtinfo
NAME    CLASS
non-global-zone supported
kernel-zone    supported
```

3.5.2 Creation and Basic Properties

Creating a simple kernel zone is a very simple process, as the few necessary properties have reasonable default settings. Here, we provide a very simple example of kernel zone configuration. The command to install a kernel zone is no different from that used to install a native zone. A more detailed example is shown in Code Sample 3.1 (found at the end of this chapter).

```
GZ# zonecfg -z potter create -t SYSsolaris-kz
```

Instead of configuring the `zonepath` property, you can specify storage that will be used for the kernel zone's root pool. If you do not explicitly specify this storage, Solaris automatically creates a ZFS volume named `rpool/VARSHARE/zones/<zonename>/disk0`. On that storage, Solaris creates a ZFS pool to be used as the zone's root pool. Within the zone, its root pool has one disk.

The default is convenient for simple situations, but prevents migration to a different Solaris instance unless the zone is stopped first. Also, there is no redundancy visible to the zone. Each of these limitations can be addressed.

To enable warm or live migration, the kernel zone must be configured to use shared, external storage for its root pool. This storage appears to the kernel zone as one or more virtual disks.

Several types of shared storage may be used for kernel zones, including NFS shares and SAN or iSCSI LUNs. If you provide one storage object, Solaris will use it for the root pool. If you configure two devices, Solaris will mirror them when it creates the root pool. Examples of storage objects are listed in `suri(5)`.

The default configuration for a kernel zone includes 4 GB of RAM. This memory is exclusively reserved for that kernel zone when the zone boots. These memory pages cannot be paged out by the system global zone—a constraint that improves the consistency of performance from one day to the next, but limits the number of kernel zones that can run simultaneously. The property used to configure the amount of dedicated RAM is `capped-memory:physical`.

A kernel zone manages its use of that area of RAM. Just like any other operating system that uses virtual memory, a kernel zone uses some storage as swap space. Just like any Solaris 11 system, the default swap device is part of the root pool. Although modern systems are usually configured to avoid any paging at all, you should consider the implications of paging on the I/O performance of other workloads in the system. If the processes in one kernel zone attempt to use more memory than the memory configured for that zone, it will begin paging to its device(s). To the system global zone, this operation is simply I/O and, therefore, consumes I/O bandwidth. The I/O transactions may be protected by encrypting I/O within the kernel zone, if desired.

3.5.3 Packaging

Solaris's package configuration for the kernel zone is completely independent of the package configuration for the system global zone. Thus, you can choose the same publisher as the global zone, or a different one. Kernel zones do not use proxies like native zones. Package management procedures are even more similar to those used with stand-alone systems than the procedures used with native zones are.

Several options exist to install a kernel zone that is a different Solaris version than the global zone. You can specify a custom manifest, use Solaris media, or use a Unified Archive.

3.5.4 Security

The security boundary around a native zone is configurable, meaning you can tailor access from the native zone to its global zone resources. In contrast, the security boundary around a kernel zone is static. The only configurable interactions between a kernel zone and its global zone are access to CPU time, RAM, and I/O.

A global zone cannot set the `file-mac-profile` property for one of its kernel zones, but you can make a kernel zone immutable. Instead of using the system's global zone to configure this property, you can access the kernel zone's own global zone and then use `zonecfg` from there. Of course, to ensure the intended level of security, this limitation cannot be reverted from within the kernel global zone. A specific option permits a sufficiently privileged user in the system global zone to modify an immutable kernel zone. For more details, see the section "3.4.3.3 Read-Only Zones" and Code Sample 3.2 at the end of this chapter.

3.5.5 Resource Controls

Although the resource consumption of kernel zones can be limited (in the same way that constraints can be placed on the resource consumption of native zones), there is less need for granular controls on kernel zones. For example, the number of processes that a kernel zone's users have created has no impact on any users of the global zone, or users of any other zones, for that matter. Consequently, you cannot set the properties `max-processes` or `max-lwps` for a kernel zone. If a kernel zone's administrator desires to cap the number of processes that a user of that zone can create, the administrator must use the standard Solaris methods to cap process use. The `solaris-kz(5)` man page provides a complete list of the properties that do not have meaning for a kernel zone.

By default, a kernel zone's processes share the system global zone's CPUs, and can run up to four of those processes at a time if sufficient CPU resources are available in the global zone. In other words, that zone is configured with four virtual CPUs. If you like, you can change the number of virtual CPUs configured for a kernel zone. Of course, the amount of work accomplished by a kernel zone's processes will still be limited by the amount of CPU time that the system global zone schedules for the kernel zone.

In addition, kernel zones can be configured to use the CPU resource controls described in Section 3.4.4. Both of these controls give a zone exclusive access to physical CPU resources, but the `dedicated-cpu` feature is easier to use.

Unlike for other types of zones, Solaris reserves a section of RAM for a kernel zone. A property stores the amount of RAM to be configured when the kernel zone boots—namely, the "physical" property of the capped-memory resource. The default value for this property is 2 GB, although that value is usually too small. Like most properties, you can set the "physical" property when you originally create the zone, or you can modify it later. For a kernel zone, this property cannot be modified with the live zone reconfiguration method.

From the perspective of the global zone, all of a kernel zone's RAM is locked and cannot be paged. A kernel zone performs its own paging, and manages its own virtual address space, just as any UNIX-type system manages its virtual memory. This includes the ability of a kernel zone to use swap space in its root pool. The default size of swap storage is 1 GB, but this size can be changed using the same method as is employed on a stand-alone Solaris system—that is, by modifying the size of the ZFS swap volume in the root pool.

3.5.6 File Systems and Devices

Because of the additional characteristics that keep a kernel zone isolated from the system global zone, file systems that are available in the global zone cannot be configured into a kernel zone. Instead, you can specify storage devices and use them to create file systems or use them as raw devices. Here is an example.

```
GZ# zonecfg -z dbzone
zonecfg:dbzone> add device
zonecfg:dbzone:device> set storage=nfs://dev:staff@fs1/export/dev/testdb
zonecfg:dbzone:device> end
zonecfg:dbzone> exit
```

Local devices may also be added, with the following syntax:

```
zonecfg:dbzone:device> set match=/dev/rdsk/c10t0d0
```

Only storage devices may be configured.

3.5.7 Networking

Kernel zones benefit from the rich set of networking features available to native zones, with a few exceptions. To maintain the level of isolation appropriate for kernel zones, these zones must use the exclusive-IP networking model.

As with other zones, a default configuration for kernel zones includes one anet—a VNIC that uses a physical NIC.

If you configure additional network devices into a zone, you should label them with id values in zonecfg. Doing so simplifies some configuration tasks, especially if you plan to migrate the zone. The id property of the default network device in a kernel zone is automatically configured to have a value of zero.

3.5.8 Management

Managing a kernel zone is very similar to managing a native zone, albeit with a few differences. Those differences are highlighted in the following subsections.

3.5.8.1 Problem Diagnosis

Earlier in this chapter, we described the ability to diagnose software issues inside a native zone, while working in the global zone, using DTrace and other tools.

Because of the additional isolation of a kernel zone, these tools cannot "see" inside a kernel zone.

To remedy this shortcoming, Solaris has the ability to generate a core dump of a kernel zone. To maximize self-consistency of the core image, the zone is paused while the image is saved. If this behavior is not appropriate for the situation, you can specify an option that permits the zone to continue running. The `coreadm(1M)` command controls the default storage location, but you can change that location when you first save the core. Here is an example:

```
GZ# zoneadm -z hungzone savecore
```

The `mdb(1)` command analyzes core images.

3.5.8.2 Suspend, Resume, and Deploy

Because a kernel zone owns a complete virtual memory map, processing can be temporarily suspended, and the entire memory image can be copied to storage. Later, this image can be copied back into RAM and processing can continue at the next instruction. This technique opens up new possibilities for managing zones.

The copy of memory created in this way contains the state of any workloads running in the zone. When you resume processing, it continues at the next machine instruction, working with the same data. Resuming a suspended image can take just a few seconds, depending on the amount of memory that had been allocated by processes running in the zone.

The suspend feature enables you to perform the following tasks:

- Temporarily pause a zone and its workload to free up RAM for some other use
- Reduce the amount of time needed to bring a workload to a state where it can operate efficiently (e.g., a static data warehouse)
- Start several kernel zones and suspend many or all of them, so that one or more of them can be resumed quickly, perhaps improving business agility

A storage location is required that will hold the memory image when processing is suspended. This location is stored in the zone property `suspend:path` or `suspend:storage`. The former is a full path name. The latter is a storage object; its syntax is described in `suri(5)`.

3.5.8.3 Migration

Another new management option possible for kernel zones is the ability to move to a different computer without stopping its workload. This ability is very useful when the goal is to balance the load of multiple systems, or to perform hardware maintenance on the computer, or maintenance operations on the system global zone.

Solaris 11 supports two slightly different types of migration: warm and live. To the users of the workload, the primary difference between these two types is the period of time during which processing does not occur. For a live migration, that time is a fraction of a second, making this method appropriate for active workloads with no convenient time for interruption. By comparison, the interruption in processing is much longer with warm migration. This technique can be used when an interruption measured in minutes is preferable to the service outage caused by rebooting the zone on the destination system, but there is insufficient bandwidth to support live migration.

Although the difference to users is simply the duration of time that the workload is paused, the requirements and the steps to perform these two types of migration are very different.

Warm migration requires a suspend resource (described in the previous section). Further, that resource must be made accessible to the destination system before the zone resumes operation. Internal storage is not appropriate for kernel zones that may be migrated.

In contrast, live migration requires the zone's root pool to exist on shared storage, available to both the original and destination global zones. Live migration also requires specific Solaris services to be running on the destination host.

Two commands are required to perform a warm migration: suspending the zone and resuming it on the other computer. Live migration does not store the zone's image as warm migration does, so it requires only one command. With live migration, the memory image is simply copied to the other computer, and then I/O and execution are transferred.

For either warm or live migration, the original and destination systems must be sufficiently similar to support these features. Incompatibilities of a destination system might potentially include older CPUs that are missing features available on the original system, a different amount of CPUs or RAM configured for the kernel zone, or missing devices.

One of the first steps performed automatically during a live migration is verification that the destination system is sufficiently compatible. Also, the command to migrate a zone has an option that tests compatibility, but does not perform the migration. The following example shows the simplicity of live zone migration:

```
carditos# zoneadm -z monarch migrate canada
```

Of course, live migration requires cooperation between the two Solaris systems. The receiving end of the live migration must be running services that authenticate the migration and receive the image, among other tasks. Those services must be enabled once, with the following command:

```
svcadm enable -s svc:/system/rad:remote svc:/network/kz-migr:stream
```

By default, live migrations of kernel zones are encrypted to prevent an outsider from capturing the image while in flight.

The incompatibilities mentioned as obstacles to live migration will also prevent successful warm migration. A failure to boot after warm migration can be followed by an attempt on another system, including the original one. Performing a warm migration requires a few commands; pay careful attention to the prompts shown here:

```
GZ1# zonecfg -z zone1 export -f /net/zonecfgs/zone1.cfg
GZ2# zonecfg -z zone1 -f /net/zonecfgs/zone1.cfg
GZ1# zoneadm -z zone1 suspend
GZ2# zoneadm -z zone1 boot
```

Both live and warm migration require that appropriate I/O resources are available on the target host. In some situations, the name of a device (e.g., a `lower-link` property for an anet resource) will be different. You can compensate for that discrepancy by configuring a zone of the same name on the remote host and making appropriate modifications before performing the migration.

3.6 Solaris 10 Zones

Thousands of SPARC systems are currently running the Solaris 10 operating system. In most cases, the desire to take advantage of innovations in Oracle Solaris 11 can be fulfilled by migrating the workload to a native zone on a Solaris 11 system. This process is usually straightforward because of the binary compatibility from one version of Solaris to the next, backed by the Oracle Solaris Binary Application Guarantee. People often place these workloads into native zones.

In other situations, such migration might prove difficult or its results uncertain. Perhaps the workload includes shell scripts that work correctly on Solaris 10 but not on Solaris 11. Perhaps your organization tuned the workload for Solaris, but retuning for Solaris 11 would require recompiling the software and the source code is no longer available. Perhaps redeployment in a Solaris 11 environment would require recertification, which is impractical for hundreds of computers that will be replaced within the next year anyway. For any of these or other reasons, you might strongly prefer to maintain a Solaris 10 environment for the workload. This raises a key question: Are other options available?

The Solaris 10 Zones feature set replicates a Solaris 10 software environment within a zone on a Solaris 11 system. All of the software from the original system runs on the Solaris 11 system without translation or emulation of binary instructions; the only translations required involve the system calls.

The original Solaris 10 environment can be a Solaris 10 system without zones, or a Solaris 10 native zone. This process works best with the last update: Solaris 10 1/13. Earlier updates may require patches for all features to work correctly. For example, the Solaris 10 package and patch tools require patches to work correctly in Solaris 10 Zones. The Solaris 11 global zone needs the package named `brand-solaris10`.

Two tools are available that can simplify the process of migration. The first tool, `zonep2vchk(1M)`, verifies that the configuration of a Solaris 10 system is suitable for conversion to a Solaris 10 Zone. Among other things, this tool attempts to find any binaries that would not work correctly in a Solaris 10 Zone. With an option, this tool will also output a suitable zone configuration file. You can find `zonep2vchk` in a Solaris 11 system, and copy it to the Solaris 10 systems that you want to examine.

In addition, a P2V tool is included that uses an archive of the file system of the original computer to populate the file system of the new zone. The entire process typically takes 30–60 minutes to complete and can be automated. After the original system is archived with the `flarcreate`, `tar`, `cpio`, or `pax` command, only four commands are needed to create, boot, and log in to the zone. The following example assumes that the Solaris 10 system is named `sol10` and that the Solaris 10 and Solaris 11 systems use `/net/server` as mount points for a shared NFS file system:

```
Sol10# flarcreate -L pax -S -n mys10 /net/server/balrog.flar
...
Archive creation complete.
```

Note that Solaris 10 sparse-root zones must be placed in the ready state before archive creation, so as to mount file systems from the global zone.

Before booting the Solaris 10 Zone, the original Solaris 10 system should be halted because it contains the same configuration information, including the same IP address.

```
GZ# zonecfg -z balrog
zonecfg:balrog> create -t SYSsolaris10
zonecfg:balrog> exit
GZ# zoneadm -z balrog install -p -a /net/server/balrog.flar
Source: /net/server/balrog.flar
...
Result: Installation completed successfully.
GZ# zoneadm -z balrog boot
GZ# zlogin -C balrog
[Connected to zone 'balrog' console]

[NOTICE: Zone booting up]

SunOS Release 5.10 Version Generic_Virtual 64-bit
Copyright (c) 1983, 2010, Oracle and/or its affiliates. All rights reserved.
Hostname: balrog
balrog console login:
```

Multiple Solaris 10 Zones can be hosted on the same system. When the migration is complete, the new system will have the structure shown in Figure 3.6.

After migration, you can use the same methods to manage the Solaris 10 Zone as you used before migration. Specifically, the Solaris 10 package and patch tools

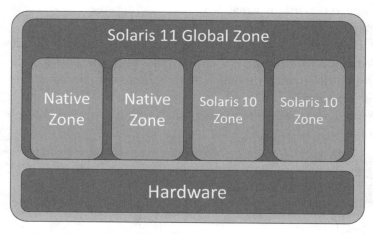

Figure 3.6 A Solaris System with Solaris 10 Zones

are still available, and they continue to be the preferred method for managing Solaris packages.

Solaris 10 Zones can also take advantage of other Solaris 11 innovations. For example, they can be placed on a ZFS file system and gain the benefits of ZFS, particularly its robustness due to its checksummed data and metadata blocks. You can also use DTrace to examine programs running in these zones.

Solaris 10 Zones can be NFS clients, but not NFS servers. They also cannot use `file-mac-profile`, which means that they cannot be immutable zones.

If the original system has Solaris 10 native zones, those zones must be migrated to other hosts *before* the global zone is migrated—migrating the global zone will disable any remaining zones. Moving these zones to Solaris 11 systems, as Solaris 10 Zones, is not difficult. Instead of using the `install` subcommand of `zoneadm`, you use the `attach` subcommand to migrate the native zones.

Finally, if the original Solaris 10 system had Solaris 8 Containers or Solaris 10 Containers, they cannot be moved to a Solaris 11 system. If you must continue to use Solaris 8 Containers, you must retain at least one Solaris 10 system.

Of course, once you have migrated a Solaris 10 system or zone to a Solaris 11 system, you must still maintain it. Although new updates to Solaris 10 are not being released, Solaris 10 patches continue to be created.

Solaris 10 introduced the concept of a boot environment (BE), which comprises all of the Solaris package content necessary to boot Solaris. One Solaris can maintain multiple BEs, with different versions of packages, and you can boot from any one BE still installed on that system. A Solaris 10 system uses one disk drive per BE. That scheme limits the BEs' usefulness, and usually requires breaking the root drive mirrored pair; in turn, this process increases risk while patching or updating Solaris.

A Solaris 10 zone benefits from multiple boot environments, but does not suffer from the need to break the mirror. The global zone uses ZFS to store the Solaris 10 zone—by default—which means that snapshots can be used to store multiple BEs per Solaris 10 zone.

The following commands show the steps to create and enable a new BE for a Solaris 10 zone:

```
z10# zfs snapshot rpool/ROOT/zbe-0@snap
z10# zfs clone -o mountpoint=/ -o canmount=noauto rpool/ROOT/zbe-0@snap rpool/ROOT/newBE
cannot mount 'rpool/ROOT/newBE' on '/': directory is not empty
filesystem successfully created, but not mounted
```

At this point you can mount and modify the newly created BE:

```
z10# zfs mount -o mountpoint=/mnt rpool/ROOT/zbe-0
z10# patchadd -R /mnt -M /var/sadm/spool 104945-02
```

Then you can activate the BE so that it is used when the zone next boots:

```
z10# zfs get com.oracle.zones.solaris10:activebe rpool/ROOT
NAME         PROPERTY                              VALUE  SOURCE
rpool/ROOT   com.oracle.zones.solaris10:activebe   zbe-0  local
z10# zfs set com.oracle.zones.solaris10:activebe=newBE rpool/ROOT
```

Solaris 10 Zones are an excellent method to move older Solaris workloads to newer, consolidated systems. Following such migrations, the workloads benefit from the increased flexibility of Solaris 11 features.

3.7 Strengths of Oracle Solaris Zones

Oracle Solaris Zones deliver all of the strengths of the OSV model:

- Compute efficiency. Zones have almost zero overhead, giving them an advantage over hypervisors, which use CPU cycles for I/O transactions, and over partitioning, which leaves CPU cycles unused even when another workload could use those resources.
- Storage efficiency. A zone can use as little as 100MB of disk space and as little as 40MB of RAM.
- Hardware independence. Zones do not depend on any hardware features and do not have any code specific to one instruction set. They are currently supported on x86/x64 and SPARC architectures, making Solaris Zones one of the few virtualization technologies available on multiple CPU architectures.
- Observability. The kernel controls access to all information regarding its zones, so tools such as DTrace can simultaneously view internal details of multiple zones and their processes.

In addition, zones offer several advantages over other forms of OSV:

- Solaris 8 Containers and Solaris 9 Containers allow you to run all of the software from an older system on a system running Solaris 10.
- The `solaris10` brand allows you to run Solaris 10 software on Solaris 11.

- The flexible and dynamic resource controls can automatically adapt to the changing needs of one or more workloads.

- A configurable security boundary provides the ability to relax or strengthen the privileges of each zone individually.

- Zones are a tightly integrated feature of Oracle Solaris, and benefit from innovations in Solaris such as ZFS, IPS, and DTrace.

3.8 Summary

Oracle Solaris Zones are a very popular, mature, and feature-rich form of system virtualization that are used in production environments in data centers all over the world. In practice, the more common uses of zones include the following situations:

- Consolidating applications from multiple servers to fewer servers, especially as a no-cost virtual server.

- Hardening an OS environment with read-only mounts and minimal privileges, especially for Internet-facing environments.

- Hosting environments such as cloud computing, Internet service providers (ISPs), and web hosting, where a homogeneous environment is preferred by the hosting organization, and where quick provisioning is important. Each customer's operations can be configured on multiple systems, ready to boot on the most lightly loaded system.

- Software development environments, which also benefit from rapid provisioning and homogeneity, giving each developer full privileges in that zone.

- Rapid provisioning for short-lived environments—for example, functionality testing. A cloned zone provides a well-defined starting point.

- High-scale virtualization, in which dozens or hundreds of VEs reside in one computer, because of the superior efficiency of Solaris Zones.

Released as a feature set of Solaris 10 in early 2005, Oracle Solaris Zones have achieved broad support from independent software vendors. Network virtualization adds a new dimension to their usefulness for Solaris and the future.

Code Sample 3.1 Detailed Creation of Kernel Zone

```
root@tesla:/export/home/jvictor# zonecfg -z potter
Use 'create' to begin configuring a new zone.
zonecfg:potter> create -t SYSsolaris-kz
zonecfg:potter> info
zonename: potter
brand: solaris-kz
autoboot: false
autoshutdown: shutdown
bootargs:
pool:
scheduling-class:
hostid: 0xa7a4b83
tenant:
anet:
    lower-link: auto
    allowed-address not specified
    configure-allowed-address: true
    defrouter not specified
    allowed-dhcp-cids not specified
    link-protection: mac-nospoof
    mac-address: auto
    mac-prefix not specified
    mac-slot not specified
    vlan-id not specified
    priority not specified
    rxrings not specified
    txrings not specified
    mtu not specified
    maxbw not specified
    bwshare not specified
    rxfanout not specified
    vsi-typeid not specified
    vsi-vers not specified
    vsi-mgrid not specified
    etsbw-lcl not specified
    cos not specified
    evs not specified
    vport not specified
    iov: off
    lro: auto
    id: 0
```

(continued)

Code Sample 3.1   Detailed Creation of Kernel Zone (continued)

```
device:
    match not specified
    storage.template: dev:/dev/zvol/dsk/%{global-rootzpool}/VARSHARE/zones/%{zonename}/disk%{id}
    storage: dev:/dev/zvol/dsk/rpool/VARSHARE/zones/potter/disk0
    id: 0
    bootpri: 0
capped-memory:
    physical: 4G
zonecfg:potter> exit
root@tesla:/export/home/jvictor# zoneadm -z potter install
Progress being logged to /var/log/zones/zoneadm.20150716T010458Z.potter.install
pkg cache: Using /var/pkg/publisher.
 Install Log: /system/volatile/install.16299/install_log
 AI Manifest: /tmp/zoneadm15783.QTaakF/devel-ai-manifest.xml
  SC Profile: /usr/share/auto_install/sc_profiles/enable_sci.xml
Installation: Starting ...

    Creating IPS image
    Installing packages from:
        solaris
            origin:  http://pkg.oracle.com/solaris/release/
    The following licenses have been accepted and not displayed.
    Please review the licenses for the following packages post-install:
      consolidation/osnet/osnet-incorporation
    Package licenses may be viewed using the command:
      pkg info --license <pkg_fmri>

DOWNLOAD                    PKGS         FILES       XFER (MB)   SPEED
Completed                   482/482    64490/64490  559.6/559.6  543k/s

PHASE                                    ITEMS
Installing new actions                 88235/88235
Updating package state database          Done
Updating package cache                   0/0
Updating image state                     Done
Creating fast lookup database            Done
Installation: Succeeded
        Done: Installation completed in 1581.112 seconds.
```

Code Sample 3.2   Configuring an Immutable Kernel Zone

```
jvictor@tesla:~$ sudo zlogin potter
[Connected to zone 'potter' pts/3]
Oracle Corporation      SunOS 5.11      11.2     August 2014
root@potter:~# zonecfg -z global
zonecfg:global> set file-mac-profile=fixed-configuration
zonecfg:global> exit
updating /platform/i86pc/boot_archive
updating /platform/i86pc/amd64/boot_archive
root@potter:~# reboot
[Connection to zone 'potter' pts/3 closed]

jvictor@tesla:~$ sudo zlogin potter
[Connected to zone 'potter' pts/3]
Oracle Corporation      SunOS 5.11      11.2     August 2014
root@potter:~# cat "10.1.1.1 myhost" >> /etc/hosts
-bash: /etc/hosts: Read-only file system
root@potter:~# zonecfg -z global
WARNING: you do not have write access to this zone's configuration file. Going into read-only mode.
zonecfg:global> info
file-mac-profile: fixed-configuration
pool:
fs-allowed:
zonecfg:global> exit
root@potter:~# exit
[Connection to zone 'potter' pts/3 closed]

jvictor@tesla:~$ sudo zlogin -T potter
[Connected to zone 'potter' pts/3]
Oracle Corporation      SunOS 5.11      11.2     August 2014
root@potter:~# echo "10.1.1.1 myhost" >> /etc/hosts
root@potter:~# zonecfg -z global
zonecfg:global> info
file-mac-profile: fixed-configuration
pool:
fs-allowed:
zonecfg:global> set file-mac-profile=none
zonecfg:global> exit
updating /platform/i86pc/boot_archive
updating /platform/i86pc/amd64/boot_archive
root@potter:~# reboot
```

4

Oracle VM Server for SPARC

Oracle VM Server for SPARC (formerly called Logical Domains) is a virtualization technology that creates SPARC virtual machines, also called domains. It permits operation of virtual machines with less overhead than traditional designs by changing the way guests access CPU, memory, and I/O resources. It is an ideal way to consolidate multiple complete Oracle Solaris systems onto a modern powerful SPARC server.

Oracle VM Server for SPARC is available on systems based on SPARC chip multithreading technology (CMT) processors. These processors include the Oracle SPARC M5-32, M6-32, M7, S7, T4, T5, and T7 servers and blades; older SPARC T3 servers; Sun SPARC Enterprise T5x20/T5x40 servers; Sun Blade T6320/T6340 server modules; and Fujitsu SPARC M10 servers. The chip technology is integral to Oracle VM Server for SPARC, which leverages the large number of CPU threads available on these servers. At this writing, as many as 4096 CPU threads can be supported in a single M7-16 server. Oracle VM Server for SPARC is available on supported SPARC processors without additional license or hardware costs.

4.1 Oracle VM Server for SPARC Features

Oracle VM Server for SPARC creates virtual machines, which are usually called domains. Every domain runs its own instance of Oracle Solaris 11 or Solaris 10, just as if each had its own separate physical server. Each domain also has the following resources:

- CPUs
- Memory
- Network devices
- Disks
- Console
- OpenBoot environment
- Virtual host bus adapters (starting with Oracle VM Server for SPARC 3.3)
- Cryptographic accelerators (optionally specified on older, pre-T4 servers)

Different Solaris update levels run at the same time on the same server without conflict. Each domain is independently defined, started, and stopped.

Domains are isolated from one another. Consequently, a failure in one domain—even a kernel panic or CPU thread failure—has no effect on other domains, just as would be the case for Solaris running on multiple servers.

Oracle Solaris and applications in a domain are highly compatible with Solaris running on a physical server. Solaris has long had a binary compatibility guarantee; this guarantee has been extended to domains, such that no distinction is made between running as a guest or on bare metal. Thus, Solaris functions essentially the same way in a domain as it does on a non-virtualized system.

4.2 CPUs in Oracle VM Server for SPARC

One unique feature of Oracle VM Server for SPARC is how it assigns CPU resources to domains. This architectural innovation is discussed in detail here.

Traditional hypervisors use software to time-slice physical CPUs among virtual machines. These hypervisors must intercept and emulate privileged instructions issued by guest VM operating systems that would change the shared physical machine's state (such as interrupt masks or memory mapping), thereby violating the integrity of separation between guests. This complex and expensive process may be needed thousands of times per second as guest VMs issue instructions that would be "free" (executed in silicon) on a physical server, but are expensive (emulated in software) in a VM. Context switches between virtual machines can require hundreds or even thousands of clock cycles. Each context switch to a different virtual machine requires purging the cache and translation lookaside buffer (TLB) contents, because identical virtual memory addresses map to different physical locations. This process increases memory latency until caches become filled with fresh content, only to be discarded at the next time slice. Although these effects have been reduced on modern processors, they still carry significant overhead.

In contrast, Oracle VM Server for SPARC leverages SPARC chip multithreading processors to improve the system's simplicity and reduce overhead. Modern SPARC processors provide many CPU *threads* (also called *strands*) on a single chip. SPARC T4 and UltraSPARC T2 and T2 Plus processors provide 8 cores with 8 threads per core, for a total of 64 threads per chip. SPARC T5 and T3 processors provide 16 cores with 8 threads per core, for a total of 128 threads per chip; the T5-8 has 8 sockets and a total of 1024 CPU threads. The M5-32 and M6-32 processors provide 6 or 12 cores per chip, respectively, with 8 threads per core, and they scale to 3072 threads per system. M7 and T7 servers are based on the M7 processor, which has 32 cores and 8 threads per core, scaling up to 1024 threads on the T7-4 and 4096 threads on the M7-16. From the perspective of Oracle Solaris, each thread is considered to be a CPU.

These systems are rich in CPU threads, which are allocated to domains for their exclusive use, rather than being doled out in a time-sliced manner, and which demonstrate native performance. The frequent context switches needed in traditional hypervisors are eliminated because each domain has dedicated hardware circuitry, and each can change its state—for example, by enabling or disabling interrupts—without causing a trap and emulation. Assigning CPUs to domains can save thousands of context switches per second, especially for workloads with high I/O activity. Context switching still occurs within a domain when Solaris dispatches different processes onto a CPU, but this behavior is identical to the way Solaris runs on a non-virtualized server. In other words, no overhead is *added* for virtualization.

SPARC systems also enhance use of the processor cache. All modern CPUs use fast on-chip or on-board cache memory that can be accessed in just a few clock cycles. If an instruction refers to data that is present in RAM but is not in the specific CPU's cache, a *cache miss* occurs and the instruction is said to *stall*. In this scenario, the CPU must wait dozens or hundreds of clock cycles until the data is fetched from RAM so that the instruction can continue.

SPARC processors avoid this idle waiting time by switching execution to another CPU strand on the same core. This hardware context switch happens in a single clock cycle because each hardware strand has its own private hardware context. In this way, SPARC processors use cache miss time—time that is wasted (stall) on other processors—to continue doing useful work. This behavior reduces the effect of cache misses whether or not domains are in use, but Oracle VM Server for SPARC attempts to reduce cache misses by allocating CPU threads so that domains do not share per-core level 1 (L1) caches. This default behavior, which represents a best practice, can be ensured by explicitly allocating CPUs in units of whole cores. Actual performance benefits will depend on the system's workload, and may be of minor consideration when CPU utilization is low.

Additionally, on T4 and later servers, Oracle VM Server for SPARC supports the Solaris "critical thread API," in which a software thread is identified as being critical to an application's performance and its performance is optimized. These software threads—such as the ones used for Java garbage collection or an Oracle Database log writer—are given all the cache and register resources of a core, and can execute instructions "out of order" so cache misses do not stall the pipeline. Consequently, critical application components may run dramatically faster. Oracle VM Server for SPARC flexibly provides better throughput performance for multiple threads while providing optimal performance for selected application components. Oracle software products increasingly make use of this powerful optimization.

4.3 Features and Implementation

Oracle VM Server for SPARC uses a very small hypervisor that resides in firmware, working with a Logical Domain Manager in the control domain (discussed later in this chapter) to assign CPUs, RAM locations, and I/O devices to each domain. Logical domain channels (LDCs) are used for communication both among domains and between domains and the hypervisor.

The hypervisor is kept as small as possible for simplicity and robustness. Many tasks traditionally performed within a hypervisor kernel, such as providing a management interface and performing I/O for guests, are offloaded to domains, as described in the next section.

This architecture has several benefits. Notably, a small hypervisor is easier to develop, manage, and deliver as part of a firmware solution embedded in the platform, and its tight focus improves security and reliability. This design adds resiliency by shifting functions from a monolithic hypervisor, which might potentially represent a single point of failure, to one or more privileged domains that can be deployed in parallel. As a result, Oracle VM Server for SPARC has resiliency options that are not available in older, traditional hypervisors. This design also makes it possible to leverage capabilities already available in Oracle Solaris, thereby providing access to existing infrastructure such as device drivers, file systems, features for management, reliability, performance, scale, diagnostics, development tools, and a large API set. It serves as an extremely effective alternative to developing all these features from scratch. Other modern hypervisors, such as the Xen hypervisor used in Oracle VM Server for x86, also use this architecture.

4.3.1 Domain Roles

Domains have different roles, and may be used for system infrastructure or applications:

- The *control domain* is an administrative control point that runs Oracle Solaris and the Logical Domain Manager services. It has a privileged interface to the hypervisor, and can create, configure, start, stop, and destroy other domains.

- *Service domains* provide virtual disk and network devices for guest domains. They are generally root I/O domains so as to have physical devices available as virtual devices. It is a best practice to use redundant service domains to provide resiliency against loss of an I/O path or service domain.

- *I/O domains* have direct connections to physical I/O devices and use them without any intervening virtualization layer. They are often service domains that provide access to these devices, but may also use physical devices for their own applications. An I/O domain that owns a complete PCIe bus is said to be a *root domain*. The control domain is a root domain and is typically also a service domain.

- *Guest domains* exclusively use virtual devices provided by service domains. Applications are typically run in guest domains.

The `virtinfo` command displays the domain type. Specifically, for control domains, it displays the output `Domain role: LDoms control I/O service root`. For guest domains, it displays `Domain role: LDoms guest`. The domain structure and assignment of CPUs are shown in Figure 4.1.

The definition of a domain includes its name, the amount of memory and number of CPUs, its I/O devices, and policy settings. Domain definitions are constructed by using the command-line interface in the control domain, or by using the graphical interfaces provided by Oracle VM Manager and Oracle Enterprise Manager Ops Center.

Each server, or each physical domain on M-series processors, has exactly one control domain: the instance of Solaris that was first installed on the system. It runs Oracle VM Server for SPARC's Logical Domain Manager services, which are accessed via a command-line interface provided by the `ldm` command or Oracle VM Manager, and may run agents that connect to Oracle VM Manager or Ops

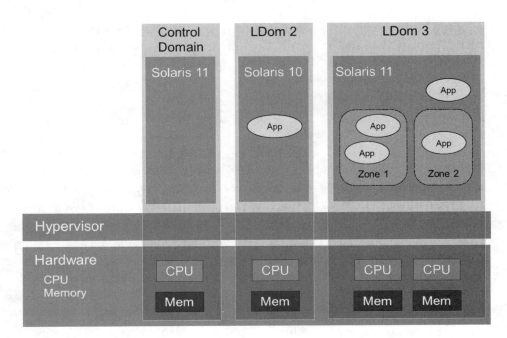

Figure 4.1   Control and Guest Domains

Center. The Logical Domain Manager includes a "constraint manager" that decides how to assign physical resources to satisfy the requirements ("constraints") specified for each domain.

I/O domains have direct access to physical I/O devices, which may be Single-Root I/O Virtualization (SR-IOV) virtual functions (described later in this chapter), individual PCIe cards, or entire PCIe bus root complexes (in which case, the domain is called a "root domain"). The control domain is always an I/O domain, because it requires access to I/O buses and devices to boot up. There can be as many I/O domains as there are assignable physical devices. Applications that require native I/O performance can run in an I/O domain to avoid virtual I/O overhead. Alternatively, an I/O domain can be a service domain, in which case it runs virtual disk and virtual network services that provide virtual I/O devices to guest domains.

Guest domains rely on service domains for virtual disk and network devices and are the setting where applications typically run. At the time of this book's writing, the maximum number of domains on a SPARC server or SPARC M-series physical domain (PDom) was 128, including control and service domains. As a general rule, it is recommended to run applications only in guest and I/O domains, and not in control and service domains.

A simple configuration consists of a single control domain that also acts as a service domain, and some number of guest domains. A configuration designed for availability would use redundant service domains to provide resiliency in case of a domain failure or reboot, or in case of the loss of a path to an I/O device.

4.3.2 Dynamic Reconfiguration

CPUs, RAM, and I/O devices can be dynamically added to or removed from a domain without requiring a reboot. Oracle Solaris running in a guest domain can immediately make use of a dynamically added CPU and memory as additional capacity; it can also handle the removal of all but one of its CPUs. Virtual disk and network resources can be added to or removed from a running domain, and a guest domain can make use of a newly added device without a reboot.

4.3.3 Virtual I/O

Oracle VM Server for SPARC abstracts underlying I/O resources to virtual I/O. It is not always possible or desirable to give each domain direct and exclusive use of an I/O bus or device, as this arrangement could increase the costs of both devices and cabling for a system. As an alternative, a virtual I/O (VIO) infrastructure provides shared access and greater flexibility.

Virtual network and disk I/O is provided by service domains, which proxy virtual I/O requests from guest domains to physical devices. Service domains run Solaris and own PCIe buses connected to the physical network and disk devices; thus they are also root domains. The control domain is typically a service domain as well, as it must have I/O abilities and there is no reason not to use that functionality.

The system administrator uses the `ldm add-vswitch` and `ldm add-vds` commands to define virtual network switches and virtual disk services, respectively. These services are then used to provide virtual network and disk devices to guest domains, and forward guest I/O operations to physical I/O devices used as "backends." In a guest domain, Solaris uses virtual network and virtual disk device drivers that perform I/O by sending I/O requests to service domains. The service domain then processes the I/O operation and sends back the necessary status information when the I/O operation is complete.

The addition of device drivers that communicate with service domains instead of performing physical I/O is one of the ways in which Solaris has been modified to run in a logical domain. Communication is done via logical domain channels provided by the hypervisor. These LDCs provide communications channels between guests, and an API for sending messages that contain service requests and responses. The number of virtual devices in a domain is limited to the number of LDC endpoints that domain can have. SPARC T4, T5, T7, M5, M6, and M7 systems can have up to 1984 LDC endpoints per domain. Older T2 systems are limited to 512 LDC endpoints per domain, while T2+ and T3 systems can have up to 768 LDC endpoints for each domain.

Virtual I/O requires some degree of overhead, but it now approaches native I/O performance for appropriately configured service domains and back-ends. In practice, service domains with sufficient CPU and memory can drive guest I/O loads, and virtual disks can be based on physical disk volumes (LUNs) or slices. Figure 4.2 shows the relationship between guest and service domains and the path of I/O requests and responses.

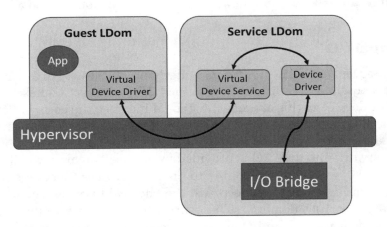

Figure 4.2   Service Domains Provide Virtual I/O

4.3.4 Physical I/O

Virtual I/O is the most flexible choice for most domains, and its performance is very close to "bare metal" performance. Physical I/O, however, may be used for applications that need the highest I/O performance, or for device types such as tape that are not supported by virtual I/O.

As mentioned previously, a service domain is almost always an I/O domain (or it would not have devices to serve out), but an I/O domain may not be a service domain: It might use its own I/O devices to achieve native I/O performance unmediated by any service layer. As an example, such a deployment pattern is used with Oracle SuperCluster, which is optimized for high performance.

The physical I/O devices assigned to a domain are one of the following types:

- **PCIe root complex.** The domain is assigned an entire PCIe bus, and natively accesses all the devices attached to it. The domain is called a "root domain."

- **Single Root I/O Virtualization (SR-IOV) "virtual function" (VF) device.** SR-IOV cards can present as multiple virtual functions, which can be individually assigned to a domain. An SR-IOV–capable card can have 8, 16, 32, or 64 separate virtual function devices, depending on the specific card. SPARC servers have built-in Ethernet SR-IOV devices, and Oracle VM Server for SPARC supports SR-IOV for Ethernet, InfiniBand, and FibreChannel. Qualified cards are listed in the Oracle VM Server for SPARC Release Notes.

- **Direct I/O (DIO).** This type is similar to SR-IOV, except that a device in a PCIe slot is presented directly to the domain—one card results in one device for one domain. SR-IOV is preferred to direct I/O, since it provides additional flexibility. Direct I/O is not supported on T7 and M7 servers. As with SR-IOV, qualified cards are listed in the Oracle VM Server for SPARC Release Notes.

To create an I/O domain, you first identify the physical I/O device to give to the domain, which depends on the server model and the resources to be assigned, and then issue the `ldm add-io` command to assign the device. Depending on the server and previous device assignments, it may be necessary to first issue an `ldm rm-io` command to remove the device from the control domain, which initially owns all system resources.

Physical devices are used by Solaris exactly as they would be in a non-virtualized environment. That is, they have the same device drivers, device names, behavior, and performance as if Solaris was not running in a domain at all.

There are some limitations to use of physical I/O. Notably, a server has only a given number of devices that can be assigned to domains. That number is smaller than the number of virtual I/O devices that can potentially be defined, since virtual I/O makes it possible to share physical network and disk devices. Also, I/O domains cannot be live-migrated from one server to another (see the discussion of live migration later in this chapter). Nevertheless, physical I/O can be the right answer for I/O-intensive applications.

4.3.5 Domain Configuration and Resources

The logical domains technology provides for flexible assignment of hardware resources to domains, with options for specifying physical resources for a corresponding virtual resource. This section details how domain resources are defined and controlled.

The Oracle VM Server for SPARC administrator uses the `ldm` command to create domains and specify their resources—the amount of RAM, the number of CPUs, and so forth. These parameters are sometimes referred to as domain *constraints*. The `ldm` command is also used to set domain properties, such as whether the domain should boot its OS when started.

A domain is said to be *inactive* until resources are bound to it by the `ldm bind` command. When this command is issued, the system selects the physical resources needed to satisfy the domain's constraints and associates them with the domain. For example, if a domain requires 32 CPUs, the domain manager selects 32 CPUs from the set of online and unassigned CPUs on the system and gives them to the domain. The domain is then *bound* and can be started by the `ldm start` command. The `ldm start` command is equivalent to powering on a physical server. The `ldm stop` command stops a domain, either "gracefully," by telling the domain to shut itself down, or forcibly (`-f` option), with the equivalent of a server power-off.

If the server does not have enough available resources to satisfy the server's constraints, the bind will fail. However, the sum of the constraints of all domains can exceed the physical resources on the server. For example, you could define 20 domains, each of which requires 8 CPUs and 4 GB of RAM on a machine with 64 CPUs and 64 GB of RAM. Only domains whose constraints are met can be bound and started. In this case, the first 8 domains could be bound. Additional domains can be defined for occasional or emergency purposes, such as a disaster recovery domain that is defined on a server normally used for testing.

4.3.6 CPUs

Each domain is assigned exclusive use of a number of CPUs, which are also called *threads*, *strands*, or *virtual CPUs* (vCPUs). Current Oracle SPARC servers have 8 CPU threads per core, with up to 32 cores per chip. The number of chips (also called sockets) depends on the server model.

Virtual CPUs can be assigned individually or in units of entire cores. They should be assigned on core boundaries to prevent "false cache sharing," which can reduce performance if multiple domains share a core and compete for the same L1 cache. The default behavior of Oracle VM Server for SPARC is to "do the right thing" and allocate different cores to domains whenever possible, even for sub-core allocations.

The best practice is to allocate virtual CPUs in whole-core units instead of on CPU thread units. The commands `ldm set-core 2 mydomain` and `ldm set-vcpu 16 mydomain` both assign 2 CPU cores with a total of 16 threads, but the first command requires that they be allocated entire cores, while the second command means that those resources could potentially be spread over more than 2 cores, which might also be shared with other domains. Allocating individual vCPUs in multiples of 8 also ensures allocation on core boundaries.

Figure 4.3 is a simplified diagram of the threads, cores, and caches in a SPARC chip.

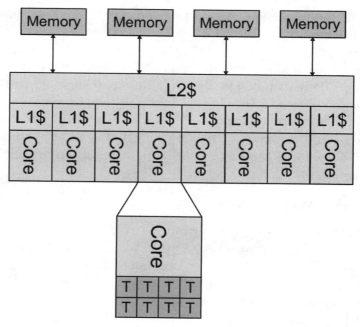

Figure 4.3   SPARC Cores, Threads, and Caches

Whole-core allocation is recommended for domains with substantial CPU load. This technique is also a prerequisite for using "hard partition licensing," in which the domain is defined to have a maximum number of CPU cores (`ldm set-domain max-cores=N mydomain`). When this type of licensing is used, Oracle licensed products in the domain need to be licensed only for the maximum number of cores in the domain, rather than for the entire server.

Allocation of an entire core may be overkill for light workloads. System administrators should not excessively worry when defining domains to accommodate the light CPU requirements needed to consolidate small, old, or low-utilization servers; they should just allocate a partial core's threads if that is all that is needed. Alternatively, multiple Oracle Solaris Zones can be consolidated within a logical domain. This is a popular method for ensuring highly granular resource allocation.

On servers with multiple CPU sockets, the Logical Domain Manager attempts to assign CPU cores and memory from the same server socket to avoid NUMA (non-uniform memory access) latency. This practice reduces latency between CPUs and memory.

Oracle Solaris commands such as `vmstat` and `mpstat` can be used within the domain to monitor its CPU utilization, just as they are used on a dedicated server. The `ldm list` command can be used in the control domain to display each domain's CPU utilization.

The number of CPUs in a domain can be dynamically and nondisruptively changed while the domain is running. Changes to the number of vCPUs in a domain take effect immediately. The Dynamic Resource Manager feature of Oracle VM Server for SPARC can be used to automatically add or remove CPUs based on a domain's CPU utilization: It adds CPUs if utilization is higher than a specified threshold value, and it removes CPUs if utilization is lower than a threshold so they can be assigned to other domains that might benefit from their capacity.

4.3.7 Virtual Network Devices

Guest domains have one or more virtual network devices connected to virtual Layer 2 network switches provided by service domains. From the guest domain's perspective, virtual network interfaces are named *vnetN*, where *N* is an integer starting from 0 for the first virtual network device. The command `ifconfig -a` or `dladm show-phys` is used to display the network interface `vnet0`, `vnet1`, and so on, rather than real device names like `ixgbe0`. Virtual network devices can be assigned static or dynamic IP addresses, just like physical devices.

4.3.7.1 Network Connectivity and Resiliency

Every virtual network device is connected to a virtual switch exported by a service domain. The virtual switch uses the service domain's physical network device or link aggregation as a back-end. Network traffic from the guest domain to the physical network proceeds from the guest's virtual network device to the virtual switch, and then over the back-end network interface or aggregation. If the back-end is a link aggregation, virtual network traffic can benefit from the bandwidth, failover, and load-balancing capabilities provided in the IEEE 802.3ad standard.

A domain's virtual network devices can be on different virtual switches so as to connect the domain to multiple networks, provide increased availability using IPMP (IP Multipathing), or increase the available bandwidth. IPMP can be used with either probe-based or link-based failure detection. To use link-based detection, specify `linkprop=phys-state` with the `ldm add-vnet` commands used to define the virtual devices. IPMP configuration is performed in the guest domain and is otherwise the same as on physical servers.

By default, network traffic between domains on the same virtual switch does not travel to the virtual switch, service domain, or physical network. Instead, it relies on a fast memory-to-memory transfer between source and destination domains. This approach reduces both latency and load on the service domain, albeit at the expense of extra LDCs between each virtual network device on the virtual switch. If a domain has a large virtual I/O configuration, then LDCs can be conserved by setting `inter-vnet-link=off` on the virtual network device. In this case, interdomain network traffic goes through the virtual switch (but not the physical network), instead of directly between domains.

Virtual network devices can be configured to exploit features such as jumbo frames, VLAN tagging, and RFC 5517 PVLANs. Virtual network devices can have bandwidth controls (`ldm set-vnet maxbw=200M net0 mydomain`) to prevent domains from monopolizing bandwidth. Network devices can be assigned an IEEE 802.1p class of service, and can be protected from MAC or IP spoofing.

4.3.7.2 MAC Addresses

Every virtual network device has one or more MAC addresses. MAC addresses can be assigned manually or automatically from the reserved address range of `00:14:4F:F8:00:00` to `00:14:4F:FF:FF:FF`. The bottom half of this address range is used for automatic assignments; the other 256,000 addresses can be used for manual assignment.

A virtual network device may need more than one MAC address. Solaris 11 network virtualization permits creation of virtual NICs (vNICs) that can be used for "exclusive IP" Solaris zones that manage their own network device properties. This scheme is supported by defining virtual network devices with an `alt-mac-addrs` setting to allocate multiple MAC addresses—a feature sometimes called "vNICs on vNets."

The Logical Domain Manager detects duplicate MAC address by sending multicast messages with the address it wants to assign, and listening for a response from another machine's Logical Domain Manager saying that address is in use. If such a message comes back, it randomly picks another address and tries again.

4.3.8 Virtual Disk

Service domains can have virtual disk services that export virtual block devices to guest domains. Virtual disks are based on back-end disk resources, which may consist of physical disks, disk slices, volumes, or files residing in NFS, ZFS, or UFS file systems. These resources could include any of the following:

- A physical block device (a disk or LUN, including iSCSI), such as `/dev/dsk/c1t48d0s2`
- A slice of a physical device or LUN, such as `/dev/dsk/c1t48d0s0`
- A disk image file residing in a file system mounted to the service domain such as `/path/to/filename`
- A ZFS volume; the command `zfs create -V 100m ldoms/domain/test/zdisk0` creates the back-end `/dev/zvol/dsk/ldoms/domain/test/zdisk0`
- A volume created by Solaris Volume Manager (SVM) or Veritas Volume Manager (VxVM)
- A CD ROM/DVD or a file containing an ISO image

Back-ends based on physical disks, LUNs, or disk slices provide the best performance. There is no difference between defining them as `/dev/dsk` or `/dev/rdsk` devices—that is, back-ends created through both of these techniques are treated identically. Virtual disks specifying an entire disk should use the "s2" slice; individual slices are allocated by using other slice numbers.

Virtual disks based on files in the service domain are convenient to use: They can be easily copied, backed up, and, when using ZFS, cloned from a snapshot. This approach provides flexibility, but has less performance than physical disk back-ends.

Files in an NFS mount can be accessed from multiple servers, though, as with LUNs, they should not be accessed from different hosts at the same time. Different kinds of disk back-ends can be used in the same domain: The system volume for a domain can use a ZFS file system back-end, while disks used for databases or other I/O intensive applications can use physical disks.

Virtual disks on a local file system, such as ZFS, cannot be used by multiple hosts at the same time, so they will not work with live migration. If you want to perform live migration, you must use virtual disk back-ends that can be accessed by multiple hosts. Those options include NFS, iSCSI, or FibreChannel LUNs presented to multiple servers.

4.3.8.1 Disk Device Resiliency

Redundancy can be provided by using virtual disk multipath groups (mpgroups), in which the same virtual disk back-end is presented to the guest by different service domains in active/passive pairs. This scheme provides fault tolerance in the event of service domain failure or loss of a physical access path. If a service domain is rebooted or its path fails, then I/O proceeds down the other member of the mpgroup. The back-end storage can be a LUN accessed by FC-AL adapters attached to each service domain, or even NFS mounted to both service domains.

The commands in Listing 4.1 show how to define a virtual disk served by a control domain and an alternative service domain. The `ldm list-bindings` and `ldm set-vdisk` commands can be used to display and set which of the mpgroup paths is the active path.

Listing 4.1   Define an mpgroup

```
# ldm add-vdsdev mpgroup=foo \
  /path-to-backend-from-primary/domain ha-disk@primary-vds0
# ldm add-vdsdev mpgroup=foo \
  /path-to-backend-from-alternate/domain ha-disk@alternate-vds0
# ldm add-vdisk ha-disk ha-disk@primary-vds0 myguest
```

This approach is the recommended and commonly used method for providing path and service domain resiliency. The administrator can display which path is active by giving the `ldm list-bindings` command, and can use the `ldm set-vdisk` command to change which member of the mpgroup is the active path. In this way, multipath groups can be used to balance loads over service domains and host bus adapter (HBA) paths.

Multipathing can also be provided within a single I/O domain with Solaris multiplexed I/O (MPXIO), by ensuring that the domain has multiple paths to the same device—for example, two FC-AL HBAs to the same SAN array. You enable MPxIO in the control or service domain by running the command `stmsboot -e`. The result of this command is a single, but redundant path to the same device. The single device is then configured into the virtual disk service, which provides path resiliency within the same service domain. This strategy, which can be combined with mpgroups to provide redundancy in case a service domain fails, is a frequently used production deployment.

Virtual disk redundancy can also be established by providing multiple virtual disks, from different service domains, and arranging them in a redundant ZFS mirrored or RAIDZ pool within the guest. The virtual disk devices must be specified with the `timeout` parameter (`ldm set-vdisk timeout=seconds diskname domain`). If any of the disk back-ends fail (i.e., path, service domain, or media), then the fault is propagated to the guest domain; the guest domain marks the virtual disk as unavailable in the ZFS pool, but the ZFS pool continues in operation. When the defect is repaired, the system administrator can indicate that the device is available again.

Insulation from media failure can be provided by using virtual disk back-ends in a redundant ZFS pool in the service domain, with mirror or RAIDZ redundancy. This technique can also be used with iSCSI LUNs or NFS-based files exported from an Oracle ZFS Storage Appliance (ZFSSA) configured with mirrored or RAIDZ, which has the advantage of permitting live migration since the storage is accessed via the network. These options offer resiliency in case of a path failure to a device, and can be combined with mpgroups to provide resiliency against service domain outage.

4.3.8.2 Virtual HBA

Oracle VM Server for SPARC 3.3, a feature delivered with Oracle Solaris 11.3, added a new form of virtual I/O by introducing virtual SCSI host bus adapters that support the Sun Common SCSI Architecture (SCSA) interface.

The virtual I/O design described earlier is flexible and provides good performance, but it does not support devices such as tape, and it does not support some native Solaris features, such as Solaris MultiPathing disk I/O (MPxIO) for active/active path management. Virtual HBA (vHBA) eliminates these restrictions.

The logical domain administrator defines virtual SANs on a physical SAN (`ldm add-vsan`), and then defines guest virtual HBAs on the virtual SAN (`ldm add-vhba`). Guests see all the devices on the virtual HBA and SAN, just as with a non-virtualized system. A single command gives access to all the devices, instead of two commands (`ldm add-vdsdev`, `ldm add-vdisk`) being required for each virtual disk.

Virtual HBAs can be defined on any supported SPARC server using domains running Solaris 11.3 or later. The administrator lists the physical HBAs on the service domain, defines a virtual SAN on the domain with the guest's devices, and then creates a virtual HBA for the guest. This can be done dynamically while the guest is running. Listing 4.2 shows creation of a virtual SAN and a virtual HBA.

Listing 4.2   Define a Virtual HBA

```
# ldm ls-hba -d primary
NAME                                                    VSAN
----                                                    ----
...snip...
MB/RISER2/PCIE2/HBA0,1/PORT0,0
...snip...
# ldm add-vsan MB/RISER2/PCIE2/HBA0,1/PORT0,0 my-vsan primary MB/RISER2/PCIE2/HBA0,1/
↪PORT0,0 resolved to device: /pci@0/pci@0/pci@9/SUNW,emlxs@0,1/fp@0,0
# ldm add-vhba my-vhba my-vsan myguest
```

The guest domain now has a host bus adapter. It sees the devices on this HBA just as if it had exclusive access to a physical HBA in a non-virtualized environment, with actual device names and features, as shown in Listing 4.3.

Listing 4.3   Guest Domain Sees Devices on Virtual HBA

```
my-guest # format
Searching for disks...done
AVAILABLE DISK SELECTIONS:
       0. c0t600144F0EDE50676000055A81BB2001Ad0 <SUN-ZFS 7420-1.0-36.00GB>
          /scsi_vhci/disk@g600144f0ede50676000055a81bb2001a
       1. c0t600144F0EDE50676000055A815160019d0 <SUN-ZFS 7420-1.0 cyl 778 alt 2 hd 254 sec 254>
          /scsi_vhci/disk@g600144f0ede50676000055a815160019
       2. c1d0 <SUN-DiskImage-40GB cyl 1135 alt 2 hd 96 sec 768>
          /virtual-devices@100/channel-devices@200/disk@0
Specify disk (enter its number): ^C
```

Virtual HBA is a major advance in Oracle VM Server for SPARC capability. It provides virtual I/O with full Solaris driver capabilities and adds virtual I/O for tape and other devices. Moreover, vHBA consumes only one LDC for all the devices on the HBA, instead of one LDC per device, which eliminates constraints on disk device scalability. The original virtual disk and physical disk architectures are not eliminated or deprecated, and can be used concurrently with vHBA.

4.3.9 Console and OpenBoot

Every domain has a console, which is provided by a virtual console concentrator (vcc). The virtual console concentrator is usually delivered by the control domain, which then runs the Virtual Network Terminal Server daemon (vntsd) service.

By default, the daemon listens for `localhost` connections using the Telnet protocol, with a different port number assigned for each domain. A guest domain operator connecting to a domain's console first logs into the control domain via the `ssh` command so that no passwords are transmitted in cleartext over the network; the `telnet` command can then be used to connect to the console. Domain console authorization can be implemented to restrict which users can connect to a domain's console. Normally, only system and guest domain operators should have login access to a control domain.

Both Oracle VM Manager and Oracle Enterprise Manager Ops Center provide a graphical user interface for managing systems. The GUI includes a point-and-click method for launching virtual console sessions, with no need to log into the control domain.

Guest console traffic is logged on the virtual console service domain in text files under `/var/log/vntsd/`*domainname*. These files, which are readable only by root, provide an audit trail of guest domain console activity. Such logging is available and on by default when the service domain runs Solaris 11 or later, but can be enabled or disabled by issuing the command `ldm set-vcons=on|off` *domainname*.

4.3.9.1 Cryptographic Accelerator

SPARC processors are equipped with on-chip hardware cryptographic accelerators that dramatically speed up cryptographic operations. Such accelerators improve security by reducing the CPU consumption devoted to encrypted transmissions, making it feasible to encrypt network transactions while maintaining performance. Live migration automatically leverages cryptographic acceleration.

This feature does not require administrative effort to activate on current servers. On older SPARC servers (T3 and earlier), each CPU core has a cryptographic unit that the administrator adds to domains with the command `ldm set-crypto` *N* `domain`, where *N* is the number of cores.

4.3.9.2 Memory

Oracle VM Server for SPARC dedicates real memory to each domain, instead of oversubscribing guest memory and swapping between RAM and disk, as some hypervisors do. On the downside, this approach limits the number and memory size of domains running on a single server to the amount that fits in RAM. On the upside, it eliminates problems such as thrashing and double paging, which can harm performance when hypervisors run virtual machines in virtual memory environments.

The memory requirements of a domain running the Oracle Solaris OS are the same as when running Solaris on a physical machine. In other words, if a workload needs 8 GB of RAM to run efficiently on a dedicated server, it will need the same amount when running in a domain. Memory can be dynamically added to and removed from a running domain without service interruption. Removing memory requires time to evacuate pages, which may even cause guest domain swapping if the memory load is high. Note that kernel data might be allocated to pages, which prevents them from being removed from the domain.

4.4 Installing Oracle VM Server for SPARC and Building a Guest Domain

This section describes the processes of setting up Oracle VM Server for SPARC, creating a simple guest domain, and installing Oracle Solaris on it.

4.4.1 Verifying and Installing Firmware

All SPARC servers and Blade Modules ship with firmware support for domains. Nevertheless, it is important to ensure that the current firmware for the server is installed—it should match the version of Solaris running in the control domain and the version of Oracle VM Server for SPARC. Current information on firmware releases can be obtained from docs.oracle.com. The Release Notes, Reference Manual, and Administration Guide for Oracle VM Server for SPARC identify the firmware levels needed on each server model. Use the instructions in the server's Installation Guide or Administration Guide for verifying and installing the firmware.

4.4.2 Installing Oracle VM Server for SPARC Software

Oracle VM Server for SPARC software must be installed in the control domain of the SPARC server or physical domain. Guest, I/O, and service domains do not need any additional software. Oracle VM Server for SPARC comes pre-installed in Solaris 11 and later, reducing the administrative effort needed to take advantage of this software.

Customers running Solaris 10 can download Oracle VM Manager for SPARC from www.oracle.com/virtualization/index.html by following the link for Oracle VM Server for SPARC downloads. The software is delivered in a .zip file; this file's contents can be unpacked by issuing the unzip command, and installed by using the `install-ldm` script in the unpacked directory. Note that Solaris 11 or higher must be used for control and service domains on SPARC T7, S7, M5, and M6 servers. Oracle VM Server for SPARC version 3.2 was the last version supporting Solaris 10 control domains; future versions will require Solaris 11 or later. Guest and I/O domains can still run Solaris 10 using update levels supported on the underlying hardware, thereby preserving application certifications.

In the factory-installed default mode, the server runs a single domain, which owns all I/O, memory, and CPU resources. The initial configuration of the server consists of defining the control domain and essential services, as illustrated in the following example taken from a SPARC T5 system. (The text of the example has been edited for brevity.) The `ldm list` command shows the initial control domain configuration: The control domain owns this server's 1024 CPU threads and 1 TB of RAM.

```
# ldm list
NAME        STATE     FLAGS    CONS   VCPU   MEMORY     UTIL   NORM  UPTIME
primary     active    -n-c--   UART   1024   1047296M   0.0%   0.0%  2d 4h 59m
```

4.4.2.1 Configuring the Control Domain

The control domain must be resized to free up the RAM and CPUs to be allocated to guest domains. Essential services for virtual disk, network, and consoles should be defined now as well. When the domain is rebooted, it will have the specified number of CPU cores and amount of RAM. The remainder of those resources will be available for allocation to other domains, as shown in Listing 4.4.

Listing 4.4   Configuring the Control Domain

```
1  # ldm add-vds primary-vds0 primary
2  # ldm add-vswitch net-dev=net0 primary-vsw0 primary
3  # ldm add-vcc port-range=5000-5100 primary-vcc0 primary
4  # svcadm enable vntsd
5  # ldm set-core 2 primary
6  # ldm start-reconf primary
7  # ldm set-memory 16g primary
8  # ldm add-config initial
9  # ldm list-config
10 factory-default
11 initial [current]
12
13 # shutdown -y -g0 -i6
```

Line 1 of Listing 4.4 defines a virtual disk server. Notice the naming convention: The name is `primary-vds0`, indicating that it operates in the domain named `primary` (the control domain) and is the initial virtual disk server (`vds0`). The last token on the line indicates which domain runs this server. Following this convention is recommended but not necessary, as the name of the service makes it self-documenting. This naming convention is separate from Solaris device naming. Note that the virtual disk service is multithreaded, so no performance advantage accrues from defining multiple virtual disk servers in a service domain.

Line 2 of Listing 4.4 defines the virtual switch `primary-vsw0`, which is associated with the network link `net0`. Multiple virtual switches can be defined and attached to different network devices or link aggregations. Line 3 defines a virtual console concentrator that listens for local connections on ports 5000 to 5100, and line 4 enables the Solaris service to start it.

Lines 5, 6, and 7 of Listing 4.4 describe the control domain: It has 2 CPU cores and 16 GB of RAM. A delayed reconfiguration is used to set the memory allocation. Thus, the memory allocation takes effect after reboot, and ensures optimal alignment of memory and CPU cores for performance. If a separate root domain is to be created, perhaps for a service domain, this would be a good time to issue an `ldm rm-io` command to remove the bus it will use from the control domain; that step can eliminate the need for a possible later reboot. The remaining lines save this initial configuration in firmware so it will persist after a power cycle and then reboot the server.

4.4.2.2 Creating a Guest Domain

In the following example, we create a simple guest domain imaginatively named `ldom1`, with a single virtual network device, and a virtual disk residing in a ZFS file system. Although it is not the best-performing virtual disk, it offers the advantage of convenience. The following commands define a ZFS file system and allocate within it an empty 10 GB file that will be used for the Solaris system disk:

```
# zfs create -o compression=on -o mountpoint=/ldoms rpool/ldoms
# zfs create rpool/ldoms/ldom1
# mkfile -n 10g /ldoms/ldom1/disk0.img
```

The preceding lines create a ZFS data set, with compression turned on to save disk space. The option to `mkfile` creates an empty file: No disk blocks are allocated until data is written to them. ZFS provides a great deal of operational flexibility—a characteristic that is helpful for a demo exercise. Virtual disks can also be allocated from other back-ends, such as physical disks, for better performance.

The commands in Listing 4.5 create the domain. Line 2 specifies the number of CPUs (1 core, equivalent to 8 threads), and line 3 sets the RAM assigned to the domain. Line 4 creates the virtual network device using the virtual switch defined previously; we could define additional network devices if we wanted the domain to reside on separate networks. Line 5 exports the empty disk image as a virtual volume `vol10@primary-vds0` from the virtual disk service. Line 6 imports this volume as a virtual disk `vdisk10` into the guest domain. The commands for adding a virtual disk are a bit more complicated than the others, but can be interpreted as defining a virtual disk resource and then assigning it to the domain. Virtual disks based on physical disks—for example, `/dev/dsk/c3t1d0s2`—provide better performance, but this example is suitable for testing and demonstration purposes. Finally, lines 7 and 8 do the same for a file containing the ISO image of an Oracle Solaris installation CD.

Listing 4.5 Creating a Guest Domain

```
1    # ldm add-domain ldom1
2    # ldm set-core 1 ldom1
3    # ldm set-mem 8g ldom1
4    # ldm add-vnet vnet1 primary-vsw0 ldom1
5    # ldm add-vdsdev /ldoms/ldom1/disk0.img vol10@primary-vds0
6    # ldm add-vdisk vdisk10 vol10@primary-vds0 ldom1
7    # ldm add-vdsdev /mnt/iso/sol-11-2_text-sparc.iso s11-2@primary-vds0
8    # ldm add-vdisk vdisk_iso s11-2@primary-vds0 ldom1
```

The domain's definition is now complete. In this example, we set an OpenBoot Prom (OBP) variable to force the domain to come to the `ok` prompt instead of booting an OS by setting the `autoboot?` property. The "\" in the command line is an escape character, so we can enter the "?" character as a literal value. We then bind the domain, which includes assigning the port used by the virtual console concentrator—in this case, 5000. Next we start the domain, which is similar to performing a "power-on" step on a real server. The OBP displays an `ok` prompt at this point.

```
# ldm set-variable autoboot\?=false ldom1
# ldm bind ldom1
# ldm list ldom1
NAME           STATE      FLAGS    CONS    VCPU   MEMORY    UTIL   NORM   UPTIME
ldom1          bound      ------   5000    8      8G
# ldm start ldom1
```

It is helpful to bring up a second terminal window to watch these steps unfold. We can issue the `telnet` command after the `ldm bind` command assigns the port number. At first, no output follows the output coming from the `telnet` command itself (the line beginning with "`Press ~?`"). When the `ldm start ldom1` command is issued, OpenBoot is loaded and outputs `{0} ok` (see Listing 4.6).

Listing 4.6   Starting a Guest Domain

```
# telnet localhost 5000
Trying 127.0.0.1...
Connected to localhost....
Escape character is '^}'.
Connecting to console "ldom1" in group "ldom1" ....
Press ~? for control options ..
SPARC T5-2, No Keyboard
Copyright (c) 1998, 2012, Oracle and/or its affiliates. All rights reserved.
OpenBoot 4.35.0.build_17, 8.0000 GB memory available, Serial #xxxxxxxx.
Ethernet address 0:xx:xx:xx:xx:xx, Host ID: xxxxxxxx.

{0} ok
```

4.4.2.3 Viewing a Domain

From the `ok` prompt, we can issue OpenBoot commands and view the domain's devices, as shown in Listing 4.7.

Listing 4.7   Viewing a Guest Domain Configuration from the OpenBoot Prompt

```
{0} ok devalias
vdisk_iso              /virtual-devices@100/channel-devices@200/disk@1
vdisk10                /virtual-devices@100/channel-devices@200/disk@0
vnet1                  /virtual-devices@100/channel-devices@200/network@0
net                    /virtual-devices@100/channel-devices@200/network@0
disk                   /virtual-devices@100/channel-devices@200/disk@0
virtual-console        /virtual-devices/console@1
name            aliases
{0} ok
```

This output shows that the domain is a virtual machine with its own devices. Notice how the device aliases are derived from the `ldm` commands that defined them.

4.4.2.4 Installing Solaris in a Domain

Even the thrill of issuing OpenBoot commands can pall after a while, so we will install Oracle Solaris in the domain. Installation can be done over the network if a Solaris Automated Installer or JumpStart infrastructure is available, and it works just as the process does on physical machines. For simplicity, we will boot from an installation ISO image. Except for the device name alias in the boot command, this process is identical to that used when installing from a DVD on a physical machine. The beginning of the boot process is shown in Listing 4.8; the remainder is identical to the bare-metal version.

Listing 4.8   Booting a Guest Domain

```
{0} ok boot vdisk_iso
Boot device: /virtual-devices@100/channel-devices@200/disk@1  File and args:
SunOS Release 5.11 Version 11.2 64-bit
Copyright (c) 1983, 2014, Oracle and/or its affiliates. All rights reserved
```

The rest of the Solaris installation proceeds as usual, and is not shown here.

4.4.2.5 Managing Domains

From the control domain, you can use the `ldm` command to start, stop, reconfigure, migrate, and observe the activity of the domain, and to see which resources are bound to it.

The next example shows short and long forms of `ldm list`. The control domain's console is identified with the "SP" notation, indicating that its console is accessed via the service processor, which is typical on a SPARC server. The line for the guest domain shows the virtual console service port number used to access the domain's console. You can also see the number of virtual CPUs and the physical CPUs to which they are bound. For instance, `ldom1`'s virtual CPU 0 is on physical CPU 8. The long format listing (Listing 4.9), which has been lightly edited for brevity, shows the utilization of each virtual CPU.

Listing 4.9   Listing a Guest Domain Configuration

```
# ldm list
NAME           STATE       FLAGS    CONS    VCPU   MEMORY    UTIL   UPTIME
primary        active      -n-cv-   SP      8      8G        1.2%   1h 3m
ldom1          active      -n----   5000    8      8G        1.8%   22m
# ldm list -l ldom1
NAME           STATE       FLAGS    CONS    VCPU   MEMORY    UTIL   UPTIME
ldom1          active      -n----   5000    8      8G        1.8%   22m

SOFTSTATE
Solaris running
UUID
    6460469f-f897-cbbb-d6b3-dbe5e3427d3a
MAC
    00:14:4f:fb:c9:76
```

```
HOSTID
    0x84fbc976
CONTROL
    failure-policy=ignore
    extended-mapin-space=on
    cpu-arch=native
    rc-add-policy=
    shutdown-group=15
DEPENDENCY
    master=
CORE
    CID    CPUSET
    2      (16, 17, 18, 19, 20, 21, 22, 23)
VCPU
    VID    PID    CID    UTIL STRAND
    0      16     2      2.3%   100%
    1      17     2      1.2%   100%
    2      18     2      1.7%   100%
    3      19     2      2.0%   100%
    4      20     2      1.3%   100%
    5      21     2      1.9%   100%
    6      22     2      1.7%   100%
    7      23     2      1.9%   100%
MEMORY
    RA                 PA                 SIZE
    0xc000000          0x36c000000        2560M
    0x40c000000        0x42c000000        1536M
    0x80c000000        0x50c000000        64M
    0xc00000000        0x810000000        1792M
    0x1000000000       0x8e0000000        704M
    0x140c000000       0xa2c000000        1536M
CONSTRAINT
    cpu=whole-core
    max-cores=unlimited
    threading=max-throughput
VARIABLES
    auto-boot?=false
    pm_boot_policy=disabled=1;ttfc=0;ttmr=0;
NETWORK
    NAME             SERVICE                    DEVICE      MAC              MODE  PVID VID    MTU
    vnet10           primary-vsw0@primary       network@0   00:14:4f:f9:2c:ac 1                1500
DISK
    NAME             VOLUME                     TOUT DEVICE   SERVER        MPGROUP
    vdisk10          vol10@primary-vds0              disk@0   primary
    vdisk_iso        s11-2@primary-vds0              disk@1   primary
VCONS
    NAME             SERVICE                    PORT
    ldom1            primary-vcc0@primary       5000
```

4.4.2.6 Viewing a Domain from the Inside

Once Oracle Solaris is installed in a domain, you can use the normal commands to operate it and view its configuration. The domain in our example, which is found on a T5220 server, has 8 CPUs and a network interface named vnet0. You can boot it from the OpenBoot command line (see Listing 4.10). A pleasant side effect of running in a domain is that the boot process is very fast, because there is no need to perform a power-on self-test (POST) or to probe physical devices. After Solaris is running, you can reboot or shut it down from the OS using the customary init, shutdown, and reboot commands. In addition, you can use the ldm stop command to shut down a domain; it sends a message to Solaris in the domain asking it to gracefully shut itself down. It is also possible to abruptly halt the domain by adding the -f flag to the command.

Listing 4.10   Booting a Guest Domain

```
{0} ok boot disk
Boot device: /virtual-devices@100/channel-devices@200/disk@0  File and args:
SunOS Release 5.11 Version 11.2 64-bit
Copyright (c) 1983, 2014, Oracle and/or its affiliates. All rights reserved.
Hostname: mydomain
vm5 console login: myself
Password:
Last login: Tue Jan 20 15:06:02 on console
Oracle Corporation      SunOS 5.11      11.2      December 2014
# hostid
884fbc976
# psrinfo -vp
The physical processor has 8 virtual processors (0-7)
  UltraSPARC-T2 (chipid 0, clock 1415 MHz)
```

At this point, the administrator can install application software and start using the domain.

4.4.2.7 Dynamic Reconfiguration

The logical domains technology lets the system administrator change the CPU, RAM, and virtual I/O resources made available to guest domains. The Solaris operating system and the Logical Domain Manager interact in a cooperative way to communicate and process requests to change resource allocations.

For example, the domain in the preceding example can be changed to use 16 CPUs (2 cores) by issuing either of these commands on the control domain: ldm add-core 2 ldom2 or ldm set-vcpu 16 ldom2. The command takes effect immediately without rebooting the guest, and the new CPU resources can be used immediately. The `psrinfo` command in the guest domain shows the new CPU configuration (see Listing 4.11).

Listing 4.11   Booting a Guest Domain

```
# psrinfo -vp
The physical processor has 2 cores and 16 virtual processors (0-15)
  The core has 8 virtual processors (0-7)
  The core has 8 virtual processors (8-15)
    UltraSPARC-T2 (chipid 0, clock 1415 MHz)
```

When new CPUs are added to a domain, Solaris receives a message from the hypervisor telling it that it has new CPUs. Solaris updates system data areas to recognize these CPUs, and can start dispatching work to them. When CPUs are removed, Solaris receives a message telling it which CPUs will be removed. Solaris responds by unbinding interrupts from those CPUs and making them ineligible for dispatching processes. When that step is finished, it tells the Logical Domain Manager that the CPUs can be removed. This cooperation ensures that a CPU is not yanked out of a domain while in use. Adding and removing CPU resources is a relatively quick operation, though it can take a substantial time (many seconds) when hundreds of CPUs are added or removed.

Memory can be added or removed from a domain in a similar manner by using the `ldm add-mem`, `ldm set-mem`, or `ldm rm-mem` command. The Logical Domain Manager tells Solaris that it has new real memory to use when adding memory, and it indicates which memory locations it would like to remove when reducing domain memory. Removing memory can take a substantial amount of time because the contents of occupied memory pages must be copied to other pages in the domain, and can even result in swapping. It may not be possible to remove all the desired memory locations because some locations may be used for nonmovable data areas. In such a case, you may see messages saying that not all the memory could be removed.

Virtual I/O devices can be added via the `ldm add-vnet` and `ldm add-vdisk` commands, and I/O can be removed using `ldm rm-vnet` and `ldm rm-vdisk` commands. As with other resource types, interaction between the Logical Domain Manager and Solaris ensures that I/O devices being removed are not in use at the time of their removal. A virtual disk with a mounted file system is not removed unless the `ldm rm-vdisk` command is issued with the `-f` flag to "force" removal. Cryptographic accelerators can also be added or removed on those older servers that use them.

These commands can easily be scripted to ensure their execution at particular times or by a resource manager.

4.4.2.8 Dynamic Resource Management

Oracle VM Server for SPARC provides a policy-based resource manager that automatically adds or removes CPUs from a running domain based on its utilization and relative priority. Policies can be prioritized to ensure that important domains obtain preferential access to resources. They can also be enabled or disabled manually, or based on time of day for different prime-shift and off-hours policies. For example, one domain might have the highest resource needs and priority during the daytime, whereas a domain running batch work might operate in a more resource-intensive manner at night.

Policy rules specify the number of CPUs that a domain has, bounded by minimum and maximum values, and based on their utilization. If CPU utilization exceeds the value of `util-upper`, virtual CPUs are added to the domain until the utilization rate falls below that threshold or the maximum CPU count `vcpu-max` is reached. Conversely, CPUs are removed if the utilization rate drops below `util-lower`, until the number of CPUs reaches the minimum setting. Collectively, the effect is to automatically transfer CPUs from low-utilization domains to high-utilization domains.

The resource manager includes ramp-up (attack) and ramp-down (decay) controls to adjust the system's response to workload changes, specifying the number of CPUs to add or remove based on changes in utilization rates, and indicating how quickly the resource manager should respond. As an example, the command in Listing 4.12 creates a policy that controls the number of CPUs for domain `ldom1`, is named `high-usage`, and is in effect between 9 a.m. and 6 p.m. The lower and upper CPU utilization settings are 25% and 75% CPU busy, respectively. The number of CPUs is adjusted between 2 and 16: One CPU is added or removed at a time (the attack and decay values). For example, if the CPU utilization exceeds 75%, a CPU is added unless `ldom1` already has 16 CPUs.

Listing 4.12 Dynamic Resource Manager

```
# ldm add-policy tod-begin=09:00 tod-end=18:00 util-lower=25 \
     util-upper=75 vcpu-min=2 vcpu-max=16 attack=1 \
     decay=1 priority=1 name=high-usage ldom1
```

4.4.2.9 Cloning a Domain

It is easy to clone domains, especially when using virtual disks residing in ZFS. A golden image instance of Oracle Solaris can be installed, patched, and customized, and then used as a master copy for multiple domains. Note that this method could be used with other storage, but ZFS makes it easy to demonstrate cloning without requiring a storage array.

ZFS administrators can take a snapshot of a virtual disk and create clones from it. Snapshots are read-only images of the data present in a ZFS file system at the time the `zfs snapshot` command is executed, while clones are read/write images based on a snapshot. ZFS snapshots save disk space because space is consumed only for changed disk contents. For example, if a snapshot is taken of a ZFS file system with 100 GB of data but only 5 MB of the data has been changed, only 5MB of additional disk space is consumed by the snapshot. A snapshot, a clone, and the file system they are based on use the same disk locations for data that they share in common. At first, the disk footprint of the new domain will be negligible, as shown in the following example, but eventually it may increase if the contents of the Solaris instance diverge from the master image.

Both physical disk back-ends and virtual disks using a file system like UFS can be easily replicated by using the low-tech `cp` command. With that approach, each copy of a disk will require the same disk space as the original disk.

Before cloning a domain, be sure to shut it down to ensure that the disk contents are stable. You may also wish to unbind the domain if its purpose is to be a template for other domains. Then, assuming use of the same domain as in the previous example, we could issue the commands shown in Listing 4.13.

Listing 4.13 Cloning a VM

```
# zfs snapshot tank/ldoms/ldom1@initial
# zfs list
NAME                              USED  AVAIL  REFER  MOUNTPOINT
...
rpool/ldoms/ldom1                 2.52G  61.6G  2.52G  /ldoms/ldom1
rpool/ldoms/ldom1@initial            0      -  2.52G  -
# zfs clone rpool/ldoms/ldom1@initial  rpool/ldoms/ldom2
# zfs list
NAME                              USED  AVAIL  REFER  MOUNTPOINT
...
rpool/ldoms/ldom1                 2.52G  61.6G  2.52G  /ldoms/ldom1
rpool/ldoms/ldom2                    0  61.6G  2.52G  /ldoms/ldom2
rpool/ldoms/ldom1@initial            0      -  2.52G  -
# ls -l /ldoms/ldom2
-rw------T  1 root     root      10737418240 Jan  2 23:19 disk_ldom.img
{Issue ldm commands to define the domain.}
{The OS is already installed; just boot it.}
{When it has finished booting: }
# zfs list
...
rpool/ldoms/ldom2                 11.2M  60.6G  2.25G  /ldoms/ldom2
```

Essentially the same outcome could be achieved by cloning LUNs, but this listing illustrates the key point. Once you have issued the `ldm` commands needed to define domain `ldom2`, you can simply bind and boot the guest domain—Oracle Solaris is already installed on the virtual disk.

A cloned Solaris instance has the same IP address and host name as the system from which it was cloned. You can choose from among several methods to give it a unique identity. One strategy is to configure the guest to use DHCP when it boots. Another technique is to unconfigure the Solaris system identity before shutting down and cloning the image. The first boot of the cloned image will then prompt (at the guest console) for system identification data, such as the time zone, IP address, and so on. Alternatively, you can configure the golden image domain with a unique host name and IP address that will not be given to any other domain. After booting a domain cloned from the golden image domain, simply log into the clone via SSH, and change its host name and IP address with the standard Solaris administrator commands.

4.4.3 Domain Migration

Domains running on one SPARC server (the source host) can be migrated to a different, compatible server (the target host) as part of planned workload migration. This strategy can be used to free up server memory and CPUs, or to vacate it for planned maintenance.

Note that Oracle VM Server for SPARC does not require domain migration for some situations where that operation is necessary on other platforms. For example, you can dynamically reallocate CPU and memory between domains instead of migrating them to free up resources. More importantly, you can use multiple service domains to provide redundancy: Instead of evacuating a server to upgrade system software, you can update and reboot redundant service domains one at a time to perform a "rolling upgrade" that does not require taking a host system out of service. Migration should not be considered a way to provide "high availability" for a failed system—you cannot migrate from a system that is already down. That said, domain migration is a useful operational tool.

In *live* migration, a running domain is moved from a source server to a target server. The domain's memory contents are transmitted over the network from the source to the target while the domain continues to run. Memory contents are compressed to reduce transmission time, and they are encrypted to prevent security exposures (memory contents might include passwords or private information). Memory contents are decrypted and decompressed on the target system.

Since the domain is still running, it continues to alter memory contents, so the migration process tracks which pages have changed during the migration and retransmits them. After several passes of transmitting memory, the domain is suspended on the source machine, remaining changed pages are transmitted, and the domain then resumes execution on the target machine without a reboot. The original domain on the source system is removed, so that it exists only on the target system.

Live migration has several prerequisites. Domains must use virtual I/O devices (I/O domains cannot be migrated), and the target system must run compatible firmware and logical domains software and have access to the virtual device backends for both the disk and network. Sufficient CPU and memory resources must be available to meet the running domain's requirements. The `ldm migrate` command can be issued with the option `-n` to conduct a dry run that tests whether the migration is possible but does not actually migrate the domain.

By default, live migration requires that the source and target systems have the same SPARC chip type (such as M7) and clock speed. Oracle VM Server for SPARC permits "cross-CPU live migration," in which domains are migrated between different SPARC server types by setting the `cpu-arch` property of each domain before the domain is started. The default value for this property is `native`, which provides optimal performance by letting Solaris exploit all the CPU chip's features. Alternatively, it can be set to `generic`, a lowest-common-denominator value that permits the widest range of live migration compatibility at the cost of eliminating chip-specific optimizations. The value `migration-class1` can be used for T4 and later processors, which permits live migration across those server types while providing access to most CPU optimization features.

In the simplest form of migration, the `ldm migrate` command is used interactively. It prompts for the password for `root` or a `userid` with the LDoms Management profile on the target system's control domain:

```
# ldm migrate ldg1 root@targethost
```

Live migration can also be done using a root-owned private password file—a technique that eliminates the challenge for a password. That option is being deprecated in favor of using SSL certificates to mutually authenticate the source and target systems—a technique that also eliminates the need for a password but offers better security and scalability. It is also possible to enable FIPS 140-2 compliant live migration, in which case both the source and target systems must be in FIPS 140-2 mode; if they are not, the migration will be rejected.

The amount of time that a migration takes depends on the domain memory size, level of activity, and network speed. Processing of migration is a multithreaded operation that uses CPU capacity in the control domain, so it is important to size the control domain with sufficient CPU cores, especially on the source host. Oracle VM Server for SPARC 3.2 added several performance enhancements that can speed up live migration, including parallel page copying, memory-mapped I/O, and LZJB compression.

In *cold* migration, the domain must be stopped and in the *bound* or *inactive* state on the source machine. Cold migration consists of verifying access to the domain's I/O resources and then moving the description of the domain to the target system. Once the domain is migrated, the domain on the source machine is unbound (if it is currently bound to resources) and removed from the source domain configuration. Cold migration can be helpful for planned migration of workloads that can tolerate the outage associated with a shutdown and reboot. It is very fast, as only descriptive information is transmitted between servers.

4.4.4 Physical to Virtual Conversion

Oracle VM Server for SPARC provides a Physical to Virtual (P2V) tool, `ldmp2v`, to automate conversion of physical Oracle Solaris systems to guest domains. This tool moves file system contents from a physical server to a domain that it creates and, if necessary, replaces packages geared toward the sun4u architecture platform (used by all UltraSPARC and SPARC64 systems) with packages for the sun4v architecture used in current SPARC platforms. The physical system can be running Solaris 8, 9, or 10, and must use UFS file systems on either plain disks, SVM metadevices, or VxVM encapsulated boot disks. Systems running Solaris 11 or Solaris 10 with ZFS root cannot be migrated using `ldmp2v`.

P2V migration consists of three phases, which are carried out with the `ldmp2v` command:

1. *Collection*: `ldmp2v collect` runs on the physical machine and collects a file system image and configuration data using `ufsdump` or `flarcreate`. The resulting file can be transmitted to the target system's control domain or stored on an NFS server that is available to both the physical system and the control domain.

2. *Preparation*: `ldmp2v prepare` runs on the control domain of the target platform. It creates a guest domain, and restores the contents of the collected file system into virtual disks.

3. *Conversion*: `ldmp2v convert` runs on the control domain of the target platform. It upgrades the guest domain to prepare it to run as a domain. This process replaces `sun4u` packages (used on older SPARC) with their corresponding `sun4v` versions for current SPARC servers.

If the physical system is running Solaris 8 or Solaris 9, the P2V process upgrades the resulting system image to Solaris 10. The migrated image will then have the same system identity version as on the physical machine. The P2V process can optionally preserve the physical system's network identity by reusing its MAC address.

The P2V process requires Solaris 10 system images to be available in either Solaris installation DVD or network install format, with the package SUNWldmp2v being installed in the control domain. The file /etc/ldmp2v.conf must be populated with variables indicating the names of the default virtual switch and virtual disk servers, and identifying the type of disk back-ends to use for virtual disks. The P2V command must be made available to the physical system, either by NFS mount or by copying the command to a local disk.

Once this process is complete, the guest domain has the same system identity and applications as it did on the original physical server. The amount of time to complete the conversion process depends on the sizes of the file systems being copied and the network bandwidth available for their transmission to the control domain. The amount of administrator effort is reduced compared to a fresh un-automated install, with only a few commands needed to carry out a complete system migration.

Existing systems can be also consolidated and moved into domains by using Oracle Solaris Zones. Zones in a domain can be created from physical system images by using methods analogous to the previously described steps—that is, by taking archives of Solaris images and then using them to create zones. Domains running Solaris 11 can host native Solaris 11 Zones and Solaris 10 Zones. Solaris 10 domains can run either native Solaris 10 Zones or Solaris 8 or Solaris 9 Containers. This attractive alternative readily handles cases (boot disks on ZFS, Solaris 11 hosts) not supported by ldmp2v. It is documented in the Oracle Solaris Administration documentation library in the manual covering Oracle Solaris Zones, Oracle Solaris 10 Zones, and Resource Management.

4.4.5 Oracle VM Manager and Ops Center

The preceding examples managed Oracle VM Server for SPARC by working through its built-in command-line interface. Such interactions can be scripted, in a process that does not require any additional software, but does require prerequisite skills and may be intimidating for the occasional user. Also, the effort required to script/automate this process does not scale well when many machines are involved.

Fortunately, Oracle VM Server for SPARC is part of the Oracle VM product family, which includes Oracle VM Server for x86. Both VM Servers can be administered using Oracle VM Manager, which provides GUI support and a sophisticated API for managing virtual machines and the storage and network infrastructure on which they run. Servers are arranged into pools that are treated as a uniform collection of compute resources, without the need to log into individual servers to control their VMs and resources. The administrator can define, start, stop, modify, clone, migrate, and delete virtual machines from the GUI interface, as well as define and control network, storage, and server resources used for virtualization. Advanced server policies can be set for balancing loads across a pool, or setting up high-availability (HA) clustering that automatically starts VMs if a server fails. Oracle VM Manager also provides an advanced CLI and web services API for automation. For a full description of Oracle VM Manager, see the documentation at `http://docs.oracle.com/cd/E50245_01/index.html`.

Figure 4.4 shows an Oracle VM Manager screen with a SPARC server pool and an x86 pool, both administered from the same window. You can see the servers and VMs in each pool, and a VM (domain) has been selected and highlighted in

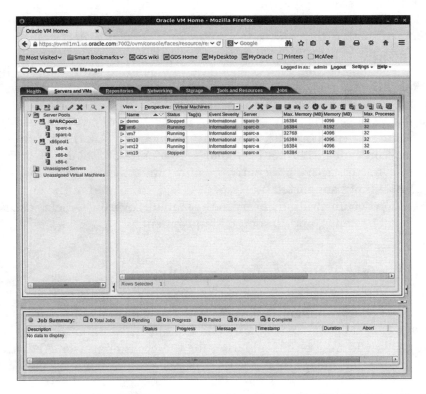

Figure 4.4   Oracle VM Manager with Two Server Pools: SPARC and x86

the SPARC pool. That activates the icons for editing the VM (the yellow slanted pencil), as well as stopping it, connecting to its console, rebooting it, live migrating it to another server in the pool, or cloning it.

Next, we will create some VMs using the Oracle VM Manager GUI. The user interface includes a Create Virtual Machine icon, which we can use to create a new VM or make clones from a pre-created virtual machine template. In this case, we will clone a Solaris 11.2 template to make three copies (see Figure 4.5). Each of these clones will have Solaris pre-installed and ready to be configured and run. Prebuilt Solaris virtual machines can be downloaded from the Oracle Software Delivery Cloud (OSDN; `https://edelivery.oracle.com/oraclevm`).

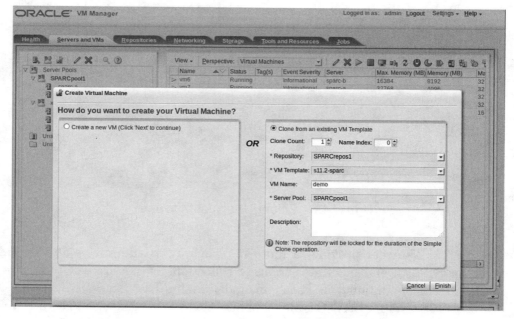

Figure 4.5   Cloning Virtual Machines from a Template

Editing a virtual machine is also straightforward: Just select the virtual machine and click on the yellow "edit" icon. A pop-up window then lets you change virtual machine attributes such as the number of CPUs and the amount of memory, or add virtual disk and network devices, as shown in Figure 4.6.

It is also easy to migrate a VM with the Oracle VM user interface: Select a VM and click on the migrate icon to bring up the dialog box shown in Figure 4.7, which lets the administrator specify a migration target.

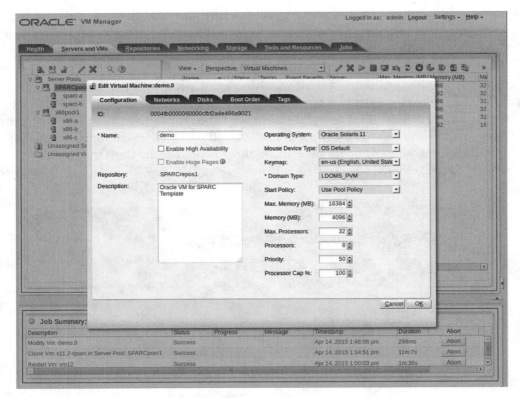

Figure 4.6   Editing a Virtual Machine

Oracle VM Manager provides a more natural way to administer Oracle VM Server for SPARC, and facilitates treating collections of servers as pools of resources instead of administering each one individually.

Oracle VM Server for SPARC is also supported by OpenStack, with a Nova driver that provides compute and virtualization, in conjunction with other OpenStack services such as Neutron (networking), Cinder (block storage), and Horizon (web-based management). OpenStack can be used to create Infrastructure as a Service (IaaS) clouds deploying guest domains. For further information, see `http://docs.oracle.com/cd/E69554_01/html/E79549/`.

Another solution is Oracle Enterprise Manager Ops Center, which provides comprehensive system management. It offers full life-cycle support for provisioning and managing systems in a data center from a single user interface, for both

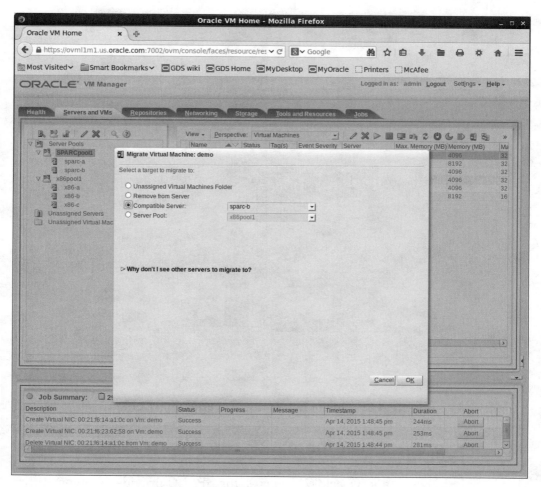

Figure 4.7   Migrating a Guest Domain

real and virtual systems. You can use Ops Center to create, delete, configure, boot, and shut down domains. It also provides monitoring and management, showing utilization charts for CPU, memory, and file systems. Ops Center manages resource pools, permitting dynamic reallocation of resources based on policies, and it provides a graphical interface for controlling domain migration. For details, see Chapter 7, and `http://www.oracle.com/software/products/opscenter/`.

Figure 4.8 shows several physical nodes that are visible in the assets tab of the Ops Center, with details provided for the resources used by several domains.

Figure 4.8   Oracle Enterprise Manager Ops Center

4.5 Oracle VM Server for SPARC and Solaris Zones

Oracle Solaris Zones and Oracle VM Server for SPARC provide complementary methods to virtualize Solaris systems, so it is natural to compare them.

Zones provide lightweight OS virtualization with excellent isolation, security, observability, fast deployment, resource granularity, and native performance. However, because multiple zones run on a single Solaris instance, native zones do not permit running multiple kernel update levels at the same time. Zones also have some restrictions, such as not providing support for live migration, and being dependent on the Solaris instance in which they run. These issues were addressed in Oracle Solaris 11.3 and later versions with the introduction of live migration of Solaris Kernel Zones.

In contrast, domains are more like "business as usual" for system administrators and application planners, and more like the industry-standard concept of virtual machines. They are individually installed, patched, used, and managed, much like physical servers, and they provide even better separation than zones. Oracle Solaris can be installed in a domain via a network install or by booting from a DVD device, just like on a physical server. Like zones, domains can also be cloned from previously installed and customized instances. Unlike zones, however, a running domain can be migrated from one server to another without rebooting the domain, and different Solaris versions can coexist on the same hosting environment.

Domains are available on all currently shipping SPARC servers, whereas zones are available on any SPARC or x86 platform that supports Solaris. Also, because domains host full OS instances on dedicated CPUs and RAM, they have a larger resource footprint than zones. Many more virtualized instances can be hosted on the same platform by using zones than by using domains.

Solaris Zones and Oracle VM Server for SPARC domains can be combined without adding overhead by running zones within domains to achieve the highest degree of flexible virtualization. Separate OS instances can be configured when different OS kernel levels are required, with each OS instance hosting many lightweight, virtualized zone environments.

4.6 Summary

Oracle VM Server for SPARC provides efficient, highly functional, and robust virtualization on SPARC servers, suitable for the most demanding applications. A domain is a separate, independent virtual machine with its own OS instance.

Compared to other virtualization technologies, Oracle VM Server for SPARC provides an extremely efficient hypervisor without the overhead of traditional hypervisors. It also eliminates the licensing costs associated with commercial virtualization products.

Oracle VM Server for SPARC is an ideal choice for migrating from older platforms to current hardware in a consolidated, energy-efficient platform. Oracle Solaris systems can be easily moved to a domain, thereby leveraging Solaris and SPARC binary compatibility. Workloads from other operating systems and platforms can also be migrated to provide an efficient virtualized solution that reduces both energy costs and server sprawl.

Physical Domains

Virtualization technologies have breathed new life into the concept of consolidated workloads, returning to this earlier model from the model of one workload per server. However, the use of virtualization can lead to an environment with "too many eggs in one basket" and the risk of a complete service outage, including all related workloads, due to one hardware failure. In that situation, a combination of virtualization and partitioning is more appropriate.

5.1 Introduction

The consolidated workload form of server virtualization relies on the ability to group multiple subsets of resources in a server. Physical domains ensure that each group is not only software fault isolated, but also fully hardware and electrically fault isolated. It is important to understand how the hardware works and how physical resources are assigned to domains, as this scheme has a direct impact on the resources available to the hypervisor that runs in each physical domain (the PDomain, or PDom for short).

PDoms are an implementation of hardware partitions, but an implementation unlike other virtualization technologies. Technologies based on hypervisors (e.g., Oracle VM Server for SPARC, also known as logical domains, or LDoms for short) depend on services running in a special LDom to configure the guest virtual environments. This special LDom is known as the control domain. When virtualized interfaces (network, disks, CPUs, consoles) are used, they must be routed through the hypervisor to the control domain, which in turn has an impact on performance. Where there is a requirement for bare-metal performance, high I/O throughput, large memory footprint, yet flexible configurability, you should consider running the application in the control domain instead of guest domains. The third virtualization technology is OS virtualization (e.g., Oracle Solaris Zones). As it runs in every guest domain, it will not be referenced in this chapter. LDoms are covered in more detail in Chapter 4, "Oracle VM Server for SPARC," while Oracle Solaris Zones are described in detail in Chapter 3, "Oracle Solaris Zones."

This chapter discusses the features of physical domains as implemented in the SPARC M6-32, M7-8, and M7-16 servers (see Figure 5.1). While the M6 or M7 notation indicates the actual SPARC processor supported in that server, the number after the dash indicates the maximum number of processors possible in a physical domain. While both the SPARC M6-32 and the SPARC M7-16 offer flexible physical domain configurations, their implementations are quite different and require different methods of setting up environments for logical domains.

Figure 5.1   SPARC M7-8, M7-16, and M6-32 Servers

5.2 SPARC M6: An Introduction

Oracle's SPARC M6 processor-based servers offer hard domain isolation and add the capability of each hard domain to run a logical domain environment (i.e., a hypervisor). There can be up to 4 such environments in the M6-32. The SPARC M6 processor supports 12 cores per processor, with an architecture that supports up to 96 threads. This architecture is ideal for today's business requirements of higher consolidation of data center services with no loss of performance, regardless of the technology being used.

While the Oracle SPARC M6 processor utilizes many of the constructs found in the SPARC T-series server lines, the concept of physical domains is unique to the SPARC M-series servers. The hallmark of the SPARC M-series server architecture is high performance and bandwidth, vertical scaling of CPUs and memory, and high availability delivered primarily through redundancy.

SPARC M-series servers are modular in design and utilize many of the same common components. On the SPARC M6-32, CPUs and memory are placed in the same board, called the CMU. The I/O is on a different board, called the IOU. For the SPARC M6-32, up to 16 CMU and 16 IOU boards are supported.

5.2.1 CPU/Memory and I/O Units

As the name indicates, a CPU and memory unit (CMU) board contains 2 processors (or CPU) and 64 DIMMs slots for memory. A separate cage called the I/O unit (IOU) provides 16 PCIe slots and 8 disk drives. On the SPARC M6-32, there must be at least one CMU for each IOU, but it is possible to have more CMU boards than IOU boards. It is important to note that the PCIe controller is actually part of the M6 processor itself. Two PCIe root complexes are found on the SPARC M6 chip. With the newer SPARC processor, M7, the PCIe controller was moved off-chip, to its own ASIC. This difference is important when setting up the I/O environment for the logical domain guests.

Figure 5.2 shows the general layout of CMUs and I/O in a domain configurable unit (DCU) on the SPARC M6-32. DCUs are the building blocks of physical domains.

Figure 5.2 depicts just one of the 4 possible DCUs in the M6-32. The DCU can have up to 8 CPUs that are balanced against the 16 PCIe slots. The ability to access all 16 PCIe slots requires 2 CMU boards at minimum.

5.2.2 Domain Configurable Units

PDoms are not constructed by combining CPUs, memory, and I/O. Rather, they are built by combining domain configurable units. In the SPARC M6-32, there are up to four DCUs, all of which are configurable. Figure 5.3 shows the possible PDoms in a SPARC M6-32.

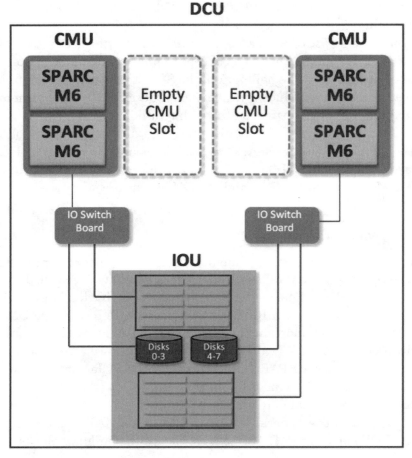

Figure 5.2 Minimum Layout for 16 PCIe Slot Configuration on the
SPARC M6-32 Server

5.3 SPARC M7: An Introduction

Oracle's new SPARC M7 processor-based servers take Oracle's very successful
SPARC processor to new levels by offering the world's first implementation of
Software in Silicon technology—a technology intended to support the "cloud" with
the most secure platforms in the world. The SPARC M7 processor also improves
density by doubling the core count of previous-generation processors: It supports
32 cores per processor, with an architecture that supports up to 256 threads in as
little as two rack units (2 RU). The SPARC M7 processor also doubles the memory

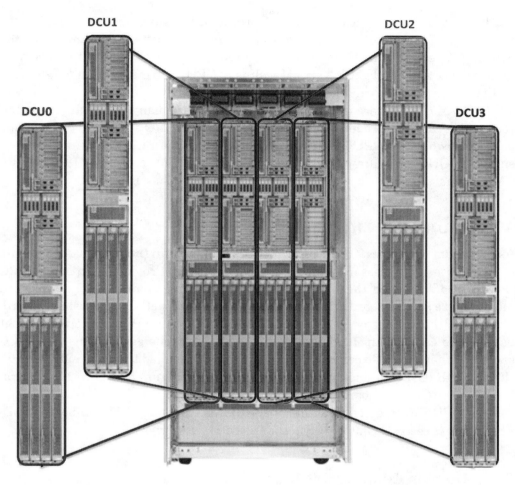

Figure 5.3   DCUs in a SPARC M6-32. Each DCU is outlined.

and I/O bandwidths of previous SPARC processors. A new cache and memory hierarchy greatly improve the processing speed of earlier systems. This architecture is ideal for today's business requirements, which include higher consolidation of data center services with no loss of performance, regardless of which virtualization technology is used. The Software in Silicon technology on the SPARC M7 processor is delivered via eight on-chip accelerators that offload database query processing and perform real-time data decompression. This acceleration, high thread count, and high performance can be delivered consistently across all of the virtualization technologies.

Although the new Oracle SPARC M7 processor is used on both the SPARC T7 and SPARC M7 server lines, the concept of physical domains is unique to the SPARC M7 servers. The hallmarks of the SPARC M7 server architecture are high performance and bandwidth, vertical scaling of CPUs and memory, and high availability delivered primarily through redundancy.

SPARC M7 servers are modular in design and utilize many of the same common components as their predecessor. All CPU, Memory and I/O are placed on the same board, known as the CPU/memory I/O unit (CMIOU). For the SPARC M7-8, up to eight CMIOU boards are placed in a CMIOU chassis. For the SPARC M7-16, two CMIOU chassis are connected together with a switch chassis.

5.3.1 CPU/Memory I/O Units

As their name indicates, CMIOUs are boards that contain the three base elements of a computer: a processor (or CPU), memory, and I/O. Previous high-end SPARC servers had separated the I/O on its own board while combining the CPU and memory on a second board. Now all three are brought together onto a single board.

Each CPU is connected to 16 memory DIMMs and three PCIe 3.0 x16 slots that use a PCIe carrier. An important change from previous generations of SPARC servers is that the PCIe control is now separate; it is called the I/O controller hub (IOH). Each IOH contains five PCIe root complexes. Figure 5.4 shows the general layout of the CMIOU board.

Each CPU is connected to 16 memory DIMMs via eight buffer-on-board (BoB) ASICs and three PCIe 3.0 x16 slots that use a PCIe carrier.

5.3.2 Domain Configurable Units

Physical domains are not constructed by combining CPUs, memory, and I/O, but rather are built by combining DCUs. Two different configurations of SPARC M7-8 exist, each with a fixed domain configuration: one with a single PDom, and the other with two PDoms. These physical domains are static, as their size cannot be altered. In contrast, the SPARC M7-16 contains up to four DCUs; these DCUs are configurable and can be combined to form PDoms.

The SPARC M7-8 with a single static PDom can be treated as a single computer without domains. We will not discuss it further in this book. The SPARC M7-8 with two static PDoms is shown in Figure 5.5; each PDom is outlined.

There is similar flexibility in the DCU layout for the M7-16. The SPARC M7-16 has four DCUs, as shown in Figure 5.6. These DCUs can be combined to form PDoms.

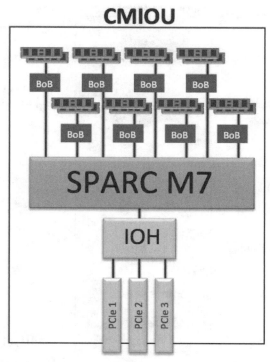

Figure 5.4 Components on a Single CMIOU Board
in SPARC M7-8 or SPARC M7-16 Server

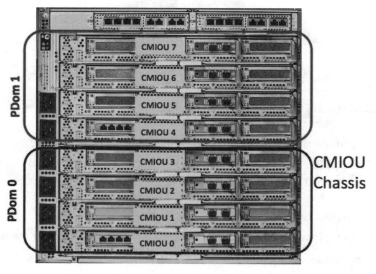

Figure 5.5 PDoms in a SPARC M7-8

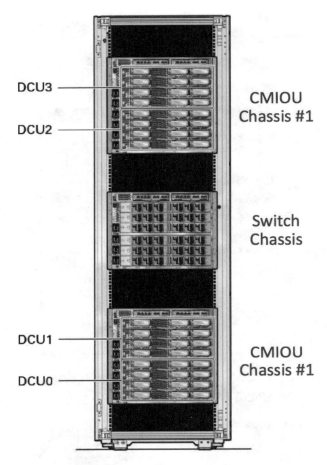

Figure 5.6   DCUs in a SPARC M7-16

5.4 Virtualization Technologies

Oracle's layered virtualization technologies can be used together to create resilient high-availability systems. Three virtualization technologies are used on Oracle SPARC Servers:

- Physical domains are used primarily to isolate hardware.
- Logical domains are used primarily to isolate the operating system.
- Oracle Solaris Zones are used primarily to isolate programs.

The most important capability of the high-end Oracle SPARC Servers is the support for layering the virtualization technologies. As physical domains are the most basic technology, they are designed to run one or more logical domains, or guest domains. Each guest domain runs an instance of Oracle Solaris, which in turn allows Solaris to support up to hundreds of individual Oracle Solaris Zones. Every zone appears to the applications running inside it as if that zone is a complete and unique instance of Solaris.

Figures 5.7, 5.8, and 5.9 show the different layers possible on different SPARC servers. The most important capability of the high-end Oracle SPARC servers is that they support all three virtualization types.

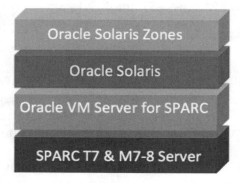

Figure 5.7 SPARC T7 and M7-8 (One PDom) Server Virtualization Layers

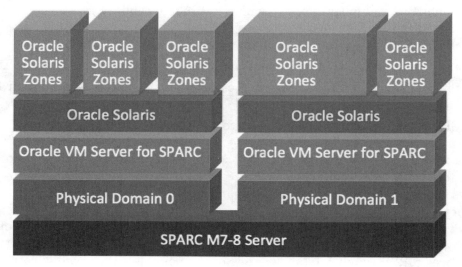

Figure 5.8 SPARC M7-8 (Two PDoms) Server Virtualization Layers

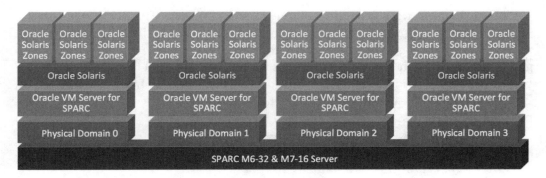

Figure 5.9   SPARC M6-32 and M7-16 Server Virtualization
Layers for Up to Four PDoms

5.4.1 Physical Domains

The physical domains on the SPARC M6 and M7 servers provide IT organizations with the ability to divide a single hardware system into multiple, fault-isolated environments. The SPARC M7-8 server supports either one or two static PDoms, though this support is provided only as a factory-installed option. By comparison, the SPARC M6-32 and M7-16 servers can be configured with one to four dynamic PDoms. With proper configuration, hardware or software faults in one domain remain isolated and unable to affect the operation of other domains.

The maximum number of processors in a PDom depends on the model:

- SPARC M6-32 servers can have up to 32 processors in a single PDom.
- Dual-PDom SPARC M7-8 servers can have up to 4 processors in each PDom.
- Single-PDom SPARC M7-8 servers can have up to 8 processors in their lone PDom.
- SPARC M7-16 servers can have up to 16 processors in a single PDom.

Because a physical domain is made from a combination of DCUs, there are several possible DCU combinations that you can use to make a PDom. Figure 5.10 shows the possible PDom configurations in the SPARC M6-32 server.

There is no requirement for the DCUs to be adjacent to each other to be part of a PDom. Figure 5.11 shows two different combinations for two PDoms, both of which work equally well.

Figures 5.12 through 5.17 show a few of the possible PDom configurations in the SPARC M7 servers.

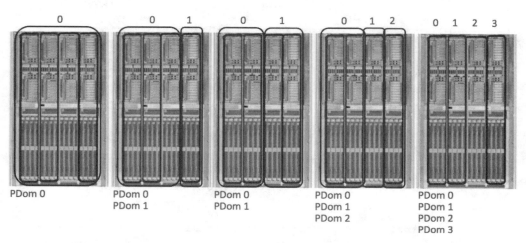

Figure 5.10   SPARC M6-32 Server: Maximum of Four PDoms

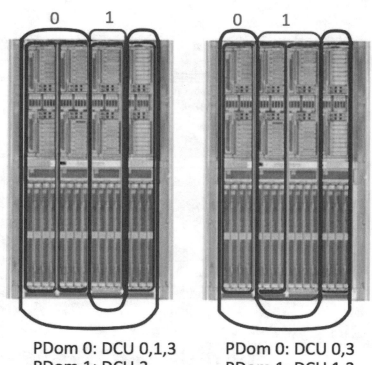

Figure 5.11   Potential Physical Domain Combinations in a SPARC M6-32 Server

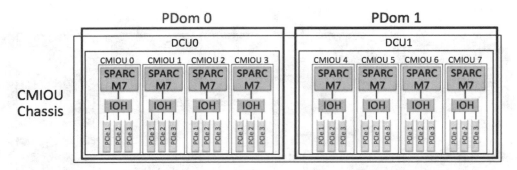

Figure 5.12   SPARC M7-8 Server with Two Static PDoms

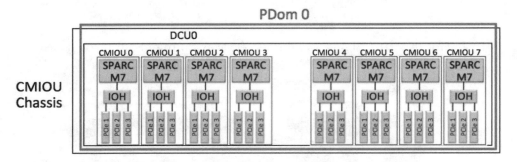

Figure 5.13   SPARC M7-8 Server with One PDom

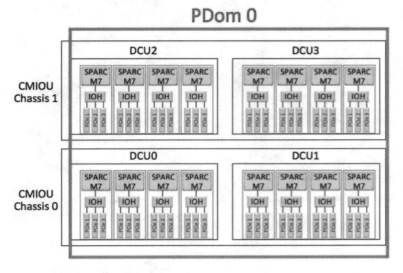

Figure 5.14   A Single PDom in the SPARC M7-16 Server

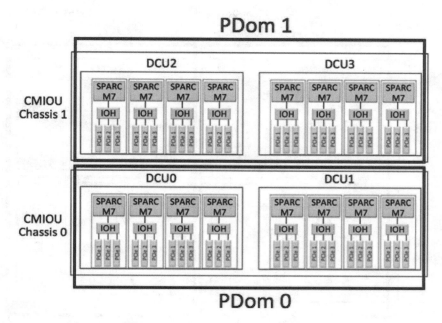

Figure 5.15   Two PDoms in the SPARC M7-16 Server

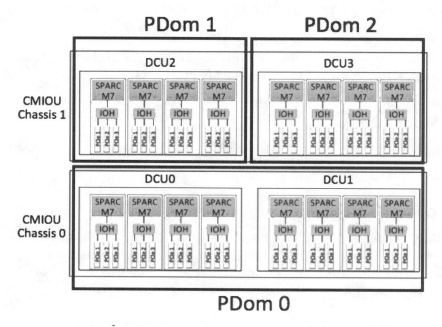

Figure 5.16   Three PDoms in the SPARC M7-16 Server

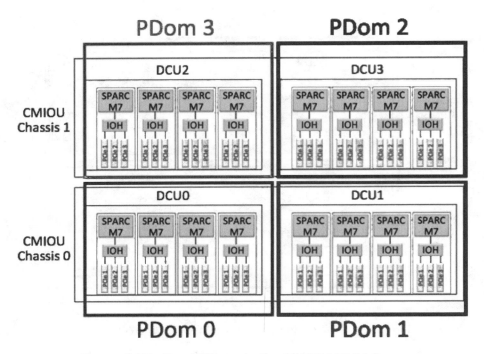

Figure 5.17   Four PDoms in the SPARC M7-16 Server

The choice of layout to use depends on the business and technical requirements of the physical environment in which the applications will be run.

5.4.2 Static PDoms

As noted earlier, the PDoms on the SPARC M7-8 are static. Thus, their DCU configurations cannot be changed.

5.4.3 Dynamic PDoms

The SPARC M6-32 and SPARC M7-16 both support dynamic PDoms. As long as a DCU has a CMU (M6) or CMIOU (M7), it can be assigned to a PDom.

In the example that follows, we will create `PDom0` on the SPARC M7-16 using the command-line interface (CLI) on the service processor (SP).

Step 1. Determine which DCUs are available:

```
show /Servers/PDomains/PDomain_0/HOST
Properties:
autorestart = reset
autorunonerror = powercycle
bootfailrecovery = poweroff
bootrestart = none
boottimeout = 0
dcus_assignable = /SYS/DCU0 /SYS/DCU1 /SYS/DCU2 /SYS/DCU3
dcus_assigned = (none)
dcus_available = /SYS/DCU0 /SYS/DCU1 /SYS/DCU2 /SYS/DCU3
```

Step 2. Assign `DCU0` and `DCU1` to `PDomain_0`:

```
set /Servers/PDomains/PDomain_0/HOST/ dcus_assigned="/SYS/DCU0 /SYS/DCU1"
Set 'dcus_assigned' to '/SYS/DCU0 /SYS/DCU1'
```

Step 3. Verify the assignment:

```
show /Servers/PDomains/PDomain_0/HOST
Properties:
autorestart = reset
autorunonerror = powercycle
bootfailrecovery = poweroff
bootrestart = none
boottimeout = 0
dcus_assignable = /SYS/DCU0 /SYS/DCU1 /SYS/DCU2 /SYS/DCU3
dcus_assigned = /SYS/DCU0 /SYS/DCU1
dcus_available = /SYS/DCU0 /SYS/DCU1 /SYS/DCU2 /SYS/DCU3
```

5.4.4 Logical Domains

Like prior generations of SPARC processors, the SPARC M6 and M7 processors support a multithreaded hypervisor that enables the creation of logical domains within a single physical domain. The hypervisor is a small firmware layer that provides a stable virtual machine architecture that is tightly integrated with the processor. Multithreading is crucial to its operation, because the hypervisor interacts directly with the underlying multicore/multithreading processor. Supported in all servers from Oracle using Oracle's multicore/multithreaded technology, Oracle VM Server for SPARC provides full virtual machines that run an independent operating system instance. Each PDom runs its own instance of the OVM for SPARC hypervisor.

The number of logical domains you can create depends on the hardware configuration of the server. By default, one domain—the primary domain (also known as the control domain)—is configured when you install the OS on a host. The primary domain cannot be removed or renamed, and all of the resources are assigned to the primary domain when the domain is configured. You can have as many as 128 guest domains per PDom, and each guest domain can operate on as few as one CPU thread. However, most workloads require more than one CPU thread.

The most critical logical domain within any PDom is the *control domain*. This administrative control point runs Solaris and the Logical Domain Manager services. By default, all virtual services are provided by this domain. Of special interest are the virtual I/O services.

An understanding of where the PCIe root complexes are provided plays a part when deciding how to best lay out the control domain and the guest domains. Figure 5.18 shows the I/O layout of PCIe slots in a fully configured DCU in the SPARC M6-32. Each PCIe root complex on a SPARC M6 processor is marked by either RC0 or RC1, since there are two root complexes per SPARC M6 processor. Each CMU has two M6 processors, identified as either M6#0 or M6#1 in Figure 5.18. Each disk controller (Dsk Ctlr) PCIe card provides control to two individual disks.

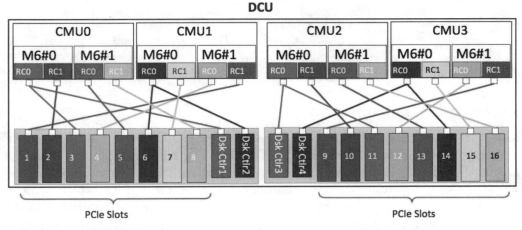

Figure 5.18   I/O Layout in a Single DCU on a SPARC M6-32

Figure 5.19 shows the I/O layout of PCIe slots for a single CMIOU in the SPARC M7-8 and M7-16 servers. As mentioned earlier, the PCIe root complex is not on the M7 processor itself, but has been moved to a separate ASIC called the I/O hub (IOH). Each IOH provides five PCIe root complexes, though only RC2 is used on the T7 servers.

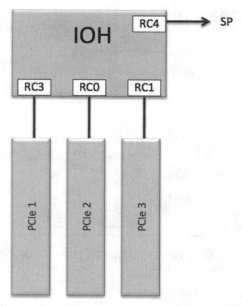

Figure 5.19   I/O Layout in a Single CMIOU on an M7-8 or M7-16 Server

Figures 5.20 and 5.21 show the I/O layout for both configurations of the M7-8. For the SPARC M7-16, the layout would resemble that in Figure 5.21 for each CMIOU chassis, except the PDoms would be identified as DCUs.

The PCIe paths through the root complex to the PCIe cards will matter when we are setting up redundant network and disk services for guest LDoms. There is an important difference between the SPARC M6-32 and the servers based on the SPARC M7 processor that changes one possible setup of LDoms—namely, the use of the configuration called direct I/O (DIO). The SPARC M6-32 supports the use of DIO because there are two PCIe root complexes are on the M6 processor itself. Since the servers based on the M7 processor use a separate ASIC for PCIe control (the IOH), they do not support DIO for LDom I/O setup. The IOH utilizes four root complexes on the SPARC M7-8 and M7-16. LDoms are covered in more detail in Chapter 4.

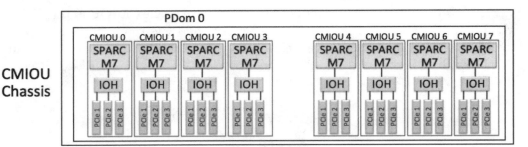

Figure 5.20   I/O Layout in a Single PDom on an M7-8 Server

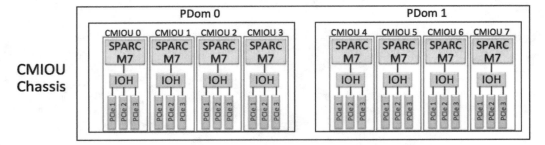

Figure 5.21   I/O Layout for Dual PDoms on an M7-8 Server

The SPARC M7-8 server supports either one or two static PDoms, which cannot be reconfigured. In contrast, the SPARC M6-32 and M7-16 contain one to four dynamic PDoms that can be configured. Each PDom is represented as `/Servers/ PDomains/PDomain_n` in Oracle ILOM, where n ranges from zero to 1 less than the maximum number of possible PDoms, depending on the number of boards in the system and the slots they occupy. Each DCU is represented as `/System/DCUs/ DCU_n` in Oracle ILOM, where n ranges from zero to 1 less than the maximum number of possible DCUs, depending on the number of boards in the system and the slots they occupy.

When referencing a physical domain, the name `HOST` must be used. For example, for `PDom0`, the name used is `/Servers/PDomains/PDomain_0/HOST`. This name must be used when assigning a DCU, powering on or off, and other operations.

5.4.5 Oracle Solaris Zones

PDoms have no direct impact on the configuration of Oracle Solaris Zones. PDoms can provide the utmost in fault isolation when the system is using zones, and they do not require the use of LDoms. Solaris Zones are covered in detail in Chapter 3.

5.5 Fault Isolation

As described earlier, PDoms are used to isolate hardware faults, LDoms are used to isolate operating system faults, and Oracle Solaris Zones are used to isolate individual processes. The priority here is the impact of those faults and then the time and process steps required to resolve them. This section will not discuss those issues here in all their gory details, but rather will give just enough information to appreciate the design choices that will be affected by the type of virtualization used on server deployment.

This is a good time to stop and recall that the computer industry acronym "RAS" is really a combination of three different words: reliability, availability, and serviceability. Availability, for example, is driven mostly through redundancy. On the SPARC M6-32, M7-8, and M7-16 platforms, hardware faults are mitigated by two types of redundant components:

- Redundant power supplies and fans
- Redundant service processors

When this type of redundancy is present, a fault in any of these components will not bring down the servers, or any of the PDoms. All of these components are hot-serviceable, which means they can be repaired while the server continues to run.

The next level of fault isolation is found within the PDom itself. The focus here is isolating the CPUs, memory, and I/O contained within the PDom. Many of the best practices used on stand-alone servers also apply to PDoms.

5.5.1 Redundant CPUs in a PDom

SPARC servers can detect hardware errors, and offline a CPU core or the entire CPU, if too many recoverable errors have been detected. The goal is to remove the faulty CPU/core before it causes any application, operating system, or hypervisor to crash.

For the LDoms running in the PDom to have good isolation and performance, it is best to assign whole cores to the LDoms. This arrangement prevents changes in the core from affecting more than one LDom. It also means that at least some cores in the PDom should not be assigned to any LDom. That way, if a core must be taken offline, a spare core can be used in place of the offlined core. This layout is easier to achieve on the SPARC M7-8 and M7-16 since each M7 processor has 32 cores. By comparison, the M6 processor in the SPARC M6-32 has only 12 cores, so there might be fewer spare cores to replace the faulty cores. It is highly recommended to have a minimum of two CMU boards in a PDom on the SPARC M6-32 and a minimum of two CMIOU boards for a PDom in the SPARC M7-8 and M7-16.

5.5.2 Redundant Memory in a PDom

All M7-based SPARC servers now support DIMM sparing. This feature is possible only when each CMIOU has all 16 DIMM slots populated. When all memory slots are populated, there is no loss of data or system services if a DIMM completely fails. When choosing between half-populated memory using a higher-density DIMM versus fully populated memory using a lower-density DIMM, choose the latter if full memory protection is needed to meet uptime requirements.

On the SPARC M6-32, there is no DIMM sparing, but pin steering is available.

5.5.3 Redundant I/O in a PDom

The Oracle VM for SPARC (i.e., the hypervisor and Logical Domain Manager) allows for very flexible I/O configurations. LDoms were covered in Chapter 4. For improved application service uptime, it is always recommended to have redundant connections to boot storage, data storage, and network services for each LDom. Figures 5.11 and 5.12 give critical details on how the processors communicate with each PCIe slot. Following the guidelines of Chapter 4, redundant virtual I/O services, redundant root domains, and redundant root complexes should be spread across CMIOU boards where possible. On the SPARC M6-32, because the PCIe controllers are on the M6 processor itself, the loss of a processor means the loss of multiple PCIe slots. Given this risk, care must be taken when setting up all I/O services. As noted earlier, the practice of assigning a single PCIe slot to an LDom (direct I/O) is supported only on servers prior to those based on the M7 processor.

5.6 Oracle Enterprise Manager Ops Center

You can monitor and manage the SPARC M6 and M7 servers, along with other servers and assets, by using the Oracle Enterprise Manager Ops Center software. You can run this software's discovery process to add information about your server to a database of physical servers, virtual systems, operating systems, networks, and storage. You can then use this software to monitor and manage all of these products from a single interface.

Figure 5.22 is a sample screenshot of Oracle Enterprise Manager Ops Center managing a SPARC M7-8 server.

Figure 5.22 Oracle Enterprise Manager Ops Center
Managing a SPARC M7-8 Server

5.7 Summary

Physical domains implement hard partitioning with extreme isolation between virtual environments. They are available in the SPARC M6 and M7 systems and provide excellent reliability, availability, and serviceability characteristics. They are appropriate for the most demanding business-critical and mission-critical workloads as well as for consolidation of many smaller workloads. Use PDoms where the business requirements call for separating business operations, or to isolate hardware faults.

For additional details on physical domains and white papers on architectures and RAS, please refer to the SPARC M6-32 and SPARC M7-8 and M7-16 documentation at `http://docs.oracle.com/en/hardware/`.

6

Oracle VM VirtualBox

Oracle VM VirtualBox is a high-performance, cross-platform virtualization engine for use on computers running Microsoft Windows, some Linux distributions, Oracle Solaris, or MacOS. Designed for use on Intel and AMD x86 systems, Oracle VM VirtualBox can be deployed on desktop or server hardware. As a hosted hypervisor, VirtualBox extends the existing operating system installed on the hardware rather than replacing it.

VirtualBox includes a hypervisor for the host platform, an application programming interface (API) and software development kit (SDK) for managing guest virtual machines (VMs), a command-line tool for managing guests locally, a web service for remote management of guests, a wizard-style graphical tool to manage guests, a graphical console for displaying guest applications on the local host, and a built-in Remote Desktop Protocol (RDP) server that provides complete access to a guest from a remote client.

As you can see in Figure 6.1, VirtualBox can run on a wide variety of host platforms. Binaries are available for these operating systems, most of them in 64-bit versions:

- Solaris (64-bit only) 10 8/11 (U10) (64-bit only) and newer (Intel only, SPARC platform not supported).
- Oracle Linux 5 and newer.
- Microsoft Windows Vista through Windows 10 and Windows Server 2008 and 2012.
- Mac OS X 10.9 and newer (Intel only).

- Linux distributions, including openSuSE (11.4 and newer), Ubuntu (10.04 and newer), Debian GNU/Linux 6 and 8, Oracle Linux (5 and newer), Red Hat Enterprise Linux (5 and newer), Fedora (6 and newer) and others. Most systems based on Linux kernel 2.6 or 3.x are supported.

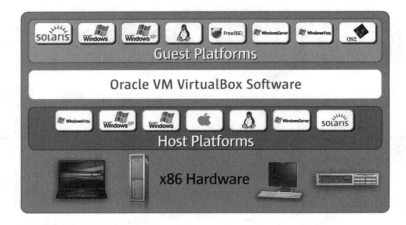

Figure 6.1   Platforms Supported by Oracle VM VirtualBox

There are no specific limitations on the guest operating system, but the supported guests include all of the host operating systems plus FreeBSD and legacy Windows versions through the most current version of the Windows operating system. No special hardware is required to run VirtualBox other than an Intel x86-compatible system and adequate memory to run the guests. If the system has Intel VT-x or AMD-V hardware virtualization extensions and they are enabled in the BIOS, VirtualBox can take advantage of them and provide even better guest operational behavior. (The VBoxManage list ostypes command, covered later in this chapter, can be used to list all of the supported guest operating systems.)

The modular design of VirtualBox provides a consistent set of features across a wide range of host platforms. As a consequence, a virtual machine or disk image created on one host can be loaded and run on any supported host. In addition, a user or administrator who is familiar with managing guest virtual machines on one type of host can manage guests on any of the other supported systems.

Advanced desktop features such as Seamless Mode and Shared Clipboard give users a uniquely intimate experience when interacting with locally running guests. The built-in Virtual Remote Desktop Protocol (VRDP) server, available by installing the Virtual Remote Desktop Extension (VDRE) described later, makes VirtualBox ideal for consolidating and hosting remote desktop systems. VRDP is a backward-compatible extension to Microsoft's Remote Desktop Protocol (RDP); thus, you can use any standard RDP client to control the remote VM. Recent improvements in disk and network performance, especially when combined with advanced resource management features in Oracle Solaris, make VirtualBox an excellent choice for hosting server workloads.

This chapter assumes general knowledge of PC hardware. It also assumes the use of VirtualBox version 5.1.4 or later.

6.1 How Oracle VM VirtualBox Works

Virtualizing an operating system on an x86 processor is a difficult task, especially without Intel VT-x or AMD-V hardware features. Before describing how VirtualBox works, we provide a quick review of the x86 storage protection model.

The Intel x86 architecture defines four levels of storage protection called *rings*, which are numbered from 0 (the most privileged) to 3 (the least privileged). These rings are used by operating systems to protect critical system memory from programming errors in less-privileged user applications. Of these four rings, ring 0 is special in that it allows software to access real processor resources such as registers, page tables, and service interrupts. Most operating systems execute user programs in ring 3 and kernel services in ring 0.

VirtualBox runs a single process on the host operating system for each virtual guest. All of the guest user code is run natively in ring 3, just as it would be if it were running in the host. This setup ensures that user code will perform at native speed when running in a guest virtual machine.

To protect the host against failures in the guest, the guest kernel code is not allowed to run in ring 0, but instead runs in ring 1 if there is no hardware virtualization support, or in a VT-x ring 0 context if there is. This presents a problem if the guest is executing instructions that are permitted only in ring 0 while other instructions behave differently when run in ring 1. To maintain proper operation of the guest kernel, the VirtualBox Virtual Machine Monitor (VMM) will scan the ring 1 code and either replace the troublesome code paths with direct hypervisor calls or execute them in a safe emulator.

In some situations, the VMM may not be able to determine exactly what the relocated ring 1 guest code is doing. In these cases, VirtualBox makes use of a QEMU emulator to achieve the same general goals. Examples include running BIOS code, real-mode operations performed early during guest booting when the guest disables interrupts, and execution of an instruction known to cause a trap that may require emulation.

Because this emulation is slow compared to the direct execution of guest code, the VMM includes a code scanner that is unique for each supported guest. This scanner will identify code paths and replace them with direct calls into the hypervisor for a more correct and efficient implementation of the operation. In addition, each time a guest fault occurs, the VMM will analyze the cause of the fault to see if the offending code stream can be replaced by a less expensive method in the future. As a result of this approach, VirtualBox performs better than a typical emulator or code recompiler. It can also run a fully virtualized guest at nearly the same speed as one that is assisted by Intel VT-x or AMD-V features.

Some operating systems may run device drivers in ring 1, which can cause a conflict with the relocated guest kernel code. These types of guests will require hardware virtualization.

6.1.1 Oracle VM VirtualBox Architecture

VirtualBox uses a layered architecture consisting of a set of kernel modules for running virtual machines, an API for managing the guests, and a set of user programs and services. At the core is the hypervisor, which is implemented as a ring 0 (privileged) kernel service. Figure 6.2 shows the relationships among all of these components. The kernel service consists of a device driver named vboxsrv that

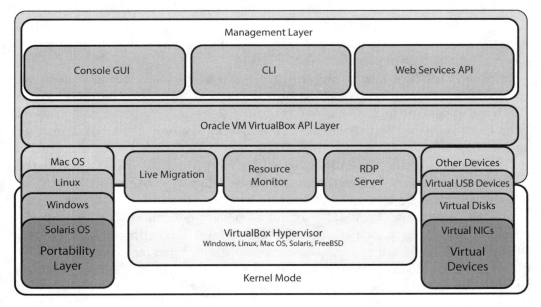

Figure 6.2 Oracle VM VirtualBox Architecture

is responsible for tasks such as allocating physical memory for the guest virtual machine, and several loadable hypervisor modules for tasks such as saving and restoring the guest process context when a host interrupt occurs, turning control over to the guest OS to begin execution, and deciding when VT-x or AMD-V events need to be handled.

The hypervisor does not get involved with the details of the guest OS scheduling. Instead, those details are handled completely by the guest during its execution. The entire guest is run as a single process on the host system and will run only when scheduled by the host. If they are present, an administrator can use host resource controls such as scheduling classes and CPU caps or reservations to ensure very predictable execution of the guest machine.

Additional device drivers will be present to allow the guest machine access to other host resources such as disks, network controllers, and audio and USB devices. It is important to understand that the hypervisor actually does very little work. Instead, most of the interesting work involved in running the guest machine occurs in the guest process. In turn, the host's resource controls and scheduling methods can be used to control the guest machine behavior.

In addition to the kernel modules, several processes on the host are used to support running guests. All of these are automatically started when needed.

- VBoxSVC is the VirtualBox service process. It keeps track of all of the virtual machines that are running on the host. It starts automatically when the first guest boots.

- VBoxZoneAccess is a daemon unique to Solaris that allows the VirtualBox device to be accessed from an Oracle Solaris zone.

- VBoxXPCOMIPCD is the XPCOM process used on non-Windows hosts for interprocess communication between guests and the management applications. On Windows hosts, the native COM services are used for this purpose.

- VirtualBox is the process that actually runs the guest virtual machine when it is started. One of these processes is present for every guest that is running on the host. If host resource limits are desired for the guest, this process enforces those controls.

6.1.2 Interacting with Oracle VM VirtualBox

There are two primary ways that a user may interact with VirtualBox: a simple graphical user interface (GUI) and a very complete and detailed command-line interface (CLI). The GUI allows the user to create and manage guest virtual machines as well as set most of the common configuration options. When a guest machine is started from this user interface, a graphical console window will open on the host that allows the user to interact with the guest as if it were running on real hardware. To start the graphical interface, type the command `VirtualBox` at any shell prompt. On an Oracle Solaris host, this command is found in `/opt/VirtualBox` with symbolic links to `/usr/bin`. On a Microsoft Windows host, the command is found in `C:\Program Files\Oracle\VirtualBox`. You must specify the full path name if the directory is not in your shell's `PATH` environmental variable.

The CLI is the `VBoxManage` command. `VBoxManage` has many subcommands and options that can be listed with the `-h` option as follows.

```
C:\Program Files\Oracle\VirtualBox> VBoxManage.exe -h
Oracle VM VirtualBox Command Line Management Interface Version 5.1.4
(C) 2005-2016 Oracle Corporation
All rights reserved.
Usage:

  VBoxManage [<general option>] <command>


General Options:

  [-v|--version]            print version number and exit
  [-q|--nologo]             suppress the logo
  [--settingspw <pw>]       provide the settings password
  [--settingspwfile <file>] provide a file containing the settings password
<output has been truncated>
```

The `VBoxManage -h` command will respond with a list of all available subcommands and options. We will look at a few of the command options in the following sections. When a `VBoxManage` command successfully completes, it will print out a banner similar to the one shown in the previous example.

If the banner fails to print, an error occurred while processing the command. In this case, diagnostic information will usually be displayed instead of the banner. In the examples in the remainder of this chapter, the banner output has been omitted for brevity.

6.2 Oracle VM VirtualBox Guest Platform

VirtualBox supports the execution of guest operating systems in fully virtualized machines. This allows the guest to run without requiring any special software or device drivers. The guest operating system is presented with a virtual motherboard that has the following features:

- 1 to 32 CPUs
- Up to 32 GB of memory
- An optional dual-channel IDE disk controller with up to 4 devices
- A Serial ATA (SATA) disk controller with up to 30 attached devices
- An optional SCSI controller with up to 16 attached devices
- An optional SAS controller with up to 255 attached devices
- NVMe Flash Storage Emulation
- Up to 8 PCI network host adapters
- Keyboard, video, and mouse (KVM) console
- Either a legacy BIOS or EFI firmware

The next several sections describe details of the VirtualBox guest platform.

For a current list of supported guest operating systems, enter the command `VBoxManage list ostypes` from the command line. To display all of the supported versions of Solaris, enter the following command:

```
Host% VBoxManage list ostypes|grep Solaris
ID:           Solaris
Description: Oracle Solaris 10 5/09 and earlier (32-bit)
Family ID:    Solaris
Family Desc: Solaris
ID:           Solaris_64
Description: Oracle Solaris 10 5/09 and earlier (64-bit)
Family ID:    Solaris
Family Desc: Solaris
ID:           OpenSolaris
Description: Oracle Solaris 10 10/09 and later (32-bit)
Family ID:    Solaris
Family Desc: Solaris
ID:           OpenSolaris_64
Description: Oracle Solaris 10 10/09 and later (64-bit)
Family ID:    Solaris
Family Desc: Solaris
ID:           Solaris11_64
Description: Oracle Solaris 11 (64-bit)
Family ID:    Solaris
Family Desc: Solaris
```

6.2.1 Virtual CPUs

Unlike Oracle VM Server for SPARC (previously called Sun Logical Domains), VirtualBox does not directly assign CPU resources to the guest domain. Instead, virtual CPUs are presented to the guest and time-sliced on real CPUs using the host system's scheduling facilities. The number of CPUs allocated for each guest can be specified in the Processor tab of the guest machine's System settings, as shown in Figure 6.3.

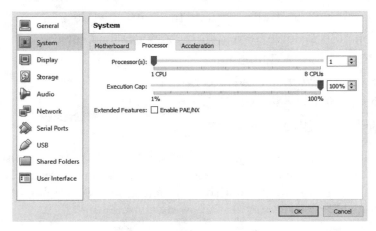

Figure 6.3   Configuring Virtual Processors

If you try to specify more CPUs than the system has, the VirtualBox graphical interface will display a warning. The guest will run, but the performance of the guest is likely to be significantly degraded.

You can also specify the number of CPUs by using the VBoxManage modifyvm command. VBoxManage will not issue a warning if the number of CPUs exceeds the capacity of the host.

```
$ VBoxManage showvminfo "Solaris 11"|grep CPU
CPU exec cap:    100%
Number of CPUs:  1
CPUID Portability Level: 0
CPUID overrides: None
$ VBoxManage modifyvm "Solaris 11" --cpus 8
$ VBoxManage showvminfo "Solaris 11"|grep CPU
CPU exec cap:    100%
Number of CPUs:  8
CPUID Portability Level: 0
CPUID overrides: None
```

VirtualBox offers support for non-executable pages (NX). This feature enables guest operating systems to mark a page that is used for data so that it cannot be executed. Such designations can help reduce the chance that a buffer overflow type of attack initiated by a worm or virus against the guest will be successful. If the guest supports the NX feature, it is recommended that this feature be enabled in the CPU settings.

Although a guest does not require hardware virtualization assistance to perform well, if the host platform supports nested page tables, enabling this feature for a guest will significantly improve performance, because most of the memory management functions can be done by the guest without requiring host intervention. Nested page tables can be enabled in the Acceleration tab of the system settings in the VirtualBox GUI.

6.2.2 RAM

Unlike Logical Domains, memory used by guests is under the control of the host platform. Although the guests can take advantage of hardware virtualization features such as nested page tables to reduce the overhead of memory management, it is still possible to request more memory for a guest than the host system has available. If a shortfall of memory occurs due to this type of oversubscription, the host operating system will start demand paging. This activity may impact the performance of the guest machines and other applications and services running on the host. VirtualBox does not yet provide a memory ballooning feature that would enable the host to take pages back from a guest in the event of a memory shortfall. Figure 6.4 shows an example of a guest with a memory allocation exceeding the recommended maximum.

To help prevent overallocation of the host memory, the VirtualBox graphical user interface will display a warning if it thinks that too much memory is being configured for a guest. In doing so, it considers only the total amount of memory on the system, not how much of that memory is actually free. It will display a warning if more than 70% of memory is allocated for a guest and a stronger warning if more than 90% of memory is being configured for a guest. If sufficient free memory is not available to meet the maximum allocated for use by a guest at the time, a guest machine may fail to start with an out-of-memory error, even if it will consume only a small amount of that memory during start-up.

Most guest systems run only a few applications or services. Because the host system performs most of the real operations on behalf of the guest, smaller memory allocations for the guest can still produce excellent results. Running a guest desktop with 512MB or less, for example, may work well as long as enough memory is allocated for the guest system to boot.

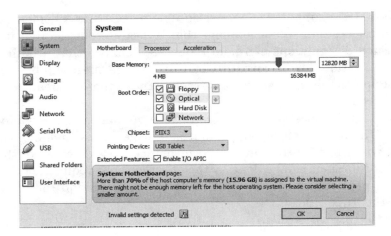

Figure 6.4   Setting Memory for an Oracle VM VirtualBox Guest

6.2.3 Virtual Disk

Because a guest operating system needs persistent storage, VirtualBox can make several different types of host storage available to the guest in the form of virtual disks. The types of host storage include:

- A file that contains a disk image
- A real disk device
- An iSCSI target
- A CD-ROM/DVD or file containing an ISO image
- A file containing a floppy disk image

All of these storage options must be presented to the guest OS using a virtual disk. To facilitate this step, the VirtualBox virtual platform can have up to seven disk controllers, depending on the guest OS being installed. Each of these controllers can have attached devices that provide access to the host storage.

Each virtual motherboard has a dual-channel IDE controller. Each channel has two devices, a master and a slave. By convention, the master device on the first IDE channel is the boot disk and the master device on the second IDE channel is a CD-ROM/DVD. Many different IDE chip sets are available, and VirtualBox can emulate an Intel PIIX3, PIIX4, or ICH6. There is no difference in the performance with these options, but if an operating system is expecting a particular

IDE controller and sees a different one, it might not operate properly. This type of problem happens most often when a virtual machine is imported from another virtualization product. To prevent such a potential conflict, you should set the IDE controller type to match that of the other virtualization product.

A virtual motherboard may also have a Serial ATA (SATA) controller, which can support up to 30 disk devices. By default, the first four devices operate in legacy IDE mode, meaning that the BIOS can use them just like any other IDE device. Once the guest operating system is up and running and has loaded the SATA drivers for these devices, they can then be accessed in SATA mode. In addition to supporting a larger number of devices, SATA is a more efficient interface both on the guest and in the emulation layer. SATA devices are preferred if the operating system supports them.

VirtualBox can also provide an LSI Logic or BusLogic SCSI controller, if necessary. This kind of controller supports up to 16 devices. LSI Logic and BusLogic SCSI controllers are appropriate for legacy operating systems that do not support SATA and need more than the 4 devices provided by the IDE controller. They can also be used to attach more than the 30 disks supported by the SATA controller.

Guest hard disks are generally mapped to files on the host platform that contain a complete image of the guest disk, including its boot sector and partition table. The disk images have a fixed geometry based on their total size. Once created, the size of the disk image cannot be altered. When a guest reads from or writes to the disk, VirtualBox redirects the I/O to the native file system services on the host.

VirtualBox supports six disk image file formats. The three common formats are available in the Guided Mode:

- VDI, the native VirtualBox disk format. It is the default when you create a new virtual machine or disk image.
- VMDK, a popular disk format used by VMware.
- VHD format used by Microsoft.

All of the preceding formats, as well as the following three additional formats, are available in Expert Mode:

- Parallels version 2 HDD format. VirtualBox does not support newer formats, but those can be converted to version 2 using tools supplied by Parallels.
- QCOW (QMU Copy-On-Write).
- QED (QEMU Enhanced Disk).

With each of these formats, VirtualBox can create fixed-size or dynamically expanding disk images. Fixed-size image files are completely allocated at creation time. This type of image file will take longer to create, because it is dependent on the write performance of the host file system. However, it will be more efficient once in use, because the system does not need to get new blocks as the guest writes to new storage areas. Dynamically expanding disk images are thin provisioned disks that start off small and then grow as the guest writes to new blocks on the virtual disk. They are faster to create, but additional work is required by the host to find new blocks the first time a guest accesses a particular part of the disk. Host file system caching strategies can hide most of the difference in performance, especially on a host that is not heavily loaded. For performance-critical applications that perform many disk writes, fixed-size disk images are recommended. For all other uses, the convenience of dynamically allocated images makes their use the preferred method.

VirtualBox maintains a library of disk, CD-ROM, and floppy disk images. Before a disk or CD-ROM image can be used by a guest, it must be registered in the Virtual Media Manager. This can be done in the VirtualBox graphical user interface or via the VBoxManage command. Once an image is registered, it can be assigned to an open port on any guest. Although a disk image may be connected to more than one guest, it can be used by only one guest at a time. A guest will fail to start if one of its disk images is connected to another guest that is already running.

Using the VBoxManage command line on a Solaris host, the following example creates a 32 GB dynamically expanding disk image, displays information about that image, and attaches it to port 3 of the SATA controller in the guest named Windows 10:

```
% VBoxManage createmedium --filename ~/VirtualBox\ VMs/Windows\ 10/Windows10_disk2.vdi
↳--size 32000 --format VDI --variant Standard
0%...10%...20%...30%...40%...50%...60%...70%...80%...90%...100%
Medium created. UUID: 42d4fd0d-2157-47e9-97ec-c69256589c8e
```

Notice that the UUID of the new device is displayed in the output from the previous command. You can also display that device by giving the VBoxManage showmedium subcommand and specifying the UUID of the device as follows:

```
% VBoxManage showmediuminfo 42d4fd0d-2157-47e9-97ec-c69256589c8e
UUID:            42d4fd0d-2157-47e9-97ec-c69256589c8e
Parent UUID:     base
State:           created
Type:            normal (base)
Location:        /root/VirtualBox VMs/Windows 10/Windows10_disk2.vdi
Storage format:  VDI
Format variant:  dynamic default
Capacity:        32000 MBytes
Size on disk:    2 MBytes
Encryption:      disabled
```

Attach the disk to the Windows 10 VM, SATA port 3 as follows:

```
% VBoxManage storageattach "Windows 10" --storagectl "SATA" --port 3 --device 0 --type
↳ hdd --medium 42d4fd0d-2157-47e9-97ec-c69256589c8e
```

The results of this command can be seen in the Storage settings of this Windows 10 guest, as shown in Figure 6.5.

Note that the actual size of the disk image is only 2MB. For a fixed-size image, add `--variant Fixed` to the `createmedium` command given earlier.

CD-ROM images are treated in a similar fashion. The Virtual Media Manager maintains a list of registered images. Because CD-ROM images are not writable

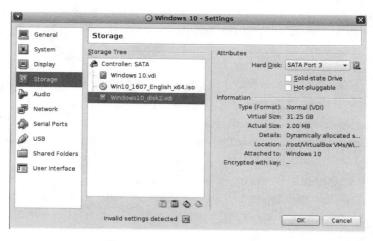

Figure 6.5   Selecting a Guest Disk Image

by the guest, they can be used by more than one guest at a time. One special image is `VBoxGuestAdditions.iso`, which can be found in the VirtualBox installation directory (e.g., `/opt/VirtualBox/additions` on a Solaris host and `C:\Program Files\Oracle\VirtualBox` on a Microsoft Windows host). The VirtualBox Guest Additions ISO contains all of the guest drivers and configuration tools that match the version of VirtualBox installed on the host. This image is automatically added by the installation program and is available to all guests.

In addition to a CD-ROM image, a guest can access real media in a CD-ROM or DVD drive on the host. By default, the guest is only allowed to read from the drive. To give the guest write access or to allow the special I/O operations required by some multimedia players, enable the `Passthrough` setting on the CD-ROM device.

6.2.4 Virtual Network Devices

VirtualBox provides up to eight Ethernet PCI devices to each guest virtual machine. The user can select the type of virtual devices that are presented to the guest as well as what the host will do with the associated network I/O. The guest adapter does not need to be the same type as that on the host. For example, a Realtek Ethernet interface on the host can be virtualized as an Intel PRO/1000 on a guest. The first four virtual network adapters can be configured using the Network settings in the graphical user interface. All eight of the devices can be configured using the `VBoxManage` command.

VirtualBox can present any of the following virtual devices to the guest operating system:

- AMD PCNet PCI II: A legacy host adapter for older guest operating systems.
- AMD PCNet FAST III: The default for most guests. This host adapter is well supported in most OS installation media, which makes it a good choice for most guests. It is also supported by the GNU GRUB bootloader, which allows network booting and installation of a guest operating system.
- Intel PRO/1000 MT Desktop: The default for newer guest operating systems such as Windows Vista and Windows Server 2008. Use this device when the PCNet adapter is no longer supported or available on the installation media.
- Intel PRO/1000 T Server: Specifically for use with Windows XP guests.
- Intel PRO/1000 MT Server: This driver is available to allow guests to be imported from other virtualization products such as VMware. The PRO/1000 MT Server virtual device is commonly used on those platforms.

- `Virt-io`: This device is used for guests that support a KVM paravirtualized (PV) network interface. Because this device is designed for virtualization, it may have performance advantages over the other emulated devices. PV drivers are available in Linux 2.6.25 or later kernels. They can be downloaded for other operating systems from the KVM project page.

In addition to choosing the virtual device for the guest, the user must configure a host networking mode to use for each device. Five different modes exist, and each offers some interesting benefits.

Not Attached is a mode similar to a network adapter that does not have a network cable attached. The device is present in the guest machine but is not reporting a positive link status. Traffic will not flow through the device in not attached mode.

Network Address Translation (NAT) hides the guest's interface behind a network tunnel. This mode is often used when the guest is a desktop system and primarily a consumer of network resources, rather than a provider of such resources. To assist guests that automatically detect their network settings, VirtualBox provides a DHCP server, router, and DNS proxy to resolve network names and correctly route packets. NAT has a few limitations that may cause applications to behave differently than they would on a real system. For example, ping may not work across the NAT tunnel. Because some VPN products use this method to determine if a network is reachable, these devices would not work with a virtual NIC in NAT mode. In addition, jumbo frames are not reliable when using NAT.

Because external systems cannot communicate directly with a guest using NAT mode, VirtualBox can provide port redirection using the host's IP address. With this approach, external systems connect to the specified port on the host, and VirtualBox then redirects all of the packets to the guest. A few restrictions are placed on the use of port forwarding, however. For example, you cannot redirect a port that is already in use by the host. Ports numbered less than 1024 require the requester to be running as root or with the `net_privaddr` privilege. Because neither of these is a recommended practice for otherwise unprivileged users, you should choose a port on the host with a number greater than 1024. The most common practice is to forward guest port 22, which allows an external system to access the guest using SSH. The following example illustrates how to establish an SSH port from the first network adapter (an Intel Pro/1000 MT Desktop) on the guest named `Solaris 11` to port 2222 on the host.

```
% VBoxManage setextradata "Solaris 11" \
      "VBoxInternal/Devices/e1000/0/LUN#0/Config/s11ssh/Protocol" TCP

% VBoxManage setextradata "Solaris 11" \
      "VBoxInternal/Devices/e1000/0/LUN#0/Config/s11ssh/GuestPort" 22

% VBoxManage setextradata "Solaris 11" \
      "VBoxInternal/Devices/e1000/0/LUN#0/Config/s11ssh/HostPort" 2222
```

The guest can be accessed by giving the command `ssh -p 2222 user@host`.

Bridged is a more advanced network mode. When this mode is used, VirtualBox installs a software network that allows the guest to share a specific host interface. A randomly generated MAC address is assigned to the guest adapter, and its full network stack is visible to external systems. All of the network operations are available to the guest, including ping and jumbo frames. Bridged mode is the recommended setting for guests running server applications and desktops requiring a VPN connection into another network.

Internal mode is used to communicate between virtual machines on the same host. It is similar to bridged mode except that all communications stay internal to the host platform. Traffic over the internal mode software network is also invisible to the host. This is the fastest and most secure method of communication between guests. The most common use for this mode is to create a private secure channel for guests to share that cannot be observed by any external system or other applications on the host system. Examples include an internal NFS server or a content provider for an externally facing web service.

Host only mode is similar to internal mode except that the host is able to communicate with the guests. All communications are internal to the host, but applications and users on the host can observe and use network services on the guests.

Basic network settings for the first four adapters, as shown in Figure 6.6, can be specified on the Network settings screen in the VirtualBox graphical interface.

6.2.5 BIOS and EFI

VirtualBox provides a virtual standard BIOS firmware that is used by the guest virtual machine during the boot process. Through the user interface, the user can select options such as boot order and support for I/O APIC.

VirtualBox also provides an Extended Firmware Interface (EFI) for operating systems such as Mac OS X that use EFI instead of the legacy BIOS. Newer versions of Windows and some Linux distributions can use either the legacy BIOS or EFI. The type of firmware is selected in the Motherboard part of the System settings. Figure 6.7 shows the BIOS and boot order settings for a guest machine.

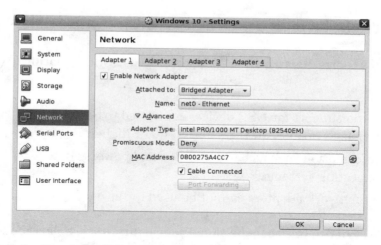

Figure 6.6 Oracle VM VirtualBox Guest Network Configuration Settings

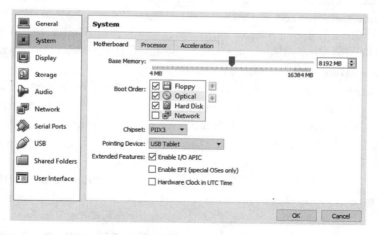

Figure 6.7 Selecting the Guest BIOS Type and Boot Order

The type of BIOS firmware can also be set using the `VBoxManage modifyvm` command line.

```
% VBoxManage modifyvm "Solaris 11" --firmware bios
```

These are just the basic features of the VirtualBox guest platform. For a complete list of all configuration options, see the *VirtualBox User Manual*, which is available in PDF format in the installation directory. This document can be found at `http://www.virtualbox.org/wiki/Downloads`.

6.3 Oracle Solaris as an Oracle VM VirtualBox Host

VirtualBox supports Solaris 10 5/09 and later as a host platform with a few restrictions:

- There is no support for USB devices connected to Solaris 10 hosts. USB support on Solaris hosts requires Solaris 11.0 or higher.
- ACPI information such as battery status and power source is not reported to guest operating systems.
- Wireless network adapters cannot be used for bridged networks.

VirtualBox can run in either the global zone or an Oracle Solaris Zone. Running in a zone provides several interesting benefits. First, it may be easier to place resource controls on an entire zone than on an arbitrary workload, especially if different people are tasked with these functions. The global zone administrator can place resource policies on the zone that may not be visible to the VirtualBox user. Further, the VirtualBox user may not have sufficient privileges to modify those policies. Migrating a zone by detaching it from one host and attaching it to another host can greatly simply the task of relocating a guest. Most of the configuration settings needed for proper operation of the guest are contained in the zone's configuration. Finally, the ability to clone a zone that contains a guest and its associated data makes it easier to rapidly deploy several copies of the same machine on the host.

To enable VirtualBox operation in a Solaris non-global zone named `solaris11zone`, download and install the VirtualBox software package in the zone as described in the next subsection, "6.3.1 Installing Oracle VM VirtualBox on a Solaris Host." After installing the VirtualBox software, shut down the nonglobal zone and add the following devices to the non-global zone:

```
global-zone# zonecfg -z solaris11zone
zonecfg:solaris11zone> add device
zonecfg:solaris11zone:device> set match=/dev/vboxdrv

zonecfg:solaris11zone:device> end
zonecfg:solaris11zone> add device
zonecfg:solaris11zone:device> set match=/dev/vboxdrvu
zonecfg:solaris11zone:device> end
zonecfg:solaris11zone> exit
```

For Solaris 11 hosts, you can enable USB support by adding the `/dev/vboxus-bmon` device as follows:

```
zonecfg:solaris11zone:device> set match=/dev/vboxusbmon
zonecfg:solaris11zone:device> end

global-zone# zoneadm -z solaris11zone boot
global-zone# zlogin -C solaris11zone
```

Finish the installation as you would any other zone, by answering the Solaris system identification questions. Once this installation is complete, VirtualBox's graphic and command-line tools can be used in the non-global zone, just as they would be in the global zone. Some of the host networking modes may require the use of exclusive IP for configuration of the guest's virtual network interface.

Another Oracle Solaris feature that can be used by VirtualBox is ZFS. Although VirtualBox has a host-independent disk cloning feature, it involves copying entire disk images, which will double the amount of storage required for the duplicated clone and places a load on the host system during the copying operation. ZFS has a fast cloning capability that takes significantly less time to complete, and the cloned disk image needs to store only those blocks that are different from the original. This approach is very efficient for deploying many copies of the same type of guest.

When running VirtualBox on a Solaris host that is also using ZFS, limiting the size of the adaptive replacement cache (ARC) is recommended. By default, ZFS can use most of the physical memory on the system: up to three-fourths on systems with 4 GB or less and up to `maxphys-1` GB on larger systems. Sometimes a guest might demand memory faster than ZFS is able to free it, which would produce one of the memory shortfall situations that we are trying to prevent. The solution is to limit the amount of memory that ZFS is able to use for the ARC. On a Solaris 10 host, this value can be set with the `zfs_arc_max` Solaris tunable parameter, which is found in `/etc/system`. The following setting will limit the ARC to 1 GB, which is a reasonable value for a 4 GB desktop hosting several virtual machines:

```
set zfs:zfs_arc_max = 0x40000000
```

As a general rule, you should not set `zfs_arc_max` to more than three-fourths of the physical memory that is left after allocating memory for all of your guests.

On Solaris 11.2 and newer hosts, the ZFS ARC cache can be controlled dynamically using the Oracle=provided script called `set_user_reserve.sh`.

See Chapter 8, "Choosing a Virtualization Technology," for an example of using both ZFS and zones for rapid provisioning of guests on an Oracle Solaris host.

6.3.1 Installing Oracle VM VirtualBox on a Solaris Host

The VirtualBox software can be downloaded from `https://virtualbox.org/wiki/downloads`. The version for Oracle Solaris 10 and 11 is provided in a single SVR4 data stream package that includes both the 32-bit and 64-bit versions of the software as well as a `README` text file describing the installation process and a package answer file named `autoresponse` for non-interactive installations. Because the package installation scripts will load kernel modules, the installation must be done in the global zone and performed either by root or by a user or role that has the `Software Installation` execution profile.

If an older version of VirtualBox is installed on the host, it must be removed before installing the new version. To check whether VirtualBox is installed on a Solaris 11 host, enter the following command:

```
# pkginfo -l SUNWvbox
   PKGINST:  SUNWvbox
      NAME:  Oracle VM VirtualBox
  CATEGORY:  application
      ARCH:  i386
   VERSION:  4.3.40,REV=2016.08.22.16.32.110317
   BASEDIR:  /
    VENDOR:  Oracle Corporation
      DESC:  A powerful PC virtualization solution
    PSTAMP:  vbox20160822163212_r110317
  INSTDATE:  Sep 10 2016 10:39
   HOTLINE:  Please contact your local service provider
     EMAIL:  info@virtualbox.org
    STATUS:  completely installed
     FILES:      345 installed pathnames
                  11 linked files
                  19 directories
                  27 executables
                   6 setuid/setgid executables
              408616 blocks used (approx)
```

The output indicates that version 4.3.40 of VirtualBox is already installed. Because we are preparing to install version 5.1.4 of VirtualBox, we must first remove the older version as follows:

```
# pkgrm -n -a autoresponse SUNWvbox
Removing VirtualBox services and drivers...
    - Unloaded: Zone access service
    - Unloaded: USB module
    - Removed: USB module
    - Unloaded: USBMonitor module
    - Removed: USBMonitor module
    - Unloaded: NetFilter (Crossbow) module
    - Removed: NetFilter (Crossbow) module
    - Unloaded: NetAdapter module
    - Removed: NetAdapter module
    - Unloaded: Host module
    - Removed: Host module
Updating the boot archive...
Done.


Removal of <SUNWvbox> was successful.
```

For versions prior to 3.1, there are two packages: SUNWbox and SUNWvboxkern.
Starting with version 3.1, there is just a single package: SUNWvbox. It is not necessary to reboot the Solaris host after the old version of VirtualBox is removed or
the new version is installed.

In the next example, a new version of VirtualBox is being installed on a system
that is already running an older release. Note the use of the included autoresponse
file for unattended package operations.

```
# ls
VirtualBox-5.1.4-110228-SunOS.tar.gz


# /usr/sfw/bin/gtar xpzf VirtualBox-5.1.4-110228-SunOS.tar.gz


# ls
autoresponse
VirtualBox-5.1.4-110228-SunOS.tar.gz
LICENSE
VirtualBox-5.1.4-SunOS-amd64-r110228.pkg
ReadMe.txt



# pkgadd -n -a autoresponse -d VirtualBox-5.1.4-SunOS-amd64-r110228.pkg

The following packages are available:
  1  SUNWvbox      Oracle VM VirtualBox
                   (i386) 5.1.4,REV=2016.08.16.19.53.110228
```

```
Select package(s) you wish to process (or 'all' to process
all packages). (default: all) [?,??,q]:
Checking package dependencies...
Done.
Checking for older bits...
Installing new ones...
Detected Solaris 11 Version 175
Loading VirtualBox kernel modules...
   - Added: Host driver
   - Added: NetAdapter driver
   - Added: NetFilter (Crossbow) driver
   - Added: USBMonitor driver
   - Added: USB driver
Configuring services...
   - Enabled: Zone access service
Installing MIME types and icons...
Installing Python bindings...
   - Installed: Bindings for Python 2.6
   - Installed: Bindings for Python 2.7
Updating the boot archive...

Installation of <SUNWvbox> was successful.
```

The default directory for the VirtualBox components is /opt/VirtualBox. The user commands VirtualBox, VBoxManage, VBoxSDL, VBoxHeadless, and VBoxDtrace are all symbolically linked into /usr/bin so that they are available for all users on the system. In general, no special privileges are required to run VirtualBox on Solaris other than appropriate file permissions for devices and disk images.

When a user runs VirtualBox, all of the machine definitions and private disk images are stored by default in a directory named VirtualBox VMs in the user's home directory. Although the machine configuration files are relatively small, disk images can grow quite large. To change the locations where these images are stored, click File → Preferences in the VirtualBox graphical interface or give the command VBoxManage setproperty machinefolder on the command line. Figure 6.8 shows how to change those preferences to a different location.

Note that changing the path for the Default Machine Folder after a virtual machine has been created will not move that machine to that new path. You must set the location before creating the machine; all new virtual machines will then be created in subdirectories located in that path.

VirtualBox disk images and machine configurations can be shared among many users. All that is required to share machine configurations and disk images is read and write file permissions to the associated files.

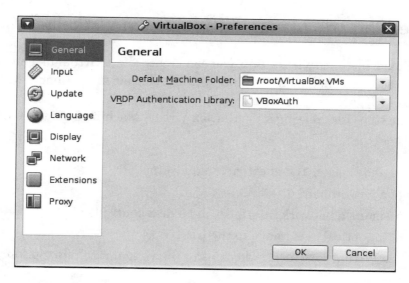

Figure 6.8   Changing the Location of Guest Disks and Machine Definitions

6.4 Oracle Solaris as an Oracle VM VirtualBox Guest

Solaris 11 is a fully supported guest OS for VirtualBox. A full complement of Guest Additions is available, including Seamless Mode and accelerated 3D graphics. For optimal performance, the following settings are recommended for a Solaris guest:

- Boot disk: SATA (one of the first four ports with IDE compatibility mode enabled)
- CD-ROM: Port 1 of the SATA controller (the default)
- Network: Intel Pro/1000MT Desktop
- Hardware acceleration: Enabled if supported by the host
- Nested page tables: Enabled if supported by the host
- PAE/NX: Enabled

Begin by downloading the Solaris 11 Installer from Oracle at `http://www` `.oracle.com/technetwork/server-storage/solaris11/downloads/` `index.html`. Then select the link titled "Installation from CD/DVD or USB."

For this example, the Solaris 11.3 x86 Text Installer ISO image was downloaded into the `/root/Downloads` folder on the Solaris host and is named `sol-11_3` `-text-x86.iso`.

6.5 Creating and Managing Oracle VM VirtualBox Guests

After you have installed VirtualBox, you can create guest virtual machines. While this can be accomplished using command-line tools, our first example will use the VirtualBox GUI installation wizard.

The basic steps for creating a VirtualBox Virtual Machine from the GUI wizard are as follows:

- Create and register the guest virtual machine.
- Create a virtual hard disk.
- Add memory, a network interface, and a disk controller.
- Mount an optical disk image to the CD/DVD.
- Add the VirtualBox Guest Additions to the virtual machine (optional).

6.5.1 Creating the Guest Machine

You can start the installation of a guest machine by launching the VirtualBox GUI tool from the command line or by clicking on the VirtualBox icon located on your desktop.

```
% VirtualBox &
```

Figure 6.9 shows the initial VirtualBox screen.

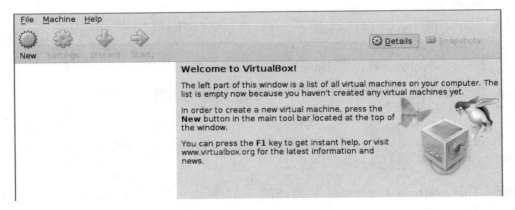

Figure 6.9   VirtualBox Main Window

To begin creating the first virtual machine, click the New button. This will launch the New Virtual Machine Wizard.

The first step is to name the new virtual machine and choose the operating system of the guest. The name of the guest is unrelated to its actual host name or network identity; those will be set later, once the guest is running. Rather, the guest's name is simply used by VirtualBox to identify the guest being managed. The operating system type determines how VirtualBox will emulate devices and which code scanning techniques to use when running the guest kernel code. The name of the guest can be changed later, but the OS type should be correct before creating the guest.

For this example the guest will be named `Windows 10` and it will run the Windows 10 operating system, as shown in Figure 6.10.

The next step is to specify the amount of memory to be allocated for the guest. The amount needed is usually less than needed for a physical system. Many operating systems manage a file cache to improve performance of disk reads. If the host OS has a file cache, the guests will not need much file cache to maintain reasonable performance, so you can configure less memory for guests. The installation wizard will suggest a minimum memory size of 2048MB based on the operating system type chosen in the previous step. Figure 6.11 shows the allocation of

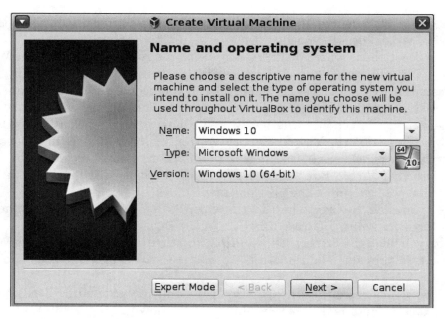

Figure 6.10   Choosing the Guest Operating System Type

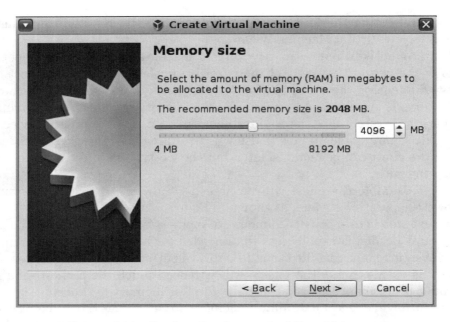

Figure 6.11   Setting the Amount of Guest Memory

4096MB for this Windows 10 guest; this amount of memory is more than enough for typical virtual desktop needs.

Every guest needs a boot disk. For simplicity, the New Virtual Machine Wizard allows you to create only a single boot disk image. It will always assign this disk as the master device on the first IDE controller. If you need a different configuration, enter the command `VBoxManage` on the command line. At this point in the guest installation, you can choose whether to create a new disk image or use one that is already registered in the Virtual Media Manager. This system does not yet contain any virtual disks, so select "Create a virtual hard disk now," as shown in Figure 6.12. Note that VirtualBox suggests a size for the disk based on the operating system that was chosen in the previous step.

When you click the Create button, the wizard will prompt you to select the hard disk type, as shown in Figure 6.13.

When you click the Expert Mode button, the Create Virtual Hard Disk Wizard will open. It provides additional disk parameters to be specified, as shown in Figure 6.14.

This disk must be either a fixed-size or dynamically expanding disk image. A dynamically expanding disk is typically used, as shown in Figure 6.14, because it does not waste real disk space and takes less time to create.

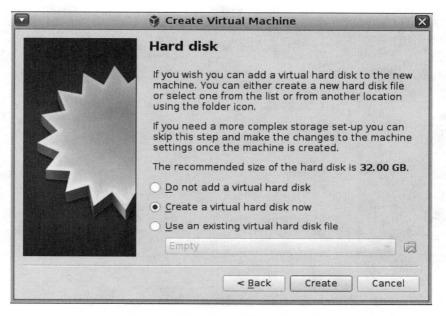

Figure 6.12   Hard Disk Wizard

Figure 6.13   Create Virtual Hard Disk Wizard

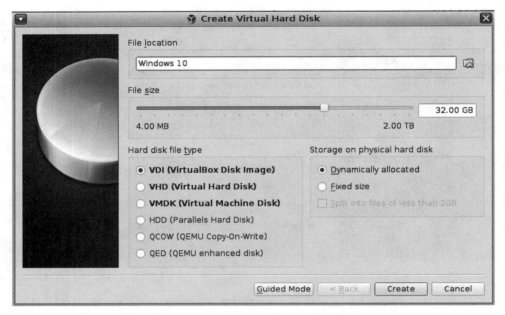

Figure 6.14   Create Virtual Hard Disk Wizard—Expert Mode

The Expert Mode Wizard allows you to name the disk image and specify its size. By default, this disk image will be stored in your home directory in a directory named `VirtualBox VMs/Windows 10`. If there is not enough space there, you can click the icon to the right of the image name and tell VirtualBox where to place the image. You will need read and write access to the directory holding the disk images.

In this example, the disk image is named `Windows 10.vdi` and has a size of 32 GB, which is the default. In practice, the name of the disk image should indicate not only which virtual machine is using it, but also how that disk is used. Figure 6.14 shows the name and size of the guest boot disk.

After reviewing the settings, click Create. At this point, the disk image will be created and registered in the VirtualBox Manager window, as shown in Figure 6.15.

You have now successfully created your first guest virtual machine. You can click the Settings button and familiarize yourself with some of the other configuration options, such as audio, video memory size, additional networks, processor accelerations, and shared folders.

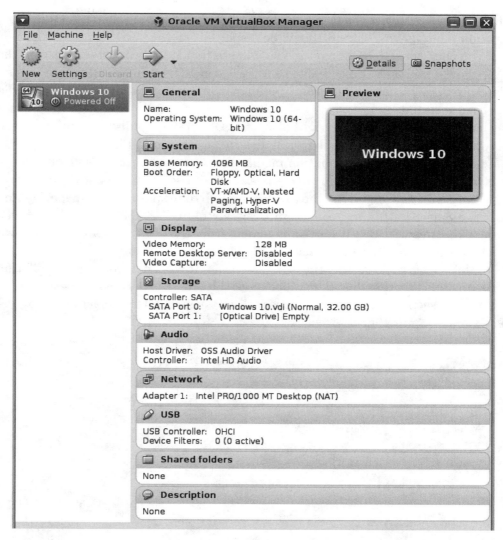

Figure 6.15 Reviewing the Guest Disk Settings

6.5.2 Installing the Guest Operating System

Once you are satisfied that the guest machine configuration is suitable for your needs, you can install the operating system on the guest boot disk. The most commonly used method is to attach a CD-ROM disk image to one of the available virtual CD-ROM devices so that the guest will boot from that device. To attach the

CD-ROM image, select the guest machine, click Settings, and then select Storage. A window similar to Figure 6.16 will be displayed.

If you click the CD-ROM device, you will see that it is the master device on the SATA Port 1 channel. It also happens to be second device in the BIOS boot order. Also note that the device is currently empty, meaning that no virtual or real media has been inserted.

Click the folder icon to the right of the CD/DVD Device pull-down menu, which allows you to select the virtual optical disk file, as shown in Figure 6.17.

To add the Windows installation media, click the Add button. Navigate to the directory where the CD-ROM image is stored and select it, as shown in Figure 6.18. Now you can highlight the appropriate virtual optical disk image file and click the Select button to insert it into the virtual CD-ROM device. Once registered, you can select this media in any guest from the CD/DVD Device pull-down menu on the guest Storage settings, as shown in Figure 6.18.

All that is left to do is start the guest machine. It will boot from the installation DVD, and you can then begin installation of the Windows 10 operating system.

The next section describes the steps to create a guest virtual machine using the `VBoxManage` command.

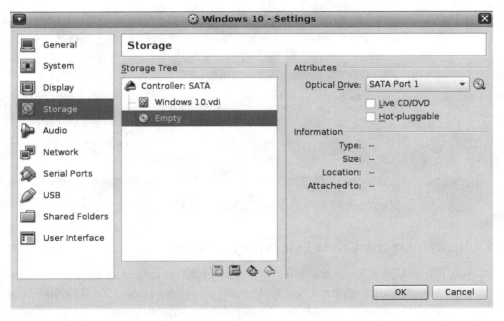

Figure 6.16 Guest Storage Configuration Before Attaching the Installation Media

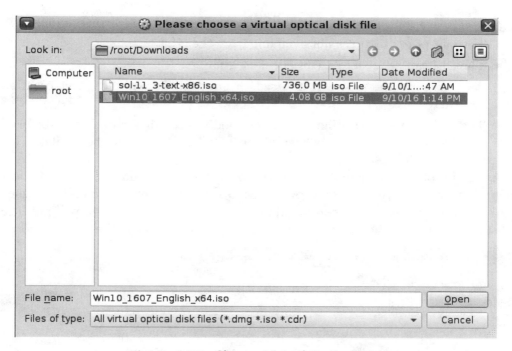

Figure 6.17   Choose Virtual Optical Disk

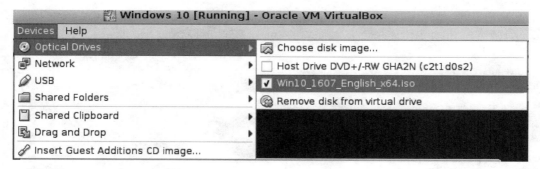

Figure 6.18   CD/DVD Device Pull-Down Menu

6.5.3 Creating a Microsoft Windows 10 Guest Machine Using the Command Line

The command-line interface for VirtualBox is more difficult to use than the GUI, but it offers several advantages:

- The CLI is more flexible than the GUI.
- The CLI offers features not available from the GUI.
- The CLI can be used to script guest creation.
- Scripts using the CLI can be used to build an automated guest creation system.
- The CLI allows the configuration and modification of VirtualBox VMs, even on a text-based or headless host where a GUI desktop is not be available.

As in the previous example, the first step is to create and register the guest virtual machine. If you do not know which OS type to select when creating your virtual machine, giving the command `VBoxManage list ostypes` will produce a list of supported options. For this example, `Windows10_64` is the correct choice.

```
% VBoxManage createvm --name "Windows 10 64" --ostype Windows10_64 \
--register
Virtual machine 'Windows 10 64' is created and registered.
UUID: e4655e95-12ad-42e3-9ffd-d5f5b18f198d
Settings file: '/root/VirtualBox VMs/Windows 10 64/Windows 10 64.vbox'


% VBoxManage showvminfo "Windows 10 64"
Name:               Windows 10 64
Groups:             /
Guest OS:           Windows 10 (64-bit)
UUID:               b09d3001-cd90-4d7f-ae09-27a658ab2e2d
Config file:        /root/VMs/Windows 10 64/Windows 10 64.vbox
Snapshot folder: /root/VMs/Windows 10 64/Snapshots
Log folder:         /root/VMs/Windows 10 64/Logs
Hardware UUID:      b09d3001-cd90-4d7f-ae09-27a658ab2e2d
Memory size:        128MB
Page Fusion:        off
VRAM size:          8MB
CPU exec cap:       100%
HPET:               off
Chipset:            piix3
Firmware:           BIOS
Number of CPUs:  1
PAE:                on
Long Mode:          on
<Output has been truncated>
```

This guest should need approximately 2048MB of memory, and 8 MB is not enough video RAM, so it will be increased to 32MB. Modify the guest virtual machine using the `modifyvm` option as follows:

```
% VBoxManage modifyvm "Windows 10 64" --memory 2048 --vram 32
```

Storage configuration requires a few commands. First you must create the SATA controller as follows:

```
% VBoxManage storagectl "Windows 10 64" --name "SATA Controller" \
--add sata --controller IntelAHCI
```

Now create the 32 GB boot disk:

```
% VBoxManage createhd --filename "Windows 10 64.vdi" --size 32000 \
--format VDI
0%...10%...20%...30%...40%...50%...60%...70%...80%...90%...100%
Medium created. UUID: d42f960e-cb3f-45cb-a3fc-4e2b6f942517
```

Attach the disk to the SATA controller:

```
% VBoxManage storageattach "Windows 10 64" --storagectl "SATA Controller" --port 0
↪--device 0 --type hdd --medium "Windows 10 64.vdi"
```

Register the DVD and attach the virtual optical image of the boot media:

```
% VBoxManage storageattach "Windows 10 64" --storagectl "SATA \
Controller" --port 1 --device 0 --type dvddrive --medium \
"/root/Downloads/Win10_1607_English_x64.iso"
```

Finally, the BIOS boot order must be set to boot from CD-ROM before the disk. Note that because the image file name is specified as a relative path name, it is relative to the VirtualBox settings, not your current working directory.

```
% VBoxManage modifyvm "Windows 10 64" --boot1 dvd --boot2 disk
```

At this point, the virtual machine is configured and ready to boot. Because Windows 10 requires a GUI interface to install the OS, you will need to connect to the host machine from a GUI-based environment such as Microsoft Windows 10 or Solaris Desktop. You can use several approaches to do so:

- Install the Oracle VM VirtualBox Extension Pack onto the VirtualBox host.
- Start up the guest Windows 10 machine with VBoxHeadless.
- Attach to the VirtualBox host with a GUI-based system (i.e., Microsoft Windows 10) using the VirtualBox Remote Display Protocol (VRDP).
- Complete the installation of the Windows OS over the VRDP connection.

6.5.3.1 VirtualBox Extensions Pack

VirtualBox Extension Packs can be downloaded to extend the functionality of the VirtualBox base package. The "VirtualBox 5.1.4 Oracle VM VirtualBox Extension Pack" is available at the VirtualBox.org downloads site (`https://virtualbox .org/wiki/Downloads`) and provides added functionality for the following components:

- The virtual USB 2.0 (EHCI) device
- The Virtual USB 3.0 (xHCI) device
- VirtualBox Remote Desktop Protocol
- Host webcam pass-through
- Intel PXE boot ROM
- Experimental support for PCI pass-through on Linux hosts
- Disk image encryption with AES algorithm

Download the extension pack and install it as follows:

```
# VBoxManage extpack install Oracle_VM_VirtualBox_Extension_Pack-5.1.4-110228.vbox-extpack
0%...10%...20%...30%...40%...50%...60%...70%...80%...90%...100%
Successfully installed "Oracle VM VirtualBox Extension Pack".
```

To check whether the Extension Pack is installed, enter the following command:

```
# VBoxManage list extpacks
Extension Packs: 1
Pack no. 0:   Oracle VM VirtualBox Extension Pack
Version:      5.1.4
Revision:     110228
Edition:
Description:  USB 2.0 and USB 3.0 Host Controller, Host Webcam, VirtualBox RDP, PXE ROM, Disk Encryption.
VRDE Module:  VBoxVRDP
Usable:       true
Why unusable:
```

VRDP is a backward-compatible extension to the Microsoft Remote Desktop Protocol (RDP) that has been available in VirtualBox since version 4.0. It is listed as part of the VirtualBox Extension Package (which was just loaded in the preceding example) and is also referred to as Virtual Remote Desktop Extensions (VRDE). To start VRDE on the Solaris host, enter the following command:

```
# VBoxManage modifyvm "Windows 10" --vrde on
```

Verify the VRDE settings by entering this command:

```
# VBoxManage showvminfo "Windows 10"|grep -i vrde
VRDE:              enabled (Address 0.0.0.0, Ports 3389, MultiConn: off, ReuseSingleConn:
↪off, Authentication type: null)
VRDE property: TCP/Ports  = "3389"
VRDE property: TCP/Address = <not set>
VRDE property: VideoChannel/Enabled = <not set>
VRDE property: VideoChannel/Quality = <not set>
VRDE property: VideoChannel/DownscaleProtection = <not set>
VRDE property: Client/DisableDisplay = <not set>
VRDE property: Client/DisableInput = <not set>
VRDE property: Client/DisableAudio = <not set>
VRDE property: Client/DisableUSB = <not set>
VRDE property: Client/DisableClipboard = <not set>
VRDE property: Client/DisableUpstreamAudio = <not set>
VRDE property: Client/DisableRDPDR = <not set>
VRDE property: H3DRedirect/Enabled = <not set>
VRDE property: Security/Method = <not set>
VRDE property: Security/ServerCertificate = <not set>
VRDE property: Security/ServerPrivateKey = <not set>
VRDE property: Security/CACertificate = <not set>
VRDE property: Audio/RateCorrectionMode = <not set>
VRDE property: Audio/LogPath = <not set>
```

Start the Windows 10 Guest virtual machine in Headless mode as follows:

```
# VBoxHeadless --startvm "Windows 10"
Oracle VM VirtualBox Headless Interface 5.1.4
(C) 2008-2016 Oracle Corporation
All rights reserved.

VRDE server is listening on port 3389.
```

From a GUI-based system that has network connectivity to the VirtualBox host system, use an RDP viewer to connect to the remote VirtualBox guest machine, as shown in Figure 6.19. The computer IP address is the IP address of the VirtualBox Host server, not the VirtualBox guest Windows 10 machine.

The installation GUI is displayed, as shown in Figure 6.20. Now you can begin installing the Microsoft Windows 10 operating system through the RDP viewer.

Figure 6.19   Remote Desktop Viewer

Figure 6.20   Microsoft Windows 10 Installer

The Solaris 11 host also has a Remote Desktop viewer, but it needs to be installed on the Solaris host. Install the Remote Desktop package on the Solaris 11 host as follows:

```
# pkg install rdesktop
          Packages to install:  1
       Create boot environment: No
Create backup boot environment: No

DOWNLOAD                              PKGS        FILES    XFER (MB)    SPEED
Completed                             1/1         49/49     0.2/0.2    324k/s

PHASE                                             ITEMS
Installing new actions                            76/76
Updating package state database                   Done
Updating package cache                            0/0
Updating image state                              Done
Creating fast lookup database                     Done
Updating package cache                            1/1
```

Connect to the VDRE Server on the Solaris host from another Solaris system by entering the following command:

```
% rdesktop 192.168.1.77:3389
```

where the IP address specified is the IP of the VirtualBox host system.

6.5.4 Creating an Oracle Solaris 11 Guest Machine Using the Command Line

To create a Solaris 11 VirtualBox guest machine from the command line on a Solaris host, you must first create and register the guest virtual machine. Use the `VBoxManage list ostypes` command as follows to display the Solaris versions that can be installed:

```
# VBoxManage list ostypes|grep -i Solaris
ID:          Solaris
Description: Oracle Solaris 10 5/09 and earlier (32-bit)
Family ID:   Solaris
Family Desc: Solaris
ID:          Solaris_64
Description: Oracle Solaris 10 5/09 and earlier (64-bit)
Family ID:   Solaris
Family Desc: Solaris
ID:          OpenSolaris
```

```
Description: Oracle Solaris 10 10/09 and later (32-bit)
Family ID:   Solaris
Family Desc: Solaris
ID:          OpenSolaris_64
Description: Oracle Solaris 10 10/09 and later (64-bit)
Family ID:   Solaris
Family Desc: Solaris
ID:          Solaris11_64
Description: Oracle Solaris 11 (64-bit)
Family ID:   Solaris
Family Desc: Solaris
```

For this example, we will install `Solaris 11_64`. First, create and register the VM on the host:

```
% VBoxManage createvm -name "solaris11" -ostype Solaris11_64 -register
Virtual machine 'solaris11' is created and registered.
UUID: b86356eb-08b9-447a-88ed-d2903be15d3a
Settings file: '/root/VirtualBox VMs/solaris11/solaris11.vbox'
```

Next, display the VM on the host:

```
% VBoxManage showvminfo "Solaris 11"
Name:            Solaris 11
Groups:          /
Guest OS:        Oracle Solaris 11 (64-bit)
UUID:            65f51db4-cf0f-401e-8585-1cd81b6b1b0d
Config file:     /root/VirtualBox VMs/Solaris 11/Solaris 11.vbox
Snapshot folder: /root/VirtualBox VMs/Solaris 11/Snapshots
Log folder:      /root/VirtualBox VMs/Solaris 11/Logs
Hardware UUID:   65f51db4-cf0f-401e-8585-1cd81b6b1b0d
Memory size:     128MB
Page Fusion:     off
VRAM size:       8MB
CPU exec cap:    100%
HPET:            off
Chipset:         piix3
Firmware:        BIOS
Number of CPUs:  1
PAE:             on
Long Mode:       on
Triple Fault Reset: off
<Output has been truncated>
```

Change to the directory where the virtual machine has been created on the host:

```
% cd ~/VirtualBoxVMs/solaris11
```

Create a hard drive in the current working directory:

```
% VBoxManage createhd --filename solaris11.vdi --size 64000
0%...10%...20%...30%...40%...50%...60%...70%...80%...90%...100%
Medium created. UUID: 36cb609d-2690-4abc-a0f6-887b954a19b4
```

Modify the guest virtual machine using the `modifyvm` option to increase the memory to 2048MB:

```
% VBoxManage modifyvm "solaris11" --memory 2048
```

Create the SATA controller:

```
% VBoxManage storagectl "solaris11" --name "SATA Controller" --add sata
```

Attach the disk to the SATA controller:

```
% VBoxManage storageattach "solaris11" --storagectl \
"SATA Controller" --port 0 --device 0 --type hdd \
--medium "solaris11.vdi"
```

Register the DVD and attach the virtual optical image of the boot media:

```
% VBoxManage storageattach "solaris11" --storagectl "SATA Controller" \
--port 1 --device 0 --type dvddrive --medium \
"/root/Downloads/sol-11_3-text-x86.iso"
```

Finally, you must set the BIOS boot order to boot from the CD-ROM before the disk. Note that because the image file name is specified as a relative path name, it is relative to the VirtualBox settings, not your current working directory.

```
% VBoxManage modifyvm "solaris11" --boot1 dvd --boot2 disk
```

At this point, the Solaris 11 virtual machine is configured and ready to boot. This particular server does not have a graphical display, so we will run the installation from a remote server using the Virtual Remote Desktop. The VRDP server is disabled by default and is enabled on a per-VM basis as follows:

```
% VBoxManage modifyvm "solaris11" --vrde on
```

Start the VirtualBox Headless Interface on the host server as follows:

```
% VBoxHeadless -s solaris11
Oracle VM VirtualBox Headless Interface 5.1.4
(C) 2008-2016 Oracle Corporation
All rights reserved.

VRDE server is listening on port 3389.
```

From a Remote Desktop viewer, we will connect to the VRDP Server as shown in Figure 6.20. The Solaris 11 Installer opens, as shown in Figure 6.21.

```
SunOS Release 5.11 Version 11.3 64-bit
Copyright (c) 1983, 2015, Oracle and/or its affiliates. All rights reserved.
Remounting root read/write
Probing for device nodes ...
Preparing image for use
Done mounting image
USB keyboard
  1. Arabic                    15. Korean
  2. Belgian                   16. Latin-American
  3. Brazilian                 17. Norwegian
  4. Canadian-Bilingual        18. Portuguese
  5. Canadian-French           19. Russian
  6. Danish                    20. Spanish
  7. Dutch                     21. Swedish
  8. Dvorak                    22. Swiss-French
  9. Finnish                   23. Swiss-German
 10. French                    24. Traditional-Chinese
 11. German                    25. TurkishQ
 12. Italian                   26. UK-English
 13. Japanese-type6            27. US-English
 14. Japanese
To select the keyboard layout, enter a number [default 27]:█
```

Figure 6.21   Solaris 11 Installer

After the installation is complete, shut down the VM and remove the Installer ISO from the CD/DVD as follows:

```
# VBoxManage controlvm "solaris11" acpipowerbutton
```

Refer to the section titled "6.5.6 Stopping a Virtual Machine" later in this chapter.

Detach the installation ISO image from the CD/DVD of the solaris11 virtual machine as follows:

```
% VBoxManage storageattach "solaris11" --storagectl \
"SATA Controller" --port 1 --device 0 --type dvddrive \
--medium emptydrive
```

6.5.4.1 VirtualBox Guest Additions: Installed Through the GUI Wizard

Although the guest operating systems do not need any special software or drivers to operate correctly, the host platform includes many additions that a guest can utilize (if they are available). VirtualBox provides a special set of drivers and utilities that can be used by the guest once the operating system has been installed. These so-called VirtualBox Guest Additions are provided in a CD-ROM disk image that is always available to the guest.

You can use one of two methods to install the Guest Additions. The first method is to attach the disk image file `VBoxGuestAdditions.iso` to one of the available virtual CD-ROM devices. Alternatively, if you are using the VirtualBox graphical console, you can choose Devices → Install Guest Additions from the guest console window. If the guest operating system does not automatically mount the media, this can be done manually from the guest.

Once the virtual media has been mounted, run the appropriate installer for your guest platform. A reboot of the guest is required only if you are upgrading an older version of the guest additions that are already installed. For a new installation, all that is required is to log out of the guest and log back in again.

Once installed, the Guest Additions provide several new features:

- Integrated keyboard and mouse. The guest no longer requires a captive keyboard and mouse. When the guest window receives focus, the keyboard and mouse are automatically attached. When the window loses focus, they are automatically released by the guest.

- Shared clipboard. A user can copy an object from an application in one guest and paste it into another application on a totally different guest, or even the host system.

- Resize guest display. The user can resize the guest display. VirtualBox will notify the guest if the resolution changes, and the drivers inside the guest will handle the changes.

- Seamless mode. VirtualBox can hide the guest display background, only displaying application windows on the host. When used with the shared clipboard, this mode hides the fact that applications are being run in virtual machines. In seamless mode, all applications appear to be running together in a single environment—creating a uniquely integrated desktop experience.

- Time synchronization: The guest clock is kept synchronized with that of the host. This prevents the type of clock skewing that is common in virtualized environments.
- High-performance graphics. If enabled in the Display settings of the guest machine, VirtualBox will allow the guest operating system to pass OpenGL and Direct3D graphics commands directly to the host's graphics adapter. The result is that the guest can perform 3D graphics operations at nearly the same speed as if those operations were running on the host. For Windows guests, 2D graphics acceleration is also available.
- Shared folders: The guest can access the host file systems as if they were local file systems. For Windows guests, these appear as network shares. For all other guests, a special file system driver is used to access the shared folders.

As with all supported guests, the Guest Additions are provided on a CD-ROM image file that is automatically installed with VirtualBox. For the Windows 10 guest that was installed in the previous section, we will install the Guest Additions after the Windows 10 OS has been installed in the guest machine. Before installing the Guest Additions, you might notice that the mouse movements in the Windows 10 virtual guest machine are erratic. Installing the VirtualBox Guest Additions in the guest machine will fix this problem.

After booting Windows 10 in the virtual guest machine, begin the installation of the VirtualBox Guest Additions by clicking on Devices from the guest machine's VirtualBox toolbar, as shown in Figure 6.22.

The VirtualBox Guest Additions icon will appear in the Microsoft Windows File Explorer, as shown in Figure 6.23.

Click on the VirtualBox Guest Additions icon to begin the installation, as shown in Figure 6.24.

Figure 6.22   Devices Pull-Down Menu

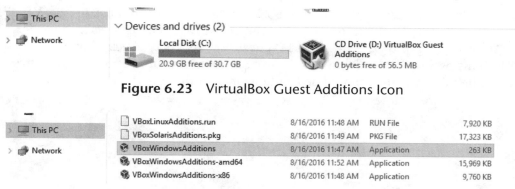

Figure 6.23 VirtualBox Guest Additions Icon

Figure 6.24 VirtualBox Guest Additions Setup

The VirtualBox Guest Additions Installation Wizard will guide you through the installation of the VirtualBox Guest Additions.

6.5.4.2 VirtualBox Guest Additions: Installed from the Command Line

The Guest Additions can also be installed in the guest virtual machine from the command line after the operating system has been installed. In an earlier example, we installed the `solaris11` VM from the command line. In this section, we will install the Guest Additions into the `solaris11` guest virtual machine from the command line.

Begin by shutting down the `solaris11` VM:

```
% VBoxManage controlvm "solaris11" acpipowerbutton
```

Detach the installation ISO image from the CD/DVD of the `solaris11` virtual machine as follows:

```
% VBoxManage storageattach "solaris11" --storagectl \
"SATA Controller" --port 1 --device 0 --type dvddrive --medium emptydrive
```

The Oracle Solaris Guest Additions are included in an ISO image that is stored in the VirtualBox installation directory and is named `VBoxGuestAdditions.iso`. Attach the `VBoxGuestAdditions.iso` image to the `solaris11` guest CD/DVD as follows:

```
% VBoxManage storageattach "solaris11" --storagectl \
"SATA Controller"  --port 1 --device 0 --type dvddrive \
--medium /opt/VirtualBox/VBoxGuestAdditions.iso
```

Boot the `solaris11` VM using `VBoxHeadless` mode, connect to the VRDP server with an RDP client, and log into the `solaris11` VM as described earlier.

After logging into the `solaris11` guest VM as root, check that the Guest Additions package is available by reviewing the contents of `/cdrom/cdrom0` directory. The following files should be available in that directory:

```
# ls /cdrom/cdrom0
32Bit                        AUTORUN.INF
cert                         runasroot.sh              VBoxSolarisAdditions.pkg
↳VBoxWindowsAdditions-x86.exe
64Bit                        autorun.sh
OS2                          VBoxLinuxAdditions.ru     VBoxWindowsAdditions-amd64.exe
↳VBoxWindowsAdditions.exe
```

As root, install the Guest Additions into the `solaris11` VM as follows and answer "`y`" when prompted:

```
# pkgadd -d /cdrom/cdrom0/VBoxSolarisAdditions.pkg all

Processing package instance <SUNWvboxguest> from </media/VBOXADDITIONS_5.1.4_110228/
↳VBoxSolarisAdditions.pkg>

Oracle VM VirtualBox Guest Additions(i386) 5.1.4,REV=r110228.2016.08.16.19.49
Oracle Corporation
Using </> as the package base directory.
## Processing package information.
## Processing system information.
## Verifying package dependencies.
## Verifying disk space requirements.
## Checking for conflicts with packages already installed.
## Checking for setuid/setgid programs.

This package contains scripts which will be executed with super-user
permission during the process of installing this package.

Do you want to continue with the installation of <SUNWvboxguest> [y,n,?] y

Installing Oracle VM VirtualBox Guest Additions as <SUNWvboxguest>

## Installing part 1 of 1.
/etc/fs/vboxfs/mount <symbolic link>
/opt/VirtualBoxAdditions/1099.vboxclient
. . . . ..
<output has been truncated>
The following message will be displayed when the installation is complete:
Installation of <SUNWvboxguest> was successful.
```

Rebooting the guest after the new additions are installed is recommended, but not required.

Once the Guest Additions are installed, all of the ancillary features such as the shared clipboard and automatic resizing of the GUI desktop display should be available for use.

One special feature of the VirtualBox Guest Additions is shared folders. This feature allows the guest to share files with other guests and the host via the host's native file system. In Oracle Solaris, the shared folders are made available as a `vboxfs` file system. Shared folders are defined per guest in the VirtualBox graphical user interface or via the `VBoxManage` command line. In this example, the directory `/export/iso` on the host is shared as `/iso` with a Solaris 11 guest.

On the host platform, shut down the solaris11 guest VM as follows:

```
% VBoxManage controlvm "solaris11" acpipowerbutton
```

On the Solaris host, issue the `VBoxManage sharedfolder` command to create the shared folder. In this example, the guest is named `solaris11` and the directory being shared from the Solaris host is `/export/public`:

```
% VBoxManage sharedfolder add solaris11 --name public \
--hostpath /export/public
```

Start up and log into the `solaris11` guest VM as `root` and mount the shared folder in the guest OS as follows:

```
# mkdir /public
# mount -F vboxfs -o uid=1234,gid=5678 public /public
# ls -la /public

total 3
-rw-r--r--   1 root     root           0 Sep 11 11:09 file1
-rw-r--r--   1 root     root           0 Sep 11 11:09 file2
-rw-r--r--   1 root     root           0 Sep 11 11:09 file3
```

Because the file permission and ownership abstractions may not translate directly between the host's OS and the guest's OS, the user starting the virtual machine in the host must have appropriate access to the files being shared. Inside the guest, the owner and group are set by mount options—in this case, user `1234` and group `5678`.

6.5.5 Starting a Virtual Machine

Oracle VM VirtualBox provides three different methods for starting a virtual machine. The most commonly used method is to work from inside the VirtualBox graphical tool itself. Select the guest and click the Green Start button. When the guest machine is started, a fully featured console window opens on the host. Until the Guest Additions are installed, the keyboard and mouse operations are captive activities. Thus, once you click inside the guest window, your cursor will be restricted to that window and the window will receive all keyboard input until told to release it, usually by clicking the Host key. The current Host key is displayed at the lower-right corner of the guest console window. Once the Guest Additions are installed, the keyboard and mouse will be seamlessly attached and detached as your mouse moves over the window. Using this method, the user on the host can control many of the operations of the guest, such as changing the size of the window, attaching CD-ROM media, or turning seamless mode on or off.

If a less complicated console is desired, a simple window with no menu decorations can be used to start a guest. The command `/usr/bin/VBoxSDL` can be given to start the guest. Instead of a fully featured window, a simple window is displayed as a result of this command. This approach is primarily used for debugging purposes, but it can also be used if a simple console is required.

A more interesting start method involves the use of a headless system. In this case, the command `/usr/bin/VBoxHeadless` is used to start the guest machine, but does not display the console on the host system. Instead, the built-in VRDP server is started. A remote system can then access the guest console using any RDP client program. For Oracle Solaris, one such program is `rdesktop`, which can be found on the Solaris Companion Software CD for Solaris 10 or can be installed from the Solaris repository on a Solaris 11 host as described earlier.

The following is an example of starting a guest machine in headless mode on a host system. This is just the type of operation that the Solaris Service Manage Facility (SMF) on a Solaris host could easily automate.

```
% VBoxHeadless --startvm "Windows 10"
Oracle VM VirtualBox Headless Interface 5.1.4
(C) 2008-2016 Oracle Corporation
All rights reserved.

VRDE server is listening on port 3389.
```

To connect to this guest from a remote system, we will use an RDP client. This example shows the use of `rdesktop` on an Oracle Solaris system to connect to the newly created Windows 10 guest machine, which is running on a host named `pandora`.

```
%  rdesktop pandora:3389
```

On the remote system, a new window opens, which shows the guest desktop that is running on `pandora`. In Figure 6.25, the guest desktop is running the Windows 10 installation program.

Figure 6.25   Displaying the Remote Desktop

6.5.6 Stopping a Virtual Machine

In most cases, a guest should be shut down by using its native method. Nevertheless, there are other options for stopping a virtual machine. Regardless of the method used to create the guest, it can be stopped from the host either through the command line or the VirtualBox graphical user interface. Both of these methods offer several mechanisms that can stop a guest.

- **An ACPI shutdown signal.** This is the recommended method. A shutdown signal is sent to the guest; if this function is supported, the guest will begin a normal shutdown. Normal shutdown includes steps such as flushing disk caches and unmounting file systems. Use of an ACPI shutdown signal is the safest of the external shutdown methods.

- **Snapshot.** The guest machine's current state will be saved and can be re-started from this point in the future. The snapshot feature is similar to the hibernation feature found on modern laptops. One difference is that you can save many snapshots and roll them back as desired—an ability that enables you to test the effects of various operations, starting with a consistent state each time.

- **Reset.** A machine reset is a hard stop that is recommended only when the ACPI shutdown does not work. In this case, the guest disk buffers are not flushed and some of the uncommitted disk data may be corrupted. Most modern operating systems feature some form of recovery in the event of a power loss, so the chances of corruption are small, but this approach should be used only when no other method works.

- **Pause.** This function will cause a virtual machine to stop execution, though it remains in memory and its operation can be resumed. The state is not saved by a pause operation.

When shutting down a VM guest, the best approach is to log into the guest operating system and use the shutdown option specific for that OS. Alternatively, you can send a shutdown signal externally to the VM guest by issuing the `VBoxManage controlvm <vmname> acpipowerbutton` command. The ACPI shutdown signal is sent to the OS and will be recognized by an ACPI-compliant chip set. As long as the VM is running a fairly modern guest operating system providing ACPI support, the ACPI shutdown signal should trigger the proper shutdown mechanism from within the guest OS.

To gracefully shut down the `solaris11` VM externally from the command line on the VirtualBox host, enter the following command:

```
# VBoxManage controlvm "solaris11" acpipowerbutton
```

No response will be displayed

Verify that the VM has been shut down by entering this command:

```
# VBoxManage list runningvms
```

If nothing is displayed, no VMs are running. If the `solaris11` VM is still running, the following output will be displayed:

```
"solaris11" {fe4ca0b4-3245-49f8-bc3f-b820d6059385}
```

From a Solaris host, running VMs can also be displayed with this command:

```
% VBoxManage list -l vms
```

Look at the state of each VM listed. A running VM will display the following state information:

```
State:                  running (since 2016-09-12T15:21:34.838000000)
```

When the VM is powered off, the following state will appear:

```
State:                  powered off (since 2016-09-10T22:26:00.000000000)
```

Each running VM also has a VirtualBox process associated with it. This information can be displayed on a Solaris host by giving the following command:

```
# ps -ef|grep -i virtual
     root  4102     1  0   Sep 10 ?              0:00 /opt/VirtualBox/VBoxZoneAccess
     root  6503     1  0 08:44:13 ?              0:29 /opt/VirtualBox/amd64/VBoxSVC
↳--auto-shutdown
     root  6501     1  0 08:44:13 ?              0:10 /opt/VirtualBox/amd64/VBoxXPCOMIPCD
     root  6755  6503  0 11:15:48 ?              1:20 /opt/VirtualBox/amd64/VirtualBox
↳--comment solaris11 --startvm fe4ca0b4-3245-49
     root  6510  4627  0 08:44:27 pts/4          1:27 /opt/VirtualBox/amd64/VirtualBox
     root  6803  5003  0 11:29:22 pts/6          0:00 grep -i virtu
     root  6766  6503  0 11:21:34 ?              5:14 /opt/VirtualBox/amd64/VirtualBox `
↳--comment Windows 10 64 --startvm e4655e95-12a
```

A last-resort method of shutting down a running VM is to reset or power off the guest externally, but this is not a graceful shutdown and is the same as pulling the power plug on a running system. Data could be lost when shutting a guest VM down in this manner. Use this option as a last resort to shut down and power off a guest VM:

```
# VBoxManage controlvm "solaris11" poweroff
0%...10%...20%...30%...40%...50%...60%...70%...80%...90%...100% that send an ACPI
```

The command `VBoxManage controlvm <vm> reset` is another "last resort" option and has the same effect on a virtual machine as pressing the Reset button on a real computer: It initiates a cold reboot of the virtual machine, which will restart and boot the guest operating system again immediately. The state of the

VM is not saved beforehand, and data may be lost. (This is equivalent to selecting the Reset item in the Machine menu of the GUI.)

6.5.7 Cloning a Virtual Machine

Two different cloning utilities are available in VirtualBox. The first is used to clone an entire VM, whereas the second is used to clone a disk. This section describes how to clone an entire virtual machine to create a second, fully independent VM.

VirtualBox supports two types of clones:

- **Full clone.** The entire target VM configuration, including all of the disks, is copied to a new VM folder. The clone can operate on its own and is not dependent on the source VM. A full clone takes much long to create because all of the data blocks are copied from the source VM to the target.

- **Linked clone.** New differencing disk images are created for the target VM in the same folder as the source VM. This type of clone takes up less space because the new disks contain only those data blocks that differ from their counterparts in the source VM. This type of clone is quicker to create because the data blocks are shared between the source and the target VM.

In this section, we consider how to create a full clone.

6.5.7.1 Clone a Virtual Machine Using the GUI Wizard

From the Oracle VM VirtualBox Manager window, select the VM to be cloned. In this example, we will clone the `solaris11` VM, as shown in Figure 6.26.

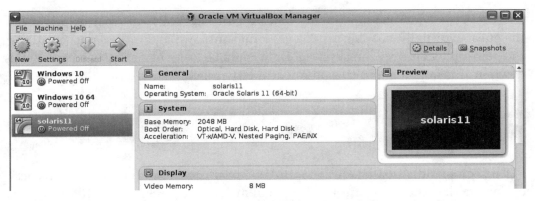

Figure 6.26   Select a Virtual Machine

In the toolbar located at the top of the Oracle VM VirtualBox Manager window, click Machine and then Clone, as shown in Figure 6.27.

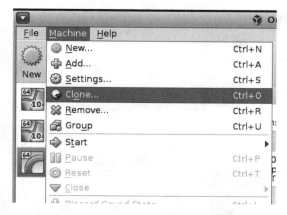

Figure 6.27   Clone a Virtual Machine

Specify a name for the new virtual machine, as shown in Figure 6.28. Select the option to "Reinitialize the MAC address of all network cards," which will assign a unique MAC address to all of the network interfaces cards. If this option is left unchecked, all network interfaces will have the same MAC address as the source VM.

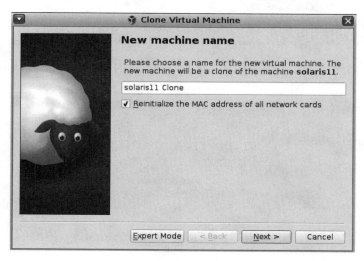

Figure 6.28   Name the New Machine

Click Next when you are finished, and the Clone Type window will appear, as shown in Figure 6.29. Choose the type of clone to create. For this example, we will select a full clone.

After you click the Clone button, the cloning process begins. A status window will open to show the progress, as shown in Figure 6.30.

During the cloning process, a new directory is created for the VM and all of the VM files are copied into that directory. When this process is finished, the status window closes and the cloned VM appears in the Oracle VM VirtualBox Manager window, as shown in Figure 6.31.

The VM can now be started.

Figure 6.29   Select the Clone Type

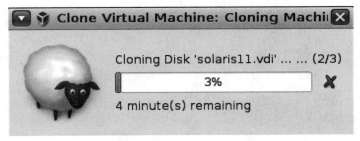

Figure 6.30   Clone Status Window

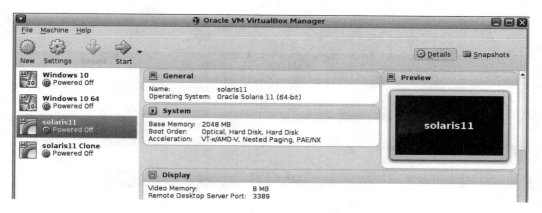

Figure 6.31 Cloned VM

6.5.7.2 Clone a Virtual Machine from the Command Line

We can also use the command line to clone the same VM that was cloned in the previous section using the GUI wizard. Begin by listing the VMs on the current host:

```
% VBoxManage list vms
"Windows 10" {26ba5f3e-d0bc-4983-b939-e168b0dcf9a0}
"Windows 10 64" {e4655e95-12ad-42e3-9ffd-d5f5b18f198d}
"solaris11" {fe4ca0b4-3245-49f8-bc3f-b820d6059385}
```

Make sure the `solaris11` VM is powered off:

```
% VBoxManage showvminfo "solaris11"|grep State
State:          powered off (since 2016-09-11T15:56:48.422000000)
```

Clone the `solaris11` VM by entering the following command:

```
% VBoxManage clonevm "solaris11" --name "solaris11_clone" --register
0%...10%...20%...30%...40%...50%...60%...70%...80%...90%...100%
Machine has been successfully cloned as "solaris11_clone"
```

A new VM named `solaris11_clone` is created and can now be listed with all of the other VMs as follows:

```
# VBoxManage list vms
"Windows 10" {26ba5f3e-d0bc-4983-b939-e168b0dcf9a0}
"Windows 10 64" {e4655e95-12ad-42e3-9ffd-d5f5b18f198d}
"solaris11" {fe4ca0b4-3245-49f8-bc3f-b820d6059385}
"solaris11_clone" {20efcaff-7336-43ed-98e9-37bc4f3fc299}
```

Start the cloned VM as follows:

```
# VBoxManage startvm solaris11_clone
Waiting for VM "solaris11_clone" to power on...
VM "solaris11_clone" has been successfully started.
```

6.5.8 Live Migration of a Guest

VirtualBox includes a feature called *teleportation* that allows a guest machine to move from one host to another while the guest machine is running. Except for some rare cases, the source and destination hosts need not run the same operating system or even the same type of hardware. In other words, you can migrate a guest running on an Oracle Solaris host to a Linux or Windows host.

The steps required to migrate a guest machine are as follows:

1. Ensure there is a TCP/IP network connection between the source and target hosts. The migration will occur over a TCP connection.

2. Configure the original guest to use some sort of shared storage (NFS, SMB, CIFS, or iSCSI) for all of its disk, CD-ROM, and floppy images.

3. On the target system, create a guest configuration that exactly matches the hardware settings (e.g., processor, memory, network) of the guest that is currently running on the source host.

4. On the target host, the guest machine must start listening for a teleportation connection request instead of actually starting. Give the `VBoxManage modifyvm --teleporter` command to apply this option.

5. Start the guest machine on the target host. Instead of starting, it will display a progress bar while waiting for the teleportation request from the source.

6. Initiate the live migration by issuing a `VBoxManage controlvm teleport` command on the source host system.

In this example, a guest machine named `Solaris10` will migrate from a host named `source` to one named `target`. The `Solaris10` guest configurations on both hosts meet the guidelines listed earlier. On the target, place `Solaris10` in teleportation mode and start it. Because it is not currently in use, port 6000 will be used for the teleportation connection.

```
target% VBoxManage modifyvm Solaris 10 --teleporter on   \
     --teleporter 6000
target% VBoxManage startvm Solaris10
```

On the host `source` where the guest `Solaris10` is currently running, initiate the live migration with this command:

```
source% VBoxManage controlvm Solaris10 teleport --host source \
--port 6000
```

The state of the guest `Solaris10` will be transferred to the host `target` and the guest will resume execution on the new host. For more information on guest teleportation, see the *VirtualBox User Manual*.

6.6 Summary

Oracle VM VirtualBox is a compact and efficient virtualization solution for Intel and AMD x86 systems. When VirtualBox is used, each guest runs in a separate virtual machine and needs no additional software or drivers to run. To improve performance and allow the guests greater access to resources within the host platform, Guest Additions are provided for all supported guest operating systems.

Although it is not as efficient as Oracle Solaris Zones, VirtualBox can take advantage of many of the resource management facilities available in Oracle Solaris to provide an excellent and well-managed environment for hosting a wide variety of applications. While features such as the internal RDP server and seamless mode windows make VirtualBox an obvious choice for virtualizing desktops, its performance and use of advanced virtualization features in modern hardware also make it a good choice for handling server workloads.

7

Automating Virtualization

Early computers were expensive, prompting their owners to squeeze all possible value out of them. This drive led to the introduction of time-share operating systems, on which many workloads may run at the same time. As per-unit cost dropped, single-user, single-workload operating systems became popular, but their adoption created the mindset of "one workload per computer," even on servers. The result was an explosion of under-utilized servers. The high costs of maintaining so many servers led to the widespread embrace of virtualization, with the goal of reducing the quantity of servers owned by organizations. Consolidation via virtualization may have reduced a company's hardware acquisition costs, but it did nothing to improve the organization's maintenance costs. Ultimately, managing VEs one at a time is no easier than managing one server at a time.

Many virtualization management tools exist on the market that can facilitate the process of automating virtualization. This chapter discusses two of them: Oracle Enterprise Manager Ops Center and OpenStack.

7.1 Oracle Enterprise Manager Ops Center

Oracle Enterprise Manager Ops Center 12c is part of the broader Oracle Enterprise Manager product. Whereas Enterprise Manager Cloud Control focuses on the higher end of the stack (i.e., database, middleware, and applications), Ops Center addresses the lower end (i.e., storage, operating systems, hardware, and virtualization).

Ops Center is designed for full life-cycle management of the infrastructure layer, which includes both Oracle hardware and operating systems. From a hardware perspective, it is capable of functions such as the following:

- Discovery of new and existing hardware
- Upgrading server firmware
- Installing the "bare metal" operating system
- Monitoring hardware components and opening service requests automatically if a hardware fault occurs
- Providing console access to the system
- Other management actions such as power-off/on, set locator lights, and others

Paramount in Ops Center's functionality portfolio is managing the two primary virtualization technologies: Oracle Solaris Zones and Kernel Zones, and Oracle VM Server for SPARC. Provisioning virtual environments (VEs) including those types includes performing any required preparation of the hardware and operating system.

7.1.1 Architecture

The architecture of Ops Center consists of three main sections:

- **Enterprise Controller:** The main server component of Ops Center. The enterprise controller delivers the user interface and stores the enterprise-wide configuration information. An organization that uses Ops Center will have at least one enterprise controller system that provides communication back to Oracle for service requests, automated patch and firmware downloads, contract validation, and other activities. However, many disaster recovery sites include their own enterprise controller so that they can continue operations management, if needed, during service outages that affect the rest of the system.
- **Proxy Controller:** The component that communicates to the managed assets, including hardware assets, operating system assets, storage assets, virtualized assets, and others. If all of the systems being managed by Ops Center are in one data center, only one proxy controller is needed, and it can run in the same server as the enterprise controller. Alternatively, you can install multiple proxy controllers per enterprise controller. Standard

configurations use one or more proxy controllers per data center, to expand the reach of the Ops Center environment to other data centers, networks, or DMZs.

- **Agent:** A proxy controller typically manages deployed software components via a software agent installed on the system. When an agent is not appropriate, an operating system can be managed without one. The Ops Center agent supports Solaris 8, 9, 10, and 11.

Figure 7.1 depicts the Ops Center architecture.

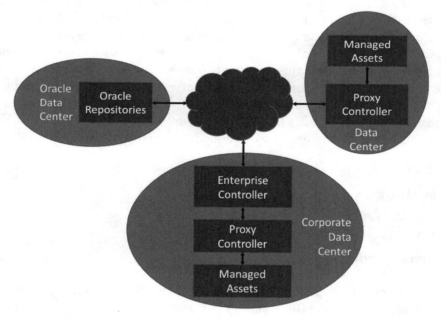

Figure 7.1   Ops Center Architecture

7.1.2 Virtualization Controllers

The Ops Center administrator can choose from two types of virtual environments. One type uses Solaris Zones; this type is simply called a global zone. The other type is a control domain, whose name refers to the use of OVM Server for SPARC. All systems that can be managed by Ops Center can be the global zone type. On modern SPARC systems, you can choose either a control domain or a global zone.

After you make that choice, Ops Center deploys the appropriate type of agent software in the management space, either the computer's control domain or global zone. This agent is called the virtualization controller (VC). Once its installation is complete, you can create the appropriate type of VEs on that server: logical domains for a control domain, or Solaris Zones for a global zone.

7.1.3 Control Domains

Control domains (CDoms) manage Oracle VM Server for SPARC logical domains (LDoms) on a computer. When you use Ops Center to provision a CDom, you choose the operating system, CDom hardware configuration (RAM, cores, and I/O), and names of virtual services provided to other domains. The service names include those for virtual disk services, network services, and console services. You can also initialize advanced Solaris features at the network layer for improved redundancy and performance, such as link aggregation. Advanced configurations, such as SR-IOV, service domains, and root complex domains, are also supported.

Once the CDom is provisioned, the Ops Center user can begin building guests. The guests must boot from either a virtual or physical disk. Using virtual disks provides the greatest flexibility at an extremely minimal performance cost. Virtual disks can reside on a number of physical media available to the CDom:

- A local file system
- A local disk
- An iSCSI LUN
- A NAS file system
- A FibreChannel LUN

When creating LDom guests, the Ops Center user creates one or more logical domain profiles that define the make-up of the guest:

- Name, CPU, core, and memory allocation
- Full core or vCPU allocation
- Architecture of the CPUs
- Networks
- Storage (local, iSCSI, NAS, FC)

When this information is combined with an operating system provisioning profile, the user can both create and provision one or more LDom guests quickly and easily by supplying a small amount of information, such as an IP address.

Further, the user can create a deployment plan to create multiple LDom guests with a single flow through the Ops Center user interface. After the deployment plan has been created, it can be used very easily to quickly create a large number of VEs, each ready to run a workload. Each of these guests will include all of the configuration details of the library image that was deployed, ensuring similarity for applications.

7.1.4 Global Zones

Global zones can be used to host applications, Solaris Zones, or any combination of those. Within the context of Ops Center, for a logical domain to include zones, the "global zone" agent must be installed in the LDom.

The Ops Center user may create a Solaris Zone profile that defines how zones will be created. Configuration options include the following:

- Dedicated or shared memory and CPU resources
- Type of zone (native or branded)
- Source of installation (e.g., operating system archive or network-based package source)
- Storage configuration (FC, iSCSI, or local disk)
- IP/Network configuration (exclusive or shared)
- DNS/Naming Services
- Time zone
- Root and administration passwords

Again, the user can create a deployment plan, based on a zone profile, to create multiple similar zones.

7.1.5 Storage Libraries

Ops Center tracks which LUNs and file systems are allocated to which guests, and ensures that more than one guest does not access the same LUN simultaneously. This constraint applies to both environments created with Ops Center and existing environments that are discovered by, and integrated into, Ops Center.

Ops Center manages this storage by using an underlying storage concept called storage libraries. Storage libraries are shared storage that is used for VEs, either for boot or data storage. Three types of storage can be used for storage libraries:

- NAS
- A static library, using LUNs created ahead of time:
  - FibreChannel
  - iSCSI
- A dynamic library, using a ZFS storage appliance, creating LUNs as needed

7.1.6 Server Pools

Ops Center includes another feature for virtualization that greatly enhances the automation, mobility, and recoverability of both LDom and zone environments—namely, a server pool. A server pool is a collection of similar VEs. It can be a group of zones or LDom hosts (CDoms), but not both types. A server pool of Solaris Zones must include servers with the same CPU technology, either SPARC or x86.

For a control domain server pool, Ops Center manages the placement of LDoms into physical computers using its own rules, guided by configuration information that the user provides and the current load on those computers. Ops Center can also dynamically balance the load periodically, among the servers in the pool.

A global zone server pool is treated the same way: Ops Center runs the zones in the servers, or LDoms, according to its rules and configuration information.

A server pool consists of the following components:

- Similar VEs
- Shared storage libraries (FC, NAS, iSCSI)
- Shared networks—a very small NAS share used to store guest metadata

The metadata comprises all of the information and resources for the guest. It is used for both migration and recovery scenarios.

Server pools enable two main mobility and recoverability features to be used in conjunction with virtualization—migration and automatic recovery.

7.1.7 Migration

Guests can migrate between hosts within a server pool. Depending on the underlying virtualization technology, this migration will either be "live" or "cold." In live migration, the guest VE is moved to the destination without any interruption of the VE's operation. In contrast, cold migration requires stopping the guest and restarting it on another host in the pool. Ops Center provides a simple way to automate the safe migration of guests from the central browser interface. It performs preflight checks to ensure that a guest can migrate and that the migration will succeed prior to initiating the actual migration step.

7.1.8 Automatic Recovery

Automatic recovery resolves a software or hardware failure without any user interaction. In the event of a server failure, guests on that member of the pool are automatically restarted on remaining, healthy hosts in the pool. Each guest that is no longer running will be automatically restarted on a healthy host in the pool.

For example, in a pool of five servers, imagine that Server 1 suffers a hardware fault and stops responding. Ops Center will restart the guest(s) that had been running on Server 1 on the remaining servers in the pool. Ops Center uses internal algorithms to determine which hosts are healthy and have sufficient resources. It uses placement rules provided when the pool was constructed to select the host on which each guest is restarted.

7.1.9 Layered Virtualization

Ops Center supports and helps automate a very popular "layered" virtualization technology. In this technology, one layer of virtualization runs underneath another layer.

The pool administrator can create a CDom server pool, where multiple LDoms are part of the pool. You can then use Ops Center to create multiple zones in one or more LDoms (see Figure 7.2). If you use layered virtualization, instead of migrating or automatically recovering at the zone level, those operations are handled at the LDom layer.

When you live migrate an LDom that has zones, the zones are automatically migrated with the LDom, and do not experience any downtime. When an LDom is automatically recovered, the zones will also be recovered and restarted automatically.

7.1.10 Summary

Virtualization technologies enable efficient consolidation, but require efficient management tools. Data center staff can use Oracle Enterprise Manager Ops Center to easily manage hundreds or thousands of VEs in multiple data centers, leveraging its efficient architecture to provision, monitor, and manage those guest VEs.

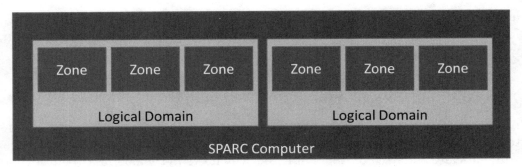

Figure 7.2 Layered Virtualization

7.2 OpenStack

A structured implementation of a private cloud would benefit from well-defined services, which are consumed by the virtual environments that self-service users deploy. One popular implementation of those services, along with the management tools necessary to deploy and use a private cloud, is OpenStack. The following subsections describe OpenStack briefly, and then discuss the integration of Oracle Solaris and OpenStack.

7.2.1 What Is OpenStack?

OpenStack is a community-based open-source project to form a comprehensive management layer to create and manage private clouds. This project was first undertaken as a joint effort of Rackspace and NASA in 2010, but is now driven by the OpenStack Foundation. Since 2010, OpenStack has been the fastest-growing open-source project on a worldwide basis, with thousands of commercial and individual contributors spread across the globe. The community launches two OpenStack releases per year.

OpenStack can be considered an operating system for cloud environments. It provides the foundation for Infrastructure as a Service (IaaS) clouds. Some new modules add features required in Platform as a Service (PaaS) clouds. OpenStack should not be viewed as layered software, however, but rather as an integrated infrastructure component. Thus, although the OpenStack community launches OpenStack releases, infrastructure vendors must integrate the open-source components into their own platforms to deliver the OpenStack functionality. Several operating system, network, and storage vendors offer OpenStack-enabled products.

OpenStack abstracts compute, network, and storage resources for the user, with those resources being exposed through a web portal with a single management pane. This integrated approach enables administrators to easily manage a variety of storage devices and hypervisors. The cloud services are based on a series of OpenStack modules, which communicate through a defined RESTful API between the various modules.

If a vendor plans to offer support for certain OpenStack services in its products, it must implement the functionality of those services and provide access to the functionality through the REST APIs. This can be done by delivering a service plugin, specialized for the product, that fills the gap between the REST API definition and the existing product feature.

7.2.2 The OpenStack General Architecture

Figure 7.3 depicts the general architecture of an OpenStack deployment. It consists of services provided by the OpenStack framework, and compute nodes that consume those services. This section describes those services.

Several OpenStack services are used to form an OpenStack-based private cloud. The services are interconnected via the REST APIs and depend on each other. But not all services are always needed to form a cloud, however, and not every vendor

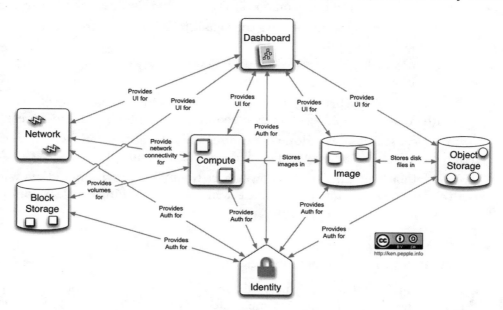

Figure 7.3 OpenStack Architecture

delivers all services. Some services have a special purpose and are configured only when appropriate; others are always needed when setting up a private cloud.

Because of the clearly defined REST APIs, services are extensible. The following list summarizes the core service modules.

- Cinder (block storage): Provides block storage for OpenStack compute instances and manages the creation, attaching, and detaching of block devices to OpenStack instances.
- Glance (images): Provides discovery, registration, and delivery services for disk and server images. The stored images can be used as templates for the deployment of VEs.
- Heat (orchestration): Enables the orchestration of complete application stacks, based on heat templates.
- Horizon (dashboard): Provides the dashboard management tool to access and provision cloud-based resources from a browser-based interface.
- Ironic (bare-metal provisioning): Used to provision bare-metal OpenStack guests, such as physical nodes.
- Keystone (authentication and authorization): Provides authentication and high-level authorization for the cloud and between cloud services. It consists of a central directory of users mapped to those cloud services they can access.
- Manila (shared file system): Allows the OpenStack instances to access shared file systems in the cloud.
- Neutron (network): Manages software-defined network services such as networks, routers, switches, and IP addresses to support multitenancy.
- Nova (compute): The primary service that provides the provisioning of virtual compute environments based on user requirement and available resources.
- Swift (object storage): A redundant and scalable storage system, with objects and files stored and managed on disk drives across multiple servers.
- Trove (database as a service): Allows users to quickly provision and manage multiple database instances without the burden of handling complex administrative tasks.

7.2.3 Oracle Solaris and OpenStack

Oracle Solaris 11 includes a full distribution of OpenStack as a standard, supported part of the platform. The first such release was Oracle Solaris 11.2, which integrated the Havana OpenStack release. The Juno release was integrated into

Oracle Solaris 11.2 Support Repository Update (SRU) 6. In Solaris 11.3 SRU 9, the integrated OpenStack software was updated to the Kilo release.

OpenStack services have been tightly integrated into the technology foundations of Oracle Solaris. The integration of OpenStack and Solaris leveraged many new Solaris features that had been designed specifically for cloud environments. Some of the Solaris features integrated into OpenStack include:

- Solaris Zones driver integration with Nova to deploy Oracle Solaris Zones and Solaris Kernel Zones
- Neutron driver integration with Oracle Solaris network virtualization, including Elastic Virtual Switch
- Cinder driver integration with the ZFS file system
- Unified Archives integration with Glance image management and Heat orchestration
- Bare-metal provisioning implementation using the Oracle Solaris Automated Installer (AI)

Figure 7.4 shows the OpenStack services implemented in Oracle Solaris and the related supporting Oracle Solaris features.

All services have been integrated into the Solaris Service Management Framework (SMF) to ensure service reliability, automatic service restart, and node

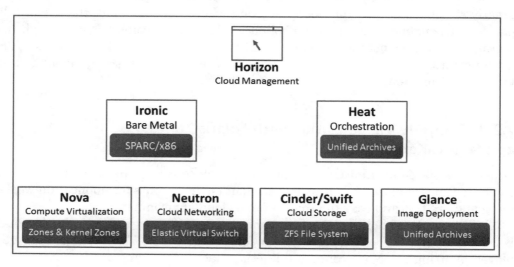

Figure 7.4 OpenStack Services in Oracle Solaris

dependency management. SMF properties enable additional configuration options. Oracle Solaris Role-Based Access Control (RBAC) ensures that the OpenStack services, represented by their corresponding SMF services, run with minimal privileges.

The OpenStack modules are delivered in separate Oracle Solaris packages, as shown in this example generated in Solaris 11.3:

```
# pkg list -af | grep openstack
cloud/openstack                    0.2015.2.2-0.175.3.9.0.2.0    i--
cloud/openstack/cinder             0.2015.2.2-0.175.3.9.0.2.0    i--
cloud/openstack/glance             0.2015.2.2-0.175.3.9.0.2.0    i--
cloud/openstack/heat               0.2015.2.2-0.175.3.9.0.2.0    i--
cloud/openstack/horizon            0.2015.2.2-0.175.3.9.0.2.0    i--
cloud/openstack/ironic             0.2015.2.1-0.175.3.9.0.2.0    i--
cloud/openstack/keystone           0.2015.2.2-0.175.3.9.0.2.0    i--
cloud/openstack/neutron            0.2015.2.2-0.175.3.9.0.2.0    i--
cloud/openstack/nova               0.2015.2.2-0.175.3.9.0.2.0    i--
cloud/openstack/openstack-common   0.2015.2.2-0.175.3.9.0.2.0    i--
cloud/openstack/swift              2.3.2-0.175.3.9.0.2.0         i--
```

To easily install the whole OpenStack distribution on a system, the `cloud/openstack` group package may be installed. It automatically installs all of the dependent OpenStack modules and libraries, plus additional packages such as `rad`, `rabbitmq`, and `mysql`.

The integration of OpenStack with the Solaris Image Packaging System (IPS) greatly simplifies updates of OpenStack on a cloud node, through the use of full package dependency checking and rollback. This was accomplished through integration with ZFS boot environments. Through a single update mechanism, an administrator can easily apply the latest software fixes to a system, including the virtual environments.

7.2.4 Compute Virtualization with Solaris Zones and Solaris Kernel Zones

Oracle Solaris Zones and Oracle Solaris Kernel Zones are used for OpenStack compute functionality. They provide excellent environments for application workloads and are fast and easy to provision in a cloud environment.

The life cycle of Solaris Zones as compute instances in an OpenStack cloud is controlled by the Solaris Nova driver for Solaris Zones. The instances are deployed by using the Nova command-line interface or by using the Horizon dashboard. To launch an instance, the cloud user selects a flavor, a Glance image, and a Neutron network. Figures 7.5 and 7.6 show the flavors available with Oracle Solaris OpenStack and the launch screen for an OpenStack instance.

Flavor Name	VCPUs	RAM	Root Disk	Ephemeral Disk	Swap Disk	ID	Public	Metadata	Actions
☐ Oracle Solaris non-global zone - tiny	1	1GB	20GB	0GB	0MB	6	Yes	Yes	Edit Flavor ▾
☐ Oracle Solaris kernel zone - tiny	1	2GB	20GB	0GB	0MB	1	Yes	Yes	Edit Flavor ▾
☐ Oracle Solaris non-global zone - small	4	2GB	40GB	0GB	0MB	7	Yes	Yes	Edit Flavor ▾
☐ Oracle Solaris kernel zone - small	4	4GB	40GB	0GB	0MB	2	Yes	Yes	Edit Flavor ▾
☐ Oracle Solaris non-global zone - medium	8	4GB	80GB	0GB	0MB	8	Yes	Yes	Edit Flavor ▾
☐ Oracle Solaris kernel zone - medium	8	8GB	80GB	0GB	0MB	3	Yes	Yes	Edit Flavor ▾
☐ Oracle Solaris non-global zone - large	16	8GB	160GB	0GB	0MB	9	Yes	Yes	Edit Flavor ▾
☐ Oracle Solaris kernel zone - large	16	16GB	160GB	0GB	0MB	4	Yes	Yes	Edit Flavor ▾
☐ Oracle Solaris non-global zone - xlarge	32	16GB	320GB	0GB	0MB	10	Yes	Yes	Edit Flavor ▾
☐ Oracle Solaris kernel zone - xlarge	32	32GB	320GB	0GB	0MB	5	Yes	Yes	Edit Flavor ▾

Figure 7.5   OpenStack Flavors

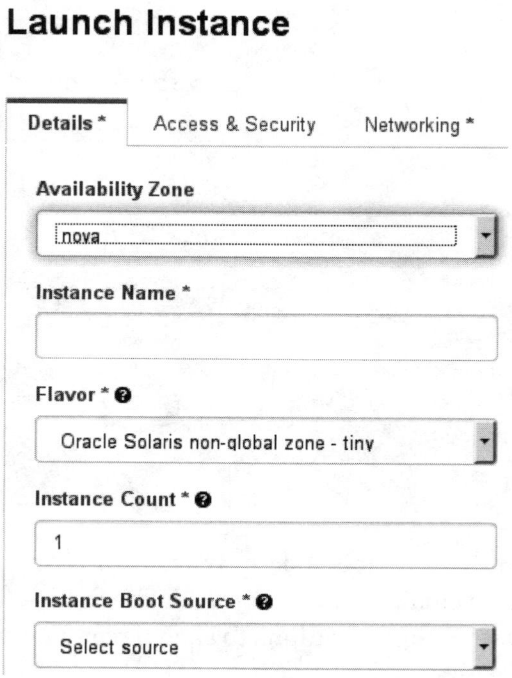

Launch Instance

Details *   Access & Security   Networking *

Availability Zone

nova

Instance Name *

Flavor * ❷

Oracle Solaris non-global zone - tiny

Instance Count * ❷

1

Instance Boot Source * ❷

Select source

Figure 7.6   OpenStack Instance Launch Screen

Oracle Solaris options specify the creation of a Solaris native zone or a Solaris kernel zone. Those special properties are assigned as `extra_specs`, which are typically set through the command line. The property's keys comprise a set of zone properties that are typically configured with the `zonecfg` command and that are supported in OpenStack.

The following keys are supported in both kernel zones and non-global zone flavors:

- `zonecfg:bootargs`
- `zonecfg:brand`
- `zonecfg:hostid`
- `zonecfg:cpu-arch`

The following keys are supported only in non-global zone flavors:

- `zonecfg:file-mac-profile`
- `zonecfg:fs-allowed`
- `zonecfg:limitpriv`

The list of current flavors can be displayed on the command line:

```
+----+-------------------------------------------+-------------------------------------+
| ID | Name                                      | extra_specs                         |
+----+-------------------------------------------+-------------------------------------+
| 1  | Oracle Solaris kernel zone - tiny         | {u'zonecfg:brand': u'solaris-kz'}   |
| 10 | Oracle Solaris non-global zone - xlarge   | {u'zonecfg:brand': u'solaris'}      |
| 2  | Oracle Solaris kernel zone - small        | {u'zonecfg:brand': u'solaris-kz'}   |
| 3  | Oracle Solaris kernel zone - medium       | {u'zonecfg:brand': u'solaris-kz'}   |
| 4  | Oracle Solaris kernel zone - large        | {u'zonecfg:brand': u'solaris-kz'}   |
| 5  | Oracle Solaris kernel zone - xlarge       | {u'zonecfg:brand': u'solaris-kz'}   |
| 6  | Oracle Solaris non-global zone - tiny     | {u'zonecfg:brand': u'solaris'}      |
| 7  | Oracle Solaris non-global zone - small    | {u'zonecfg:brand': u'solaris'}      |
| 8  | Oracle Solaris non-global zone - medium   | {u'zonecfg:brand': u'solaris'}      |
| 9  | Oracle Solaris non-global zone - large    | {u'zonecfg:brand': u'solaris'}      |
```

The `sc_profile` key can be modified only from the command line. This key is used to specify a system configuration profile for the flavor—for example, to preassign DNS or other system configurations to each flavor. For example, the following command will set a specific system configuration file for a flavor in the previously given list (i.e., "Oracle Solaris kernel zone – large"):

```
$ nova flavor-key 4 set sc_profile=/system/volatile/profile/sc_profile.xml
```

Launching an instance initiates the following actions in an OpenStack environment:

- The Nova scheduler selects a compute node in the cloud, based on the selected flavor, that meets the hypervisor type, architecture, number of VCPUs, and RAM requirements.

- On the chosen compute node, the Solaris Nova implementation will send a request to Cinder to find suitable storage in the cloud that can be used for the new instance's root file system. It then triggers the creation of a volume in that storage. Additionally, Nova obtains networking information and a network port in the selected network for an instance, by communicating with the Neutron service.

- The Cinder volume service delegates the volume creation to the storage device, receives the related Storage Unified Resource Identifier (SURI), and communicates that SURI back to the selected compute node. Typically this volume will reside on a different system from the compute node and will be accessed by the instance using shared storage such as FibreChannel, iSCSI, or NFS.

- The Neutron service assigns a Neutron network port to the instance, based on the cloud networking configuration. All instances instantiated by the compute service use an exclusive IP stack instance. Each instance includes an anet resource with its `configure-allowed-address` property set to `false`, and its `evs` and `vport` properties set to UUIDs supplied by Neutron that represent a particular virtualized switch segment and port.

- After the Solaris Zone and OpenStack resources have been configured, the zone is installed and booted, based on the assigned Glance image. This uses Solaris Unified Archives.

The following example shows a Solaris Zones configuration file, created by OpenStack for an iSCSI Cinder volume as boot volume:

```
compute-node # zonecfg -z instance-00000008 info
zonename: instance-00000008
brand: solaris
tenant: 740885068ed745c492e55c9e1c688472
anet:
        linkname: net0
        configure-allowed-address: false
        evs: a6365a98-7be1-42ec-88af-b84fa151b5a0
        vport: 8292e26a-5063-4bbb-87aa-7f3d51ff75c0
rootzpool:
        storage: iscsi://st01-sn:3260/target.iqn.1986-03.com.sun:02:...
capped-cpu:
        [ncpus: 1.00]
capped-memory:
        [swap: 1G]
rctl:
        name: zone.cpu-cap
        value: (priv=privileged,limit=100,action=deny)
rctl:
        name: zone.max-swap
        value: (priv=privileged,limit=1073741824,action=deny)
```

7.2.5 Cloud Networking with Elastic Virtual Switch

OpenStack networking creates virtual networks that interconnect VEs instantiated by the OpenStack compute node (Nova). It also connects these VEs to network services in the cloud, such as DHCP and routing. Neutron provides APIs to create and use multiple networks and to assign multiple VEs to networks, which are themselves assigned to different tenants. Each network tenant is represented in the network layer via an isolated Layer 2 network segment—comparable to VLANs in physical networks. Figure 7.7 shows the relationships among these components.

Subnets are properties that are assigned much like blocks of IPv4 or IPv6 addresses—that is, `default-router` or `nameserver`. Neutron creates ports in these subnets and assigns them together with several properties to virtual machines. The L3-router functionality of Neutron interconnects tenant networks to external networks and enables VEs to access the Internet through source NAT. Floating IP addresses create a static one-to-one mapping from a public IP address on the external network to a private IP address in the cloud, assigned to one VE.

Oracle Solaris Zones and Oracle Solaris Kernel Zones, as OpenStack instances, use the Solaris VNIC technology to connect to the tenant networks. All VNICs are bound with virtual network switches to physical network interfaces. If multiple

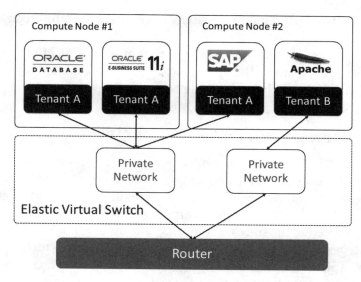

Figure 7.7 OpenStack Virtual Networking

tenants use one physical interface, then multiple virtual switches are created above that physical interface.

If multiple compute nodes have been deployed in one cloud and multiple tenants are used, virtual switches from the same tenant are spread over multiple compute nodes, as shown in Figure 7.8.

A technology is needed to control these distributed switches as one switch. The virtual networks can be created by, for example, VXLAN or VLAN. In the case of Oracle Solaris, the Solaris Elastic Virtual Switch (EVS) feature is used

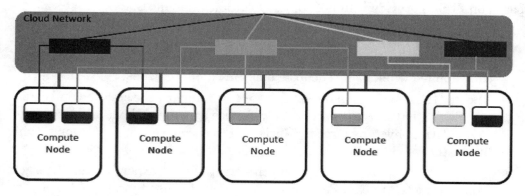

Figure 7.8 Virtual Switches

to control the distributed virtual switches. The back-end to OpenStack uses a Neutron plugin.

Finally, EVS is controlled by a Neutron plugin so that it offers an API to the cloud. In each compute node, the virtual switches are controlled by an EVS plugin to form a distributed switch for multiple tenants.

7.2.6 Cloud Storage with ZFS and COMSTAR

The OpenStack Cinder service provides central management for block storage volumes as boot storage and for application data. To create a volume, the Cinder scheduler selects a storage back-end, based on storage size and storage type requirements, and the Cinder volume service controls the volume creation. The Cinder API then sends the necessary access information back to the cloud.

Different types of storage can be used to provide storage to the cloud, such as FibreChannel, iSCSI, NFS, or the local disks of the compute nodes. The type used depends on the storage requirements. These requirements include characteristics such as capacity, throughput, latency and availability, and requirements for local storage or shared storage. Shared storage is required if migration of OpenStack instances between compute nodes is needed. Local storage may often be sufficient for short-term, ephemeral data. The cloud user is not aware of the storage technology that has been chosen, because the Cinder volume service represents the storage simply as a type of storage, not as a specific storage product model.

The Cinder volume service is configured to use an OpenStack storage plugin, which knows the specifics of a storage device. Example characteristics include the method to create a Cinder volume, and a method to access the data.

Multiple Cinder storage plugins are available for Oracle Solaris, which are based on ZFS to provide volumes to the OpenStack instances:

- The `ZFSVolumeDriver` supports the creation of local volumes for use by Nova on the same node as the Cinder volume service. This method is typically applied when using the local disks in compute nodes.

- The `ZFSISCSIDriver` and the `ZFSFCDriver` support the creation and export of iSCSI and FC targets, respectively, for use by remote Nova compute nodes. COMSTAR allows any Oracle Solaris host to become a storage server, serving block storage via iSCSI or FC.

- The `ZFSSAISCSIDriver` supports the creation and export of iSCSI targets from a remote Oracle ZFS Storage Appliance for use by remote Nova compute nodes.

In addition, other storage plugins can be configured in the Cinder volume service, if the storage vendor has provided the appropriate Cinder storage plugin. For example, the `OracleFSFibreChannelDriver` enables Oracle FS1 storage to be used in OpenStack clouds to provide FibreChannel volumes.

7.2.7 Sample Deployment Options

The functional enablement of Oracle Solaris for OpenStack is based on two main precepts. The first aspect is the availability and support of the OpenStack API with various software libraries and plugins in Oracle Solaris. The second aspect is the creation and integration of OpenStack plugins to enable specific Oracle Solaris functions in OpenStack. As discussed earlier, those plugins have been developed and provided for Cinder, Neutron, and Nova, as well as for Ironic.

Deploying an OpenStack-based private cloud with OpenStack for Oracle Solaris is similar to the setup of other OpenStack-based platforms.

- The design and setup of the hardware platform (server systems, network and storage) for the cloud are very important. Careful design pays off during the configuration and production phases for the cloud.
- Oracle Solaris must be installed on the server systems. The installation of Oracle Solaris OpenStack packages can occur with installation of Solaris—a process that can be automated with the Solaris Automated Installer.
- After choosing between the storage options, the storage node is installed and integrated into the cloud.
- The various OpenStack modules must be configured with their configuration files, yielding a full functional IaaS private cloud with OpenStack. The OpenStack configuration files are located in the /etc/[cinder, neutron, nova, ..] directories. The final step is the activation of the related SMF services with their dependencies.

The design of the hardware platform is also very important. Besides OpenStack, a general cloud architecture to be managed by OpenStack includes these required parts:

- One or multiple compute nodes for the workload.
- A cloud network to host the logical network internal to the cloud. Those networks link together network ports of the instances, which together form

one network broadcast domain. This internal logical network is typically composed with VxLAN or tagged VLAN technology.

- Storage resources to boot the OpenStack instances and keep application data persistent.

- A storage network, if shared storage is used, to connect the shared storage with the compute nodes.

- An internal control network, used by the OpenStack API's internal messages and to drive the compute, network, and storage parts of the cloud; this network can also be used to manage, install, and monitor all cloud nodes.

- A cloud control part, which runs the various OpenStack control services for the OpenStack cloud like the Cinder and Nova scheduler, the Cinder volume service, the MySQL management database, or the RabbitMQ messaging service.

Figure 7.9 shows a general OpenStack cloud, based on a multinode architecture with multiple compute nodes, shared storage, isolated networks and controlled cloud access through a centralized network node.

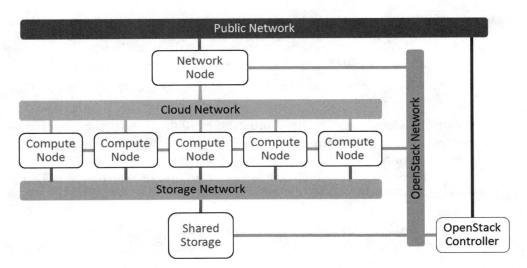

Figure 7.9   Single Public Network Connection

7.2.8 Single-System Prototype Environment

You can demonstrate an OpenStack environment in a single system. In this case, a single network is used, or multiple networks are created using etherstubs, to form the internal network of the cloud. "Compute nodes" can then be instantiated as kernel zones. However, if you use kernel zones as compute nodes, then OpenStack instances can be only non-global zones. This choice does not permit application of several features, including Nova migration. This single-node setup can be implemented very easily with Oracle Solaris, using a Unified Archive of a comprehensive OpenStack installation.

Such single-system setups are typically implemented so that users can become familiar with OpenStack or to create very small prototypes. Almost all production deployments will use multiple computers to achieve the availability goals of a cloud.

There is one exception to this guideline: A SPARC system running Oracle Solaris (e.g., SPARC T7-4) can be configured as a multinode environment, using multiple logical domains, connected with internal virtual networks. The result is still a single physical system, which includes multiple isolated Solaris instances, but is represented like a multinode cloud.

7.2.9 Simple Multinode Environment

Creating a multinode OpenStack cloud increases the choices available in all parts of the general cloud architecture. The architect makes the decision between one unified network or separate networks when choosing the design for the cloud network, the internal network, and the storage network. Alternatively, those networks might not be single networks, but rather networks with redundancy features such as IPMP, DLMP, LACP, or MPXIO. All of these technologies are part of Oracle Solaris and can be selected to create the network architecture of the cloud.

Another important decision to be made is how to connect the cloud to the public or corporate network. The general architecture described earlier shows a controlled cloud access through a centralized network node. While this setup enforces centralized access to the cloud via a network node, it can also lead to complicated availability or throughput limitations. An alternative setup is a flat cloud, shown in Figure 7.10, in which the compute nodes are directly connected to the public network, so that no single access point limits throughput or availability. It is the responsibility of the cloud architect to decide which option is the most appropriate choice.

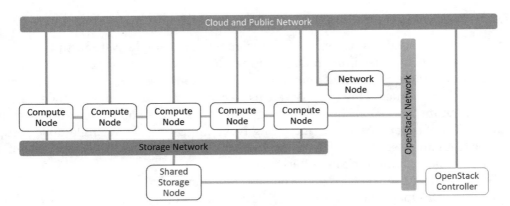

Figure 7.10   Multiple Public Network Connections

For the compute nodes, the decision can be made between SPARC nodes (SPARC T5, T7, S7, M7, or M10 servers), x86_64 nodes, or a mixed-node cloud that combines both architectures. Oracle Solaris OpenStack will handle both processor architectures in one cloud. Typically, compute nodes with 1 or 2 sockets with medium memory capacity (512 GB) are chosen. More generally, by using SPARC systems, compute nodes ranging from very small to very large in size can be combined in one cloud without any special configuration efforts.

The cloud storage is typically shared storage. In a shared storage architecture, disks storing the running instances are located outside the compute nodes. Cloud instances can then be easily recovered with migration or evacuation, in case of compute node downtime. Using shared storage is operationally simple because having separate compute hosts and storage makes the compute nodes "stateless." Thus, if there are no instances running on a compute node, that node can be taken offline and its contents erased completely without affecting the remaining parts of the cloud. This type of storage can be scaled to any amount of storage. Storage decisions can be made based on performance, cost, and availability. Among the choices are an Oracle ZFS storage appliance, shared storage through a Solaris node as iSCSI or FC target server, or shared storage through a FibreChannel SAN storage system.

To use local storage, each compute node's internal disks store all data of the instances that the node hosts. Direct access to disks is very cost-effective, because there is no need to maintain a separate storage network. The disk performance on each compute node is directly related to the number and performance of existing local disks. The chassis size of the compute node will limit the number of spindles able to be used in a compute node. However, if a compute node fails, the instances on it cannot be recovered. Also, there is no method to migrate instances. This omission can be a major issue for cloud services that create persistent data. Other cloud services, however, perform processing services without storing any local data, in which case no local persistent data is created.

The cloud control plane, implemented as an OpenStack controller, can consist of one or more systems. With Oracle Solaris, typically the OpenStack controller is created in kernel zones for modular setups. Scalability on the controller site can then be achieved just by adding another kernel zone. The OpenStack control services can all be combined in one kernel zone. For scalability and reliability reasons, the services can be grouped into separate kernel zones, providing the following services:

- RabbitMQ
- MySQL management database
- EVS Controller
- Network Node
- The remaining OpenStack Services

7.2.10 OpenStack Summary

Running OpenStack on Oracle Solaris provides many advantages. A complete OpenStack distribution is part of the Oracle Solaris Repository and, therefore, is available for Oracle Solaris without any additional cost. The tight integration of the comprehensive virtualization features for compute and networking—Solaris Zones, virtual NICs and switches, and the Elastic Virtual Switch—in Oracle Solaris provide significant value not found in other OpenStack implementations. The integration of OpenStack with Oracle Solaris leverages the Image Packaging System, ZFS boot environments, and the Service Management Facility. As a consequence, an administrator can quickly start an update of the cloud environment, and can quickly update each service and node in a single operation.

7.3 Summary

At least in IT, perfection cannot be achieved: Every solution inevitably yields new problems. In keeping with this pattern, virtualization was a solution, but it created a problem—the unbridled proliferation of virtual environments, a herd of invisible horses that must somehow be corralled.

In some cases, software intended to manage physical computers was extended with the ability to manage both physical computers and VEs. OEM Ops Center is an excellent example. New software such as OpenStack was also designed from the ground up to manage VEs and their surrounding infrastructure. Understanding these tools is a prerequisite to successful deployment of virtualization.

Choosing a Virtualization Technology

The preceding chapters described different forms of server virtualization, each with its own strengths and limitations. But which is the right combination to use?

No one answer applies equally well in all situations. Each form of virtualization has both strengths and weaknesses, which must be weighed against each other. One approach might provide great value in one situation, but offer little value in another scenario. Some virtualization solutions can be combined, making it possible to benefit from the advantages of more than one virtualization technology at the same time.

This chapter discusses potential advantages and disadvantages of layering virtualization technologies. It also provides guidelines for selecting the right virtualization technologies for different requirements.

8.1 Review of Strengths and Limitations

This section summarizes the distinguishing characteristics of the technologies discussed previously, focusing on aspects that are central to the selection process. First we will discuss the benefits of these characteristics.

A key component of virtualization is workload isolation. This takes three forms: hardware, software, and security isolation. Hardware isolation prevents a hardware failure from affecting more than one virtual environment (VE). Software isolation prevents a software failure from affecting multiple environments; it also provides separate namespaces for files, users, and processes. Security isolation permits the establishment of separate security contexts, with separate user identities, roles, and authentication and authorization mechanisms for each VE. The effect is containment of intrusions to just one VE. Although security isolation often focuses on web-facing workloads exposed to public networks and on systems housing sensitive financial, medical, or government data, it is important to secure all environments in a computing infrastructure to prevent attacks against the weakest link. Thus, organizations are well advised to architect and integrate security on a systematic basis, rather than reserving it for "high-value" targets.

Those features providing the most isolation can add significantly to the costs of a system. Nevertheless, business-critical workloads are most in need of comprehensive isolation and can often justify the extra expense of supporting independent VEs. Any additional expenses may be offset by the savings provided by consolidation.

Different forms of virtualization offer different levels of software compatibility. With some approaches, there are few or no incompatibilities: Software runs essentially the same in a virtualized environment as it does in a non-virtualized system. With others, the virtualization infrastructure performs some operations on behalf of a VE that are implemented differently than the corresponding operations on non-virtualized systems, or functionality is limited in some way. These considerations were discussed in previous chapters and will be reviewed later in this chapter as needed. In all cases, incompatibilities should be analyzed and software retested to ensure that no problems will arise in system functioning.

Recertification of software products, if necessary, should be performed by the software vendor. In such cases, in-house testing should be minimal. Software developed in-house should be analyzed or retested if it is to be used on the types of virtualization that affect program behavior.

Most forms of virtualization create at least some level of performance overhead. This overhead stems from the time that hypervisor spends running on a CPU to prevent unwanted interactions between VEs; inefficiencies caused by emptying the CPU cache after one guest runs for a time slice, before the next guest runs on that CPU; and virtual I/O, which performs many additional steps to prevent prohibited actions. The precise amount of overhead depends on the type of virtualization and on the workload. CPU-intensive workloads are the least affected because they require the least effort from the virtualization technology. The simplest case is containers (e.g., Oracle Solaris Zones) because their processes interact with the operating system kernel just as they would in a non-virtualized environment. No additional code or effort is required on the part of other components, so there is no performance overhead. In other simple cases, a VE gets a time slice on a CPU without further assistance from the virtualization technology. By comparison, I/O-intensive workloads experience performance overhead in some virtualization solutions due to resource contention and an increased number of state-changing operations, especially when I/O devices are shared. Latency-sensitive workloads should not be installed in VEs that suffer from such performance overhead without testing to ensure they can still meet their performance objectives.

VE scalability is a related performance topic. Some types of virtualization can host only a limited number of VEs with acceptable performance. Most can theoretically run dozens or even hundreds of VEs. In practice, however, most of those solutions do not scale well: They may need terabytes of RAM, they may be limited by the scalability limits of the hardware architecture to which they are tied, or their current implementation may create so much performance overhead that they can scale to only 10–20 VEs. Others can effectively handle more than 100 VEs. This effect is often mitigated by the common practice of consolidating physical systems from old, slow, low-utilization platforms onto new processors. In such circumstances, the modest resource requirements and the significant increase in processor speed may compensate for the possible overhead. To maximize the cost savings achieved from consolidation, an organization should choose the most scalable virtualization solution.

The resource requirements for many workloads change over either short or long periods of time. An ability to dynamically change the amount of resources available to those VEs is necessary to maintain appropriate throughput and response times.

Most applications are able to run on more than one version of an operating system. Some are tied to a specific version of the OS or to a specific version of an OS package or a patch level. Such applications can benefit from the freedom to run different VEs at different OS levels, thereby permitting applications with different OS requirements to coexist on the same server. Also, VEs with independent OS levels can use different patch windows for updating system software. Virtual environments that share a common OS software level may need a synchronized patch window. Unfortunately, this strategy may be difficult to realize on a practical level when different applications and different application owners share the same physical system.

Similarly, while many applications can run on different operating systems, others are available only for a particular OS. The ability to run different operating systems at the same time (e.g., Microsoft Windows and Apple Mac OS) also has value, and in some situations is an absolute necessity.

Some virtualization features enhance business agility and operational flexibility—key considerations that are discussed in Chapter 7, "Automating Virtualization." Dynamic data centers, whose workloads regularly grow and shrink, will benefit the most from these features. Cloning, for example, is the ability to create an exact copy of a VE. It accelerates provisioning when many similar workloads will exist, and can even be performed as a programmed response to a request for a new instance of an application. Likewise, VE mobility can be used to move an application from one computer to another. This capability is very valuable in dynamic data centers where workloads grow and shrink regularly, and it facilitates ongoing availability of applications during maintenance periods for physical server hardware.

Virtualization has enabled the rapid proliferation of cloud computing environments. Both public and private clouds are possible because of the ease with which VEs can be created. This computing model greatly reduces the effort involved in managing a data center, and it increases business agility by shortening the time from making a decision to run an application and having a suitable environment in which to run it.

Architects choosing virtualization technologies to meet an application's requirements must take all of the previously mentioned factors into consideration, mapping requirements onto those combinations of technologies that will best satisfy them. The following sections describe the virtualization technologies under discussion in this context.

8.1.1 Oracle Solaris Zones

As described in Chapter 3, "Oracle Solaris Zones," Oracle Solaris provides OS virtualization (OSV) in the form of Solaris Zones. Zones provide multiple virtual Solaris environments within a single Solaris instance. This technology offers the following advantages:

- **Fault isolation.** Software service and application failures in one zone have no effect on other zones.
- **Security.** Zones remain securely isolated from one another. This separation permits extremely granular privilege assignments. Further, features are provided to configure immutable zones—that is, "locked-down" environments that are protected from modification. Tamper-proof execution environments are very difficult to achieve with other virtualization methods.

- **A high level of compatibility with non-zone Solaris environments.** Zones have some functional limitations. For example, a zone cannot modify a physical device's tuning parameters.

- **Native performance.** The use of zones does not affect application performance because zones require no hypervisor or other virtualization software. The code paths of the OS and applications are unchanged, so there is no performance overhead. This outcome is typical for OSV, but unlike that for virtual machine implementations.

- **Maximum scalability, permitting the largest number of VEs per computer.** The theoretical maximum is 8191 zones per OS instance. Production systems with more than 100 running zones exist in data centers.

- **Highest resource granularity.** This characteristic permits fine-grained assignment of CPU capacity, RAM use, and allocation of other system resources.

- **Low overhead.** Besides a lack of performance overhead (mentioned earlier), native zones require the smallest amount of additional RAM, and they do not waste resources by reserving them and leaving them idle.

- **More predictable performance than hypervisors.** Because only one scheduler is making scheduling decisions, performance is more consistent.

- **Independence from processor family.** Zones are available on any SPARC-, Intel-, or AMD-based computer that runs Solaris 11. This platform independence lets planners select a virtualization architecture without being locked into a chip family.

- **Centralized observability.** Solaris tools enable you to examine all activities of all processes in all zones without buying or learning new tools. This is not possible with other virtualization methods.

- **Coexistence with Solaris versions.** Solaris 11 environments can coexist with Solaris 10 VEs.

- **No extra license fees needed.** Zones are simply a feature of the OS. Some hypervisors require a fee for their use, or a fee for support in addition to the support fees for the operating systems.

- **Business agility and operational efficiency.** Zones' features and flexibility exceed those of hardware partitions, owing to their advanced features such as VE cloning, mobility, live migration, and dynamic resource management.

Solaris kernel zones differ from native zones, leading to slightly different advantages for the former:

- **Solaris version isolation.** Applications that require different versions of Solaris can run in different kernel zones, unlike native zones.

- **Fault isolation.** Software fault isolation is greater than that of native zones.

- **A high level of compatibility with non-zone Solaris environments.** Kernel zones provide even more consistency with non-zoned environments. System tuning decisions may be made for each kernel zone.

- **Low overhead.** Kernel zones have low computational and memory overhead, albeit not as low as native zones. Each kernel zone uses more RAM than a native zone, and some virtual operations incur a performance penalty.

Solaris Zones were introduced with Solaris 10 in 2005, and have been continually enhanced and widely adopted since then. They permit robust, scalable, and highly flexible virtualization without committing to a particular chip architecture.

The benefits of Solaris Zones can be combined with the benefits of other virtualization technologies, thereby enabling the creation of highly functional and flexible virtualization architectures. When an Oracle Solaris system is hosted in a physical domain, logical domain, or other type of virtual machine, deploying application environments inside zones nested within those virtual environments provides additional benefits. Security is enhanced by zones' ability to provide a locked-down environment. Zones can be quickly and easily cloned, which simplifies the provisioning of additional virtual environments. Perhaps most importantly, the low resource requirements and scalability make it possible to locate many isolated virtual environments within the same domain or virtual machine—with the end result being better scalability than would be possible with domains or hypervisor technology alone.

One way to realize the most benefits from this combination is to deploy a new domain or virtual machine when a virtual environment needs a dedicated operating system instance, and to deploy Solaris Zones within the virtual environment for Solaris virtual environments with compatible OS software levels. That combination exploits the advantages of both forms of virtualization.

8.1.2 Oracle VM Server for SPARC

As described in Chapter 4, "Oracle VM Server for SPARC," logical domains are SPARC virtual machines that are available on SPARC servers. Like physical domains, each logical domain runs its own instance of Oracle Solaris. This technology offers several advantages:

- **Strong fault isolation.** A software failure in one domain cannot affect another domain, and domains remain isolated from failure of CPU threads and other hardware resources assigned to other domains. The fault isolation characteristics of domains are better than those of both software-based hypervisors and OSV, as they permit redundancy with multiple service domains. Nevertheless, this level of fault isolation is not as good as that offered by hardware partitioning, especially when shared I/O resources are in use. Even so, the level of fault isolation available with logical domains is appropriate for almost all workloads.

- **Security isolation.** A security penetration or compromise in one domain has no effect on other domains. Logical domains can be used to store sensitive data.

- **An extremely high level of compatibility with non-domained environments.** Only a few incompatibilities exist, such as the specific behavior of a virtual disk or network device, as documented in the current version of the domains reference material. Except for those differences, software performs the exact same steps as on a stand-alone system.

- **Native CPU performance compared to non-domained environments for many workloads.** I/O performance may suffer under shared I/O configurations, which can reduce the scalability for some workloads. Because CPU hardware threads are assigned to each domain, scalability is limited by the number of available threads on specific server models. This virtual machine technology premiered in 2007, on SPARC computers with 4 to 8 cores and 4 threads per core, for a maximum of 32 addressable CPU threads. At most 32 domains were possible, including the control domain. Newer products utilizing the SPARC M7 chip, such as the SPARC M7-16 server, now provide 32 cores with threads per core for every M7 processor. Now environments can run as many as 128 logical domains per system. This exclusive assignment of CPUs eliminates the need to time-slice guest environments onto CPUs, thereby avoiding the performance penalty experienced with other hypervisors.

- **A large number of completely separate Oracle Solaris instances.** Each domain can have its own patch levels and maintenance windows without conflict with or interference from other domains. This approach compares favorably to most OS virtualization configurations, which may require keeping patch levels synchronized across some or all guests.

- **High resource granularity.** Oracle VM Server for SPARC permits fine-grained assignment of CPU threads and RAM. The granularity associated with this approach is more flexible than with hardware partitions but less flexible compared to OS virtualization.

- **No extra license fees needed.** The logical domains technology is included with all SPARC systems. Some hypervisors require a fee for their use or support in addition to acquisition and support fees for the operating systems and hardware.

- **Excellent support for business agility and operational efficiencies.** Advanced features, such as domain cloning and mobility, support both flexibility and cost-effectiveness.

Oracle VM Server for SPARC has proved to be one of the most popular features of the SPARC server product line, with rapid uptake in its adoption and feature growth occurring since its introduction. This technology is widely used for server consolidation, especially when replacing multiple small, horizontally scaled servers from previous SPARC product families.

8.1.3 Hard Partitioning and Physical Domains

As described in Chapter 5, physical domains are a feature of certain SPARC-based servers providing isolated hardware environments, each of which runs its own hypervisor. This technology has the following strengths:

- **Best fault isolation.** No failure in one domain or in its infrastructure can affect another. Other solutions carry at least some risk that a failure occurring in one VE will affect other VEs, perhaps even causing all of them to halt.

- **Security isolation.** A security penetration or compromise in one domain has no effect on other domains.

- **Complete compatibility in every respect with non-domained environments.** There is no concern about incompatibility or non-supportability of software.

- **Native performance compared to non-domained environments.** There is no virtualization layer. The CPU code path of an application is not elongated by virtualization, and no additional firmware is needed to assist with virtualization. This advantage, compared to software hypervisors, is greatest for I/O-intensive applications. Nevertheless, domain scalability remains limited by hardware capabilities. The highest scalability is provided by SPARC M6-32 systems, which currently can have a maximum of 24 physical domains.

- **Completely separate Oracle Solaris instances.** Each instance can potentially have its own OS version, patch levels, and maintenance windows without any conflict or interference. Management of a single domain is the same as management of a single system. This is similar to hypervisor solutions, but is often an advantage compared to OS virtualization.

- **Reconfigurability.** On the SPARC M6-32 and M7-16, the sizes of the physical domains can be changed to meet business requirements. Although upgrading from a two-CPU SPARC T7-2 to a four-CPU SPARC T7-4 requires replacing the entire computer, physical domains on the high-end servers can be reconfigured from a 2-CPU partition to a 4-CPU partition, or even larger—up to a 32-CPU partition.

- **No extra license fees needed.** The physical domains technology is included with all domain-capable systems. Some hypervisors require a fee for their use, or a fee for support in addition to support fees for the guest operating systems.

- **Well-established and accepted history.** The SPARC product line benefits from two decades of partitioning development and deployment experience.

Physical domains are widely deployed in enterprise environments, especially for large applications. In such applications, ability to scale and the highest degree of isolation and availability are necessary for a relatively small number of vertically scaled virtualized environments.

8.1.4 Oracle VM VirtualBox

Oracle Solaris runs on x86 systems as well as SPARC systems, and VirtualBox can host many different operating systems, including Solaris, Microsoft Windows, and many Linux distributions. Because of this flexibility, VirtualBox plays an important role in development environments that will deliver software to multiple operating systems. VirtualBox provides the following advantages for such environments:

- **Type 2 hypervisor.** The user benefits from the rich set of tools supported on the underlying operating system, and use of that host OS does not suffer from any performance degradation because it is not running on top of a hypervisor.

- **Fault isolation.** No software failure in one virtual machine can affect another VE, although a failure of the hypervisor may halt all of the VEs.

- **Security isolation.** A security penetration or compromise of one guest has no effect on other guests. Given that most hypervisors are managed across a network, however, this creates an opportunity for an intruder to access a hypervisor directly; penetration of the hypervisor could theoretically give access to each guest, as demonstrated in the VENOM vulnerability.

- **High resource granularity compared to hardware partitions, permitting fine-grained assignment.** Hypervisors often permit oversubscription of CPU threads and RAM for enhanced consolidation ratios.

- **Coexistence of multiple operating environments that run on the x86 platform.** Use of VirtualBox provides an opportunity to leverage infrastructure investments for more heterogeneous OS mixtures. In contrast, most OS virtualization implementations support only guests of the same OS type, version, and patch level. Solaris is an exception: It supports Solaris 8 Containers and Solaris 9 Containers in Solaris 10 systems, and Solaris 10 Zones in Solaris 11 systems. All of these are VEs that mimic different versions of Solaris.

8.2 Choosing the Technology

Understanding the attributes of the virtualization choices is the first step in making wise virtualization decisions. These attributes should be matched to the corresponding data center and workload requirements.

8.2.1 Start with Requirements

Application and organizational requirements drive virtualization technology selection, just as with any architectural decision. The process of choosing any technology should begin with an assessment of the required systemic properties. Each of these requirements can suggest or preclude one or more virtualization technologies:

- Are full fault and service isolation needed with no single points of failure?
- What are the availability requirements of the workloads being virtualized?
- Is there additional budget for licensing add-on virtualization technologies?
- Are there business needs for automation and sophisticated management such as cloud provisioning, cloning, and mobility?

- Does the solution require a large number of virtualized environments with highly granular resource assignment, or are only a few environments required?

- Are workloads dynamic in nature, requiring the ability to easily change resource assignments?

- Is maximum performance needed? This consideration is important for workloads that are I/O intensive or make many system calls, because some virtualization technologies introduce performance penalties for those operations.

- Is an automated process needed for migrating from legacy unconsolidated environments or older operating system levels to a more current system?

While platform architecture may drive virtualization choices, this is not a one-way process: The virtualization capabilities of each platform can influence platform selection as well. For example, standardizing on Solaris makes it possible to leverage Solaris Zones regardless of the chip architecture employed. This approach provides a solution without extra costs, which takes advantage of the best resource granularity and scalability of the available technologies, and which makes it possible to use either SPARC or x86 systems. Conversely, selecting SPARC makes it possible to leverage the built-in domaining capabilities of modern SPARC processors without incurring additional licensing expenses.

8.2.2 Preferences

Once you have used your list of requirements to reduce the set of useful options, consideration of preferences may suggest one choice over the others. For example, perhaps a workload requires isolation of compute resources. Physical domains offer this level of isolation. Oracle VM Server for SPARC also offers such isolation when virtual I/O is not used and each CPU is assigned to a specific logical domain. Further, imagine that you would prefer to be able to move the workload while it runs. This preference suggests a need for the live migration feature that is supported for logical domains, but is not available for physical domains.

The outcome may be different if the requirements and preferences are reversed. For example, a requirement for live migration limits your choices to logical domains and Solaris kernel zones. That requirement would not limit the features that could be used with logical domains, whereas a preference for hardware isolation would remove kernel zones from the list, and would require the aforementioned configuration restrictions.

After an initial technology choice has been made, you can apply additional features offered with the technology. Continuing with our example, suppose there is a requirement to consolidate and run unmodified Solaris 8 or 9 binaries on recent SPARC servers: this could be accomplished for legacy workloads by running Solaris 8 or Solaris 9 Containers in a Solaris 10 guest domain. Alternatively, existing Solaris 8, Solaris 9, or Solaris 10 systems could be consolidated into guest domains using the logical domains physical to virtual (P2V) tool; alternatively, they could be converted into branded or native zones, which in turn run in a domain. If there are a large number of low-utilization environments to consolidate, then multiple host systems could be consolidated into zones in the same Solaris guest domain, with the fine-grained resource controls available with Solaris Zones then being leveraged.

8.2.3 Virtualization Decision Tree

By working from requirements to preferences, the visualization architect can create a decision tree. This method documents an orderly process leading to an optimal solution. The following decision trees illustrates this process, based on some of the preceding considerations. Note that real-world decision trees will be more complex than these examples.

- If the highest priorities include vertical scale, complete hardware redundancy, and complete fault isolation for separate Oracle Solaris instances, then physical domains are the only choice.
- If the highest priorities include granular, dynamic, resource allocation for multiple Solaris instances, but you also prefer separate hardware for each VE, then use logical domains.
- If the maximum number of virtual instances with the most flexible control of resources is important, then use Solaris Zones as the primary virtualization technology.
- If you want to maximize workload density inside physical domains or logical domains, deploy applications in zones within each domain. This approach increases operational flexibility without adding cost, and it permits multiple Solaris virtual environments to reside within a single domain, perhaps using different versions of Solaris. You can also use Solaris Zones to harden the workload's operating environment against intruders.
- When using logical domains with physical domains, you should assign only a single domain configurable unit to a physical domain. This minimizes the number of logical domains that will be affected by a board failure in a physical domain.

- If you require a mix of operating systems for developers, VirtualBox is an excellent choice.

8.2.4 Examples

This section uses the decision tree method described previously with some examples.

8.2.4.1 Consolidating Large Mission-Critical Workloads

In your data center, you need to increase the workload density of high-scale, mission-critical workloads (20 or more cores per workload). This situation has the following specific needs:

- Mission-critical workloads should be placed in the lowest-risk environments. Consolidation adds risk, while isolation reduces it, with isolation being a primary factor in determining the level of risk. Hard partitions are strongly suggested, and perhaps required.
- High-scale workloads need high-scale hardware. x86 systems may not scale high enough, while SPARC systems are ideal. A high-scale operating system, such as Oracle Solaris, will also play a key role.
- Because large workloads tend to have stricter availability requirements, large computer systems typically have better RAS (reliability, availability, and serviceability) characteristics, of which availability is the most important. SPARC M6-32, M7-8, and M7-16 servers excel here, offering full hardware redundancy and excellent system reliability. The ability to service many components while the servers are running is another reason why large workloads run best on the high-end servers.
- Consolidated systems benefit from dynamic resource flexibility. The flexibility of physical domains will meet this need. A mid-range or high-end SPARC system with 256 or more CPU cores is the ideal solution in this scenario. The amount of RAM in the system should be slightly more than the sum of RAM needed by all of the workloads. If you are consolidating on a SPARC server that uses a SPARC M7 processor, consider populating all the DIMM slots on the CPU boards. This will enable the DIMM sparing feature, delivering greater uptime in the event a memory DIMM completely fails.

8.2.4.2 Hosting an ISP Web Service

For an ISP, the goal is to sell the services of its web servers. The business model of an ISP web service includes the desire to maximize the density of customers and minimize acquisition and maintenance costs. The customer service contract might indicate an intent to achieve 99.9% uptime, yet include a "best effort" clause regarding service uptime. Several configurations may be offered in the service catalog, distinguished by CPU capacity and RAM. "Cost units" merely show the relative user cost per year.

- Very small: 0.5 CPU core, 512MB RAM, 4 GB disk: 1× cost units
- Small: 1 CPU core, 1 GB RAM, 16 GB disk: 2× cost units
- Medium: 4 CPU cores, 2 GB RAM, 64 GB disk: 4× cost units
- Large: 8 CPU cores, 8 GB RAM, 128 GB disk: 10× cost units
- Very large: 16 CPU cores, 16 GB RAM, 256 GB disk: 25× cost units

These factors will help you choose the virtualization best solution:

- The highest density of VEs per server requires the greatest efficiency—that is, the least amount of RAM and disk space per VE, and the least performance overhead per VE. Zones provide the highest density of virtualization solutions and are a good choice in such a case. With applications running, the Oracle Solaris kernel will use hundreds of megabytes of RAM, but each VE will consume only dozens of megabytes, plus the memory needed for the web server applications. A single-CPU server, either x86 or SPARC, can easily handle 50 small customers, or two very large customers.
- System memory is a significant portion of the cost of the system. Maximizing customer density means reducing the RAM needs as much as possible and, therefore, reducing acquisition costs. This consideration also leads to the choice of Solaris Zones. We will ignore the memory needed for the web server software, which is independent of virtualization technology. Instead of a minimum of 1 GB RAM being required for each of 50 VEs, which is typical in a hypervisor environment, only approximately 100MB is needed for each zone. Instead of a total of 50 GB RAM, plus memory for the applications, the system will need only 50 GB RAM plus application space.

8.2.4.3 Consolidation of Mixed Workloads

Consider the same situation as described previously for consolidating mission-critical workloads, with the extra constraint that the system includes multiple Solaris versions, potentially administered by different business units, and with a mixture of resource requirements. In this case, different OS instances are needed, with more resource granularity than is available with physical domains, thereby permitting both small and large virtual environments to coexist in the same system. This model also provides other benefits:

- Costs are reduced through the use of virtual devices, which share physical infrastructure over multiple clients.
- Agility is provided by dynamic resource allocation, which makes it possible to add and remove CPU, memory, and I/O devices in a running domain.
- Legacy support is enhanced by the ability to run Solaris 10 in guest domains on recent servers that are supported by Solaris 11 and later for physical instances.

8.2.4.4 Cloud Environments

Cloud adoption is causing major changes in data center and computer deployment, and depends heavily on virtualization to provide agility, flexible resource deployment, and rapid implementation. Building on the methodology of mixed workload consolidation, cloud environments can be built using Oracle VM Server for SPARC, permitting the use of different Solaris versions with different application loads and resource configurations. Development of this kind of environment can be accelerated through the use of "virtual appliances"—prebuilt virtual machine templates containing OS and application software in a ready-to-run format. In the cloud model, that approach helps reduce the time to dynamically deliver a new service. It can be implemented using Oracle VM Manager or Oracle Enterprise Manager for complete cloud functionality.

8.3 Summary

A wide range of virtualization technologies can be used to provide more efficient, agile, and lower-cost computing infrastructure. This chapter has summarized some of the important distinguishing characteristics of the virtualization technologies described in this book, and offered a methodology for selecting the best choices to meet your business and technical requirements.

9

Applications of Oracle Virtualization

Most of this book describes Oracle Solaris virtualization technologies. This chapter illustrates the application of these technologies in several strategic use cases. Rather than simply show examples of applications running in virtualized environments, which is obvious, we show interesting cases where the unique capabilities of Oracle Solaris virtualization are leveraged. Examples include Oracle's use of virtualization to build strategic products, and illustrations of actual but anonymous customer deployments.

9.1 Database Zones

Multiple database instances can be isolated in a variety of ways. Extreme isolation can be achieved by running them in different servers, or different data centers. Solaris Zones achieve a good balance of isolation and flexibility, providing an effective security boundary around each zone, and creating individual namespaces. This software and security partitioning does not use a hypervisor, so it does not reduce performance as software hypervisors do. Database zones are appropriate to consolidate multiple databases in single Solaris systems, SPARC or x86, and Database as a Service (DBaaS) clouds.

The inherent characteristics of Solaris Zones, as well as their comprehensive features, are described in Chapter 3, "Oracle Solaris Zones." The following subsections describe several of the features specific to Solaris and Solaris Zones that are particularly relevant to the use of Oracle Database software.

9.1.1 Identity and Naming Services

Each Solaris Zone has its own set of Solaris configuration files. These provide per-zone naming and naming services, including separate host names, IP addresses, naming services such as LDAP, and users.

A database zone cannot detect other database zones or interact with them, unless those zones use normal network methods to communicate with each other.

9.1.2 Security

Several security features lend themselves well to databases. A few of them are discussed here.

The configurable security boundary of Solaris Zones is implemented with Solaris privileges. Further, those privileges can be used by the system administrator to enable specific nonprivileged users to manage specific zones. For example, a user account within a database zone can be given all of the privileges available within the zone, and that user account can be assigned to a database administrator (DBA). The DBA would then effectively have superuser privileges within the zone. In addition, a user account in the global zone can be assigned to the DBA. The system administrator could then delegate administrative abilities to the DBA, enabling the DBA to boot that zone and perform some other administrative tasks.

Oracle Transparent Data Encryption uses the Solaris 11 encryption framework, which works exactly the same way in a zone as on bare metal. Combined with the individual namespaces of Solaris Zones, this framework enables a zone to protect its own data without risk of disclosure by the global zone administrator or other DBAs—a security factor that is particularly important in a cloud environment.

9.1.3 Resource Management

Although most types of Solaris Zones share all resources, a comprehensive set of resource management features enables the platform administrator to control per-zone resource consumption. This makes the boundary around a zone an effective resource management boundary.

Properly managed consolidated environments prevent "resource hogs"—that is, workloads that consume so much of a resource that others "starve" and cannot work properly. Resource management controls are required in any consolidated environment, including cloud computing.

9.1.3.1 CPU

For database zones, you can use any of the CPU management methods available to zones. Nevertheless, two factors are worth highlighting in conjunction with CPU management: computing efficiency and software license cost.

Unless you oversize the server, or assign hardware resources to a database zone, CPU performance may be inconsistent in regard to databases. For example, adding a new database may reduce the available computing capacity, in turn reducing the performance of all databases. To ensure consistent performance and optimal efficiency, one or more whole cores should be assigned to a database zone. This method reduces the opportunities for CPU contention.

By assigning whole cores with a dedicated-cpu or capped-cpu setting, you can also limit software license costs. Solaris Zones are one of the virtualization methods that can be used as "hard partitions" by Oracle for software license purposes.

9.1.3.2 Memory

One goal when using database zones is to prevent paging, thereby ensuring consistent, optimal performance. Any workload that is paged out to swap disk will experience greatly degraded performance when its pages are brought back in from swap disk. A second goal is to prevent one or more zones from using so much RAM that other zones starve, leading to paging or—even worse—an inability to allocate RAM.

You can configure a system's zones to avoid paging in any of them, but you must understand their memory requirements. The goal is to limit the RAM usage of each zone, so that the aggregate memory usage is less than the amount of RAM available to them. One method to accomplish this is to configure a virtual memory cap for each zone. Chapter 3, "Oracle Solaris Zones," describes this feature, which is known as the `swap` property. Recall that the virtual memory cap refers to the sum of RAM plus the amount of swap disk. For each zone, the `swap` property should be set to the same size as the sum of RAM and swap disk, when the workload runs in a non-virtualized environment. Be sure that this cap is large enough: If the zone attempts to allocate more memory than configured, software will fail. By constraining the use of RAM by each zone, you implicitly ensure that there is enough RAM for each other zone; see Figure 9.1. If you might deploy zones in the same server in the future, you should limit the set of zones and the amount of RAM in use.

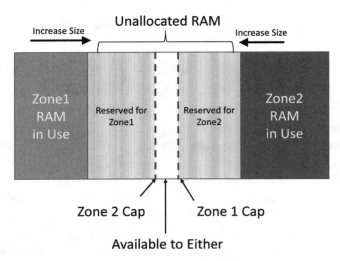

Figure 9.1   Capping Aggregate RAM Use

A slightly more complicated method allows some paging, and the ability to control the amount of swap space that can be consumed per zone. Assigning a value to both the `physical` and `swap` properties of the `capped-memory` resource will limit the amount of RAM used by each zone, and also limit the amount of virtual memory used by each zone.

Kernel zones are a special case, because each has its own preallocated physical memory pages in RAM, along with a separate swap disk area. You can mimic the previously described configuration by setting the `physical` property of the `capped-memory` resource to the amount of virtual memory that the database processes will need.

Once you understand the memory needs of each database, you can assign a few database zones that will fit into a particular server. For example, a server with 512 GB of RAM could be used to run five databases, each of which needs 100 GB. More than 100 GB of RAM will still be left for use by the global zone, and by another, similar database zone that you might add in the future.

9.1.3.3 Network

Virtual NICs (vNICs) add both flexibility and security. For example, one physical Ethernet port can be connected to your database management network, enabling you to access all of the database zones via their vNICs. This feature can also be used to reduce the number of IP addresses used by database zones, which are visible on the data center network.

Multiple ports can be used to isolate different types of network access, such as client access and RAC interconnects. Databases that are not protected by RAC would not have access to the RAC interconnect networks.

The use of redundant vNICs provides for efficient sharing of a small number of physical network ports, by multiple database instances. Each database zone should use two vNICs, each connected to one of two physical network ports that are configured for redundancy.

If desired, bandwidth consumption can be managed to prioritize some database instances over others.

9.1.3.4 Storage

Internal storage may be used with database zones, or remote storage may be accessed via the usual methods: NFS, FC, and iSCSI. Storage bandwidth may be controlled using Solaris features, if the storage is connected to the system with Ethernet.

Storage access is similar to a non-zoned environment. Redundant connections help here, too.

Although ZFS works well for database storage, it does not provide all of the performance and data ecosystem features available with ASM. ZFS is a good choice for most development databases, as well as low to medium I/O-rate databases.

9.1.3.5 Shared Memory

Although most types of Solaris Zones share all resources, a comprehensive set of resource management features allow the platform administrator to control per-zone resource consumption. This makes the boundary around a zone an effective resource management boundary.

9.1.4 Administrative Boundary

Booting a zone is faster than booting the entire computer, so start-up of a database instance in a zone is faster, too. This is also true if a zone reboot is needed, which means less downtime for the database.

Several methods can be used to create many zones that are almost identical in configuration. In development environments, this kind of technique makes it easier to ensure that developers are using the same tool sets. It is even more useful in test environments, where maintaining a consistent environment may be crucial both to successful production deployments and to problem resolution.

Using zones reduces confusion regarding Oracle Homes, because each zone will have its own home. Other zones' homes will not be visible to that zone, thereby eliminating the possibility of naming conflicts.

Both native zones and kernel zones may be reconfigured while they run, including the devices that have been assigned to them. This strategy further reduces the need for downtime, as storage devices may be added to a running zone.

The ability to migrate a zone improves the flexibility of consolidated environments, including databases. The method of migration, however, depends on the type of zone. Solaris 10 Zones and Solaris 11 native zones may be halted and then moved. Kernel zones may be moved while they are running, without any modification to application software. Nevertheless, live migration of huge-memory virtual environments (VEs) may take a very long time, even though users will not notice a disruption of service. In extreme situations, the disruption may be noticeable, or even cause other software to time out. When availability is a primary concern, Oracle RAC may be a better solution than live migration.

9.1.5 Fault Isolation

Solaris Zones are not as effective at isolating faults as logical domains are, because multiple zones rely on one Solaris kernel. Even so, they do provide effective software fault isolation, including the naming services mentioned earlier. A failure of a database software component within one zone will not affect other zones.

Zones can be RAC nodes—an approach that protects against hardware failure as well as software failures.

9.1.6 Conclusion

Database consolidation, including a DBaaS cloud environment, requires sufficient isolation between databases to comply with corporate policy and government regulations. Oracle Solaris Zones provide a complete security and identity boundary, along with comprehensive resource controls, thereby satisfying the needs of almost all consolidated database environments. Further, these goals are achieved without negative performance impact or additional cost.

9.2 Virtualization with Engineered Systems and Oracle SuperCluster

Oracle Engineered Systems are designed to provide performance and scale for enterprise applications, and are typically optimized for a particular workload category. Examples include Oracle Exadata, which is designed for high-performance Oracle databases in OLTP and DSS environments; Oracle Exalogic, which provides complementary benefits for middleware applications; and Oracle Exalytics, which is designed for data analytics. Oracle Engineered Systems share common design patterns, and they leverage engineering between layers of the Oracle hardware, networking, virtualization, OS, and application software stack for optimal and predictable performance.

One member of the Oracle Engineered Systems family is Oracle SuperCluster. This product provides unique value for multi-tier enterprise services that require high performance, scale, and availability.

9.2.1 Oracle SuperCluster

Oracle SuperCluster shares many properties associated with other members of the engineered system family. It differs from Exadata and Exalogic, however, in that it supports high-performance database *and* application tiers; it also permits a heterogeneous mix of database and application versions, whereas Exadata and Exalogic tightly integrate and certify specific application versions. Oracle SuperCluster is especially distinct in that it leverages SPARC, Solaris, and the related virtualization technologies of Oracle VM Server for SPARC and Solaris Zones instead of the x86 servers and Oracle Linux used in most Oracle Engineered Systems.

Oracle SuperCluster has been evolving over SPARC and Solaris product generations with several consistent themes. SuperCluster systems are delivered in a fixed number of preplanned configurations containing SPARC "compute nodes" with logical domain and Solaris Zones virtualization, shared general-purpose storage and specialized Exadata storage cells, an InfiniBand communications backbone, and a common management infrastructure and toolset.

The first SuperCluster systems used the SPARC T4 system as the compute node building block, with successive generations being based on later SPARC platforms. At the time of this writing, the latest version is SuperCluster M7, which is based on the M7-8 server platform. This section will focus on the M7-8 version, though many of the principles described here also apply to its predecessors.

SuperCluster heavily leverages virtualization, and it uses SPARC physical domains, Oracle VM Server for SPARC, and Solaris Zones for isolation, multitenancy, and resiliency, and to permit concurrent operation of different Solaris OS versions.

9.2.2 Hardware Architecture

Oracle SuperCluster M7 contains the following components:

- One or two SPARC M7 chassis, with two physical domains per chassis, each containing 1 to 4 processors with 32 cores each, with up to 8 TB of RAM per rack. The M7 servers are powerful systems with software-in-silicon hardware features that accelerate database operations, support encryption, and protect data integrity against storage corruption and overlays. Each M7 server can be subdivided into 4-socket "physical domains" (PDoms), as discussed in Chapter 5, "Physical Domains," each of which can be treated as a stand-alone server that can independently fail, reboot, or be serviced. Up to 18 SuperCluster M7 systems can be connected together on the same InfiniBand network.

- ZS3 (ZFS storage appliance) with 160 TB (raw) capacity for virtual machine and application use.

- Exadata storage servers for Oracle Database data, with between 3 and 11 servers, each of which has 96 TB disk and 12.8 TB flash memory capacity. Besides raw capacity and speed, Exadata storage servers are "intelligent storage" that offload database functions such as database scans, filtering, joins, and row selection. Queries that might require hosts to read millions of records, and then discard rows that do not match the query, are offloaded and filtered in storage, with only relevant rows being returned. This technique reduces server CPU utilization and core requirements, minimizes the amount of data movement, and speeds up database operations beyond what can be accomplished with regular storage. Costs are further reduced by horizontal columnar compression performed on the storage device.

- QDR 40 Gb/s InfiniBand network. This permits high-speed communication between SuperCluster components.

Scale is enhanced by adding incremental storage and by scaling to a multi-rack configuration, all composed as a single system. Additionally SuperCluster can use external storage, typically based on FibreChannel arrays, that may already exist in an enterprise architecture.

9.2.3 Virtualization Architecture

Oracle SuperCluster uses layered virtualization based on physical domains, Oracle VM Server for SPARC, and Solaris Zones. Zones run within logical domains, which themselves run within physical domains. Each of these virtualization technologies runs with zero or near-zero overhead, making it possible to leverage virtualization without incurring a performance penalty.

General-purpose (non-engineered) systems also use these virtualization technologies, and can organize them into a variety of combinations depending on user requirements. This flexibility permits different levels of performance, availability, cloud capability, live migration, consolidation levels, workload mixes, resource sharing, and dynamic resource management.

A design goal of Oracle SuperCluster is to yield the highest possible performance, with predictable behavior for each workload. To meet that goal, it uses a small number of preplanned configurations with optimal performance and pretested, validated, deterministic behavior.

9.2.4 Physical Domains

Each SuperCluster M7 compute node is divided into two physical domains for maximum isolation and independence. Each physical domain acts as a separate computer system in the same M7 chassis, and has half the CPU, memory, and I/O resources of the M7 compute node.

A chassis can have two, four, or eight CMIOU (CPU, memory, I/O) boards, depending on whether the chassis is quarter, half, or fully populated.

9.2.5 Logical Domains

Each PDom uses Oracle VM Server for SPARC logical domains with specific preset domain configurations and roles. Compared to general-purpose deployments that are oriented toward flexibility and convenience, this design emphasizes static resource assignment in fixed configurations to provide maximum performance.

SuperCluster PDoms host a small number of high-performance logical domains. An Oracle SuperCluster M7-8 PDom can have as many logical domains as CMIOUs: A PDom with one CMIOU board (in a quarter-populated chassis) can have one logical domain, while a PDom with four CMIOUs can have up to four logical domains. By comparison, general-purpose SPARC systems can have as many as 128 logical domains on the same server or physical domain, with resource granularity down to the individual CPU thread.

SuperCluster logical domains use physical I/O and static domain allocation when optimal performance is needed. General-purpose Oracle VM Server for SPARC deployments provide very good performance while offering flexibility and the benefits of virtual I/O (live migration, dynamic reconfiguration), while SuperCluster ensures native or near-native I/O performance under all circumstances.

SuperCluster optimizes performance by aligning domain CPU, memory, and I/O resource allocations to eliminate non-uniform memory access (NUMA) latency. NUMA effects can sharply reduce performance on vertically scaled, multi-socket servers. SuperCluster uses topology-aware rules to arrange assignment of CPUs, RAM, and PCIe buses to ensure local memory access. This can have a substantial effect on ensuring maximum performance and eliminating overhead and variability due to NUMA latency.

SuperCluster domains have specific application-oriented roles that are superimposed on the standard logical domain types.

9.2.5.1 Dedicated Domains

Dedicated domains are statically defined at SuperCluster installation time. They own PCIe root controllers, with direct physical access to 10 GbE NICs and to InfiniBand HCAs for storage and Exadata private networks. This setup ensures bare-metal performance for I/O, and it eliminates dependencies on other domains.

Dedicated domains run Oracle Solaris 11, and are further designated as being either database domains or application domains. The primary difference between these types is that database domains access Exadata storage cells over the private Exadata InfiniBand network for optimized Oracle Database 11*g* Release 2 or Oracle Database 12c performance. Application domains can run arbitrary applications (hence the name) as well as older versions of Oracle Database or other database software.

The number and configuration of dedicated domains is established at installation time, and can be changed on a post-installation basis by Oracle staff. Resource granularity is provided in increments of 1 CPU core and 16 GB of RAM.

9.2.5.2 Root Domains

Root domains run Oracle Solaris 11 and host SR-IOV physical functions (PFs) to provide virtual functions (VFs) for I/O domains, as described later in this chapter. SR-IOV devices may be Ethernet, InfiniBand, or FibreChannel.

Root domains are also Oracle VM Server for SPARC service domains, which provide I/O domains with virtual devices for iSCSI boot disks.

Applications are not run in SuperCluster root domains, so as to avoid compromising performance or availability in the I/O domains depending on them. This is consistent with best practices for service domains in general-purpose Oracle VM Server for SPARC environments.

Root domains are kept small so as to make resources available to the other domain types, yet should be large enough to drive virtual I/O requirements. A root domain with one InfiniBand HCA and 10 GbE NIC typically has two cores and 32 GB of RAM; double the resources are available if it has two HCAs and 10 GbE NICs. This scale is consistent with the general-purpose Oracle VM Server for SPARC practice of balancing service domain performance with the additional consideration of static allocation and heavy use of physical I/O.

Like dedicated domains, root domains are configured at installation time and can be subsequently reconfigured by Oracle staff.

9.2.5.3 I/O Domains

I/O domains run Oracle Solaris 11 and use SR-IOV virtual functions for applications. Corresponding SR-IOV physical functions are served by the root domains, as described previously. This scheme provides near-native I/O performance for Ethernet, InfiniBand, and FibreChannel devices. I/O domains use virtual I/O devices for iSCSI boot devices; these devices are provided by root domains using disk back-ends in the SuperCluster's built-in ZFS storage appliance. The use of the term "I/O domains" in SuperCluster is somewhat different than that in standard logical domains: I/O domains in SuperCluster use virtual I/O device resources from root domains, but when discussing logical domains outside the context of SuperCluster, I/O domains have direct connections to physical I/O devices.

Unlike the other domain types, I/O domains can be dynamically created and then destroyed in the post-installation environment using the I/O Domain Creation tool, which lets data center administrators define the domain and associate CPU, memory, and I/O resources—in particular, assigning InfiniBand and 10 GbE virtual functions from designated root domains. Resources are drawn from "parked" (unassigned) resources in CPU or memory repositories, and returned to the repositories when domains are removed.

As with dedicated domains, I/O domains can be further characterized as either database domains or application domains. There are physical distinctions between the two: Dedicated domains own PCIe root buses for direct physical I/O, whereas I/O domains use SR-IOV and implement static resource assignment to avoid NUMA effects.

9.2.5.4 Domain Considerations

Databases and other applications are hosted in dedicated domains or I/O domains. Dedicated domains are recommended for larger applications using more than one 32-core processor (sometimes referred to as a socket), while I/O domains are better suited for smaller applications needing up to one 32-core processor. That reflects the higher I/O capacity available to dedicated domains, and it maximizes the benefit from NUMA optimizations that permit scalable performance over multiple CPU chips. Further, dedicated domains own the physical resources for their I/O and are subject to neither variations in performance from competing use of a physical I/O resource nor availability dependencies on a root domain.

I/O domains provide native or near-native performance for a single application of moderate size. A chief benefit of I/O domains is that they can be dynamically created or destroyed as needed by using the `osc-setcoremem` administrative tool. They depend on root domains for their I/O. While I/O performance is expected to be near-native, there can be competition between I/O domains for physical I/O resources they share.

In practice, when starting or stopping SuperCluster systems, root domains must be started up before I/O domains to make the necessary services and SR-IOV functions available. The reverse is true when shutting systems down: The I/O domains should be stopped first, and then the root domains on which they depend.

Root domains should be considered infrastructure domains for the purpose of hosting I/O resources needed by the I/O domains. Applications should not run there to avoid compromising their availability and performance.

All domains on SuperCluster M7-8 run Solaris 11.3 or later. Branded zones, described in the next section, can be used in dedicated or I/O domains for applications certified with Solaris 10. Earlier versions of SuperCluster can run Solaris 10 and earlier versions of Solaris 11.

9.2.6 Oracle Solaris Zones

Dedicated domains and I/O domains can host Solaris Zones—an arrangement that permits increased virtualization density compared to the number of logical domains supported on a SuperCluster system. Solaris Zones have no overhead, so there is no performance penalty for adding zones to logical domains within physical domains. Layered virtualization with zones provides granular resource allocation, workload isolation, and security between workloads.

Zones are recommended when additional resource sharing and fine-grained allocation are needed. As a default, zones are defined without dedicated CPU and memory resources, so resources not used by an idle zone are available to other zones without any administrative effort. CPU allocations to zones can be controlled with the Fair Share Scheduler (FSS), with the exception of database zones, which also should not use `rcapd` for memory controls (these rules apply in non-SuperCluster environments, too). It is also possible to define zones with dedicated CPU and memory resources, as with general-purpose Solaris deployments, for applications. The same Solaris administrative tools for zones (`zoneadm`, `zonecfg`) are used as on general-purpose systems.

Both dedicated domains and I/O domains can use native Solaris 11 zones. In each of those categories, application domains can optionally use Solaris 10 branded zones. Solaris 10 branded zones provide the appearance of running an application in a Solaris 10 system for applications that have not been validated against Solaris 11, or have been imported from physical Solaris 10 instances elsewhere. Earlier SuperCluster editions support running Solaris 10 directly, and also permit Solaris 8 and Solaris 9 branded zones to support even older software stacks on more recent hardware.

9.2.7 Summary of Oracle SuperCluster Virtualization

Oracle SuperCluster uses layered virtualization based on physical domains, logical domains, and Solaris Zones. It provides zero or near-zero overhead virtualization to deliver maximum performance and scalability. SuperCluster takes advantage of virtualization where it is appropriate, but avoids it when desirable. A notable example is the use of physical I/O to avoid virtualization overhead, and static allocation to provide optimal assignment of CPU, memory, and I/O for lowest latency. Compared to general-purpose systems that leverage logical domains, this kind of virtualization is static in nature, and designed for a relatively small number of large, high-performance OS instances, rather than a large number of small OS instances. This design choice is consistent with its goal of being the optimal platform for large enterprise applications and databases.

9.3 Virtualization with Secure Enterprise Cloud Infrastructure

Virtualization concepts open the door to a bewildering array of choices. Oracle Optimized Solutions focus on a small set of workloads, or a specific type of deployment, delivering proven guidance that reduces the number of choices to a manageable set. These solutions then yield balanced integration and flexibility. This section describes the application of virtualization to one of those solutions: Secure Enterprise Cloud Infrastructure.

9.3.1 Introduction

Oracle researches practical compute architectures, with the intention of reducing the amount of research, testing, and risk associated with "do it yourself" data center projects. Its findings are documented as Oracle Optimized Solutions, which include detailed descriptions of hardware and software configurations. One of these designs is the Secure Enterprise Cloud Infrastructure (SECI) solution. This section describes the role that virtualization plays in SECI, the technologies chosen, and the rationale for those choices.

Many corporations have benefited from public cloud computing environments. Advantages include reduced capital expenditure costs and increased business agility. However, public cloud computing is not appropriate for every workload. Government regulations, for example, require in-house storage of certain types of data. Some corporations also have concerns regarding information security; these concerns are fed by the occasional high-profile attack as well as aggregate data about attacks that are not publicized.

To benefit from the advantages of cloud computing, while avoiding the known and perceived weaknesses of this approach, many corporations are creating "private clouds"—that is, collections of compute, networking, and storage equipment that can be used as easily and flexibly as public clouds, while allowing the organization to maintain in-house control over the data and processes. Private clouds also deliver an interim solution for corporations that want to take a phased approach to public cloud adoption.

Private clouds are often used for development and test, and for smaller production workloads, especially when many people are performing these tasks and must use an isolated compute environment for a short period of time—on a scale of hours to days. Large production workloads are not so dynamic and require the best performance and scalability, which is not always compatible with the cloud computing model, either public or private.

As a private cloud solution, SECI is able to provide multiple cloud computing service models, as defined by the National Institute of Standards and Technology (NIST): Software as a Service (SaaS), Platform as a Service (PaaS) (including Database as a Service [DBaaS]), and Infrastructure as a Service (IaaS). The SECI Implementation Guide details the steps to create an IaaS cloud. Other documents describe other service models for SECI.

The SECI design enables typical IaaS capabilities, greatly simplifying the provisioning of virtual environments and operating system instances running in those VMs. The features in Oracle Enterprise Manager Ops Center use a simple point-and-click interface that is aware of compute nodes, storage devices, and network configurations. It can deploy VEs, both Oracle Solaris Zones and Oracle VM Logical Domains, and also deliver Solaris packages into those VEs.

With OEM Cloud Control, you can also automate provisioning of database environments into those VEs. The SECI DBaaS guide adds another layer of functionality. DBaaS is one type of PaaS, giving self-service users such as database administrators and database testers the ability to quickly instantiate a database environment. An element in a service catalog might be a simple database instance, or it might include data protection, business continuity, and archival features. In simpler configurations, users specify just the quantity of basic compute resources, such as CPU cores, RAM, and amount of disk storage.

Similar functionality exists for integrated development environments (another type of PaaS), as well as for Oracle Fusion Middleware, Oracle SOA Suite, and others.

Finally, Oracle Enterprise Manager delivers automated provisioning of SaaS software such as Oracle and ISV applications, which can also be deployed in an SECI environment.

9.3.2 SECI Components

Like most Oracle Optimized Solutions, SECI includes hardware and software specifications as well as architecture details so that you can build a configuration that has already been tested with specific combinations of software. This solution is built on SPARC computers that use the new SPARC M7 processors, the Oracle Solaris operating system, and Oracle storage systems.

Because a basic environment consists of servers in one data center rack, either a small number of larger systems or a large number of smaller systems can be configured. The compute nodes in an SECI environment are SPARC systems that use one, two, or four SPARC M7 processors, resulting in a maximum of 640 compute cores per base rack. Each rack also includes two ZFS storage appliances, storing petabytes (PBs) of data.

Two types of expansion racks exist. Compute racks hold up to 20 servers, with up to 1024 CPU cores for each rack. Storage racks can combine SSDs and HDDs. Eight racks may be connected together, creating one cloud with thousands of cores and thousands of terabytes of data.

At the time of this book's writing, the smallest compute node in an SECI environment was a SPARC T7-1 system, which includes one SPARC M7 processor and 512 GB of RAM. The midsize node was a SPARC T7-2, and the largest was a SPARC T7-4, including two and four SPARC M7 CPUs, respectively.

A data center rack configured for SECI can hold up to 14 T7-1 computers, yielding 448 cores per rack. An expansion rack may be added that holds 20 of these computers. The other computer models lead to different quantities of systems per rack and cores per rack, with a maximum of 640 cores per rack using SPARC T7-4 nodes.

The SECI documents refer to these compute nodes as "virtualization servers." Because these systems use the same hardware, operating system, and infrastructure software in an SECI private cloud as they do when set up as individual systems, the performance of workloads in virtualization servers should be the same in the two different configurations.

Each virtualization server runs the Oracle Solaris 10 or 11 operating system in logical domains using the Oracle VM Server for SPARC features described elsewhere in this book. Workloads that require the use of Solaris 8 or 9 can run in Solaris "branded zones" that maximize software compatibility. Branded zones are described in Chapter 3, "Oracle Solaris Zones."

Oracle Enterprise Manager Ops Center, described in Chapter 7, "Automating Virtualization," is the primary infrastructure management interface to SECI environments. Ops Center creates server pools, which are groups of logical domains or Solaris Zones configured to run a specific set of workloads. These VEs are housed on the storage systems, enabling them to boot on any compute node in their server pool. Figure 9.2 shows the high-level components of a server pool.

Ops Center also provides tools to manage the servers and VEs, including provisioning and updating software and firmware. Monitoring tools are also included, enabling you to observe utilization and investigate changes in performance over time.

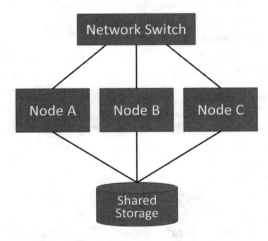

Figure 9.2 A Server Pool

9.3.3 Service Domains

If you choose to create logical domains that use only physical I/O, the number of domains that you can create is limited by the quantity of PCIe slots in the computer. To create more logical domains, you must use virtual I/O. Chapter 4, "Oracle VM Server for SPARC," described service domains—that is, logical domains that "own" PCIe slots and use them to provide virtual I/O services to guest domains. These services include virtual network devices and virtual disks.

SECI uses control domains and other logical domains to act as service domains. The use of guest domains that access storage and the network via service domains increases the workload density of one rack.

In the context of SECI, VEs in server pools are guest domains or zones in guest domains. In other words, these VEs rely on the virtual I/O provided by service domains. Achieving the performance and availability goals of server pools requires proper configuration of the service domains they will use.

Server pools that use logical domains require the use of one or two service domains that provide virtual I/O services to the guest domains that run user workloads. These service domains should be configured with sufficient CPU and RAM so that they can efficiently deliver their services. As a general rule, we recommend that service domains have at least two CPU cores. If a service domain uses more than one 10 GbE port or FC card, an additional core should be configured for each port in use, subject to measured CPU load and memory consumption.

Generally, service domains should be configured with 16 GB of RAM. In environments that plan for low workload density and do not use ZFS or NFS for virtual disk back-ends, 8 GB of RAM may be sufficient.

9.3.4 Server Pools

A core concept of Secure Enterprise Cloud Infrastructure is the "server pool." This logical design element represents a set of VEs that are configured to run in a set of computers. These computers are called "virtualization servers" in this context. You use OEM Ops Center to configure each VE.

After a server pool has been created, self-service users can use OEM Cloud Control to specify the desired characteristics such as the quantity of cores. Based on the user-provided information, Cloud Control chooses an unused VE that satisfies the need at hand. The infrastructure software then performs any necessary configuration changes such as logical storage connections, and starts the VE and any requested additional workload. It also restarts VEs after software or hardware failure.

A server pool uses a variety of physical resources, including compute and storage assets. When a VE is not running, it uses only storage space. While the VE is running, its workload uses CPUs, RAM, and network devices associated with that VE. The cloud administrator controls the amount of those resources allocated to the VE, and determines whether a VE will share resources or use dedicated resources, in conjunction with Ops Center and Cloud Control.

All VEs are stored on the ZFS storage appliances. Storage for logical domains is typically accessed from the VE via NFS, but Solaris Zones use iSCSI or FC protocols. Storage for application data is not limited to the SECI hardware, but can be connected by standard methods and protocols.

In addition, Ops Center includes availability and load-balancing policies. These features reduce the amount of downtime usually associated with updates and upgrades of hardware and software, and minimize the amount of downtime caused by software or hardware failures. Load-balancing features ensure adequate performance of all workloads, or of the most important workloads, if resource consumption of one or more VEs changes over time.

The process of updating a computer's firmware may require rebooting the computer. When performing this administrative operation, SECI uses existing virtualization features to minimize or eliminate downtime for workloads. Ops Center supports live migration features of the SPARC platforms. In an SECI environment, VEs are installed on shared storage, allowing the user to move a running VE from one computer in a pool to another in the same pool, without any disruption of the workload running in that VE. After all workloads have been migrated to other physical nodes, the firmware may be updated. As mentioned earlier, this ability has many other practical applications.

SPARC systems have very robust uptime characteristics. Sometimes, however, a VE may fail, or the virtualization server it was using may fail. In that case, Ops Center automatically restarts the VE, using a different server if necessary. If the failure of a virtualization server leads to restart of several VEs, Ops Center restarts them in order of their importance—a parameter that you choose when configuring VEs.

In addition, you can configure a server pool so that it periodically compares the resources being used by the VEs, resulting in automated live migrations of one or more VEs. Several parameters control the details of this load-balancing feature. You can also manually initiate a load-balancing operation.

9.3.5 Security

SECI benefits from encryption in VEs, with no additional performance impact compared to a non-virtualized environment. The encryption technologies used in SECI do not require any modification of software. The network and storage configuration can use encryption, in a manner that remains transparent to the application.

Oracle Solaris contains a diverse set of security features, such as Role-Based Access Control (RBAC). These features offer fine-grained administrative permissions and improve administrative accountability, VLANs to isolate network traffic, and ZFS data encryption to protect data at rest. SECI is able to leverage all of those features.

SECI environments typically use separate networks for management, storage, and workload data to further isolate access. Separate networks make it easier to achieve the proper balance between security and functionality in each context.

9.3.6 Planning of Resources and Availability

You can consider an SECI environment to be one large server that has been partitioned—albeit without the high price point typically associated with large systems. When planning VEs and server pools as part of this environment, several factors should be considered.

Compute and memory resources will be configured for a VE, but not assigned until the VE is booting on a virtualization server. Conversely, a VE begins consuming persistent storage—hard disk drives or flash storage devices—when it is provisioned, and it continues to use that storage until the VE is destroyed. Each VE will be stored on an NFS share or a FC or iSCSI LUN. To meet the typical requirements, storage of the operating system should be mirrored, either within the share or LUN or by mirroring two shares or LUNs.

For Solaris Zones, we recommend a minimum of 1 vCPU (a hardware thread) and 2 GB of RAM for each zone. Each logical domain should be assigned at least 1 core and 16 GB of RAM. For each type of VE, the maximum quantities are limited only by the amount of physical resources in each server. Generally, the hardware resources needed in a VE are the same as those needed in a non-virtualized environment.

Planned hardware and software maintenance will require the migration of VEs to other server(s) in the set of nodes in a server pool. Although it is not necessary to configure each physical node so that it can run all of workloads, you should plan for at least one or two computers to be unavailable. For example, perhaps you will choose a group of eight nodes, sized so that six of them together are able to comfortably run all of the workloads. Then, if the environment experiences a hardware failure in one node while you are performing planned maintenance on another node, there will be no outage of the service provided to your customers.

Traditional high availability (HA) of services can be achieved with the optional Oracle Solaris Cluster software. Solaris Cluster can perform very fast detection of application or VE failover; when it identifies such a state, it can perform an automated failover to another physical node.

Physical node connectivity (I/O: storage and network) must be large enough to handle the largest aggregate demands of the VEs that may run on it. Also, the I/O connections must provide availability appropriate for the most demanding VE that will run on it.

The back-end storage characteristics must be appropriate for all of the VEs. For example, if one or more workloads are databases that require a certain I/O worst-case transaction latency, the virtual storage, including the back-end, must deliver that latency or better.

The ability to react to changes in workload demand suggests that a good default assignment of VEs to computers should consist of one very important workload, plus a few other less important workloads. If one or more of the workloads unexpectedly increases, one or more of the less important workloads can be moved to other computers in the server pool. If the increase involves the critical workload, the other workloads can be moved and the resources available to the critical one can be increased. If the increase is in another workload, it can be moved to a computer with spare capacity, or other small workloads can be moved, freeing up resources that can be reassigned.

9.3.7 Conclusion

SECI uses virtualization to achieve flexible, highly automated consolidation. The ease of VE migration enables greater business agility, such that the system can more easily respond to changes in business volume. Some of those changes are predictable: A quarter-end workload, for example, might be expanded in one node after moving other workloads to other nodes. Other changes are unexpected. For example, a consumer product may become much more popular than expected, leading to a rapid increase in online ordering from a retailer. With SECI, you can quickly adapt to this shift in demand for compute resources.

9.4 Virtualization in Oracle Exalytics

Another example of Oracle Engineered Systems is the Oracle Exalytics In-Memory Machine (Exalytics, for short). Exalytics is designed for the problem domain of business analytics and decision support. It places special emphasis on in-memory processing, which is important for efficient processing of the ad-hoc queries seen for business analytics and decision support.

Exalytics comes in two varieties: (1) an x86 version and (2) a SPARC version based on the T5-8 server. Virtualization is used in both products, with each using the version of Oracle VM for its chip architecture.

The SPARC version of Exalytics is based on the T5-8 server platform, with 128 CPU cores (1024 CPU threads) and 4 TB of RAM. I/O uses solid-state disks, InfiniBand, 10 GbE networking, and FibreChannel. Exalytics provides enterprise-wide analytic processing for an institution that needs vertical scale and high performance, as well as a consolidation platform to prevent server sprawl caused by departmental solutions in multiple business units.

As with SuperCluster, the T5-8 Exalytics system can be configured using one of a preset number of logical domain configurations, with Oracle Solaris Zones supporting higher-granularity virtualization in each domain. This configuration permits concurrent operation of production and testing on the same platform, or co-residence of multiple business units, with ensured isolation, security, and non-interference.

The virtual environments host the Oracle analytic software: Oracle Business Intelligence EE Accelerator, Oracle In-Memory Data Caching, Oracle BI Publisher Accelerator, Oracle Business Intelligence Foundation Suite including Essbase, and Oracle Times-Ten In-Memory Database for Analytics.

The special advantage of this platform is the "in-memory acceleration" exploited by the application components. In-memory processing is essential for large business analytics and decision support applications, and the T5-8 platform provides this memory capacity and CPU capacity. Logical domains and zones permit multitenancy, yet add zero overhead to the solution stack. As with SuperCluster, the engineered system benefit is provided by a predefined set of configuration options, and deployment with solid-state disk and InfiniBand interconnects. That configuration lets the applications efficiently leverage the large memory of the T5-8 platform.

9.5 Consolidating with Oracle Solaris Zones

Solaris Zones are excellent environments for consolidating many kinds of applications. For example, consolidating multiple Oracle Solaris web servers into zones on one system is a straightforward process, but you can also consolidate web servers from other operating systems. Consolidating into zones provides better isolation and manageability than simply collapsing the contents into one web server.

Benefits of using zones in this situation include workload isolation, comprehensive resource controls, delegated administration, and simple mobility, among others.

This section demonstrates the simplicity of migrating Apache web server environments from multiple UNIX and Linux systems to one Oracle Solaris 11 system. This example is relatively simple because Apache's configuration files use the same syntax, for any one version, on any UNIX or Linux system.

Nevertheless, slight differences in file system layout must be taken into account during this consolidation. On most Linux distributions, the default location for Apache's configuration file is `/etc/httpd/conf/httpd.conf`, while on Solaris it is `/etc/apache2/2.2/httpd.conf`. Further, the default home of web pages is `/var/www/html` on most Linux systems, but is `/var/apache2/2.2/htdocs` on Solaris 11 systems.

To further simplify this example, we will assume that the web servers are delivering static web pages that exist in one NFS file system. Migrating scripts that deliver dynamic content may require more effort.

The web servers in our example have equal importance. We will use resource controls to ensure that each web server has sufficient and equal access to system resources. Each zone will be assigned 100 CPU shares and allowed to use 1 GB of RAM, 2 GB of virtual memory, and 100MB of locked memory.

The commands shown in this section assume that the original web servers have been stopped. If you must minimize the service outage, you can choose different IP addresses for the zones and change the DNS maps after you have tested the zones. If the original Apache servers are part of a single load-balanced configuration, you can perform a rolling upgrade from the original systems to the new zones.

In the command examples shown here, the prompt `GZ#` indicates that you should enter the command from a shell running in the global zone. The prompt `web01#` indicates that you should enter the command from a shell running in the non-global zone named `web01`.

This example assumes that you are familiar with the content covered in Chapter 3, "Oracle Solaris Zones."

9.5.1 Planning

The first step in the consolidation process is gathering the necessary information. For our example, there are five web servers, each with its home page in `/web-pages/index.html`. These servers are named `web01` through `web05`. The new system, running Oracle Solaris 11, will have five zones named `web01` through `web05`. Each original system had one IP address: 10.1.1.101 through 10.1.1.105. Those IP addresses will move to their respective zones, as shown in Figure 9.3.

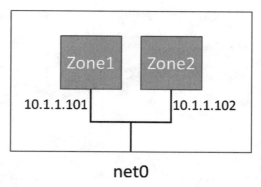

Figure 9.3   Consolidating Web Servers

Each web server mounts a shared NFS file system at `/webpages`. This directory is used in the Apache configuration file, `/etc/apache2/2.2/httpd.conf`, with the following directive:

```
DocumentRoot "/webpages"
```

9.5.2 Configure CPU Utilization

It is possible to enable the Fair Share Scheduler as the default scheduler for the system, for each zone, or for any combination of those. However, to effectively assign CPU shares to a zone, you must also make FSS the default scheduler for the system and assign shares to the global zone. To make the system boot with FSS as the default scheduler on subsequent reboots, enter this command in the global zone:

```
GZ# dispadmin -d FSS
```

To change the default scheduler to FSS without rebooting, enter this command:

```
GZ# priocntl -s -c FSS -i all
```

To immediately make FSS become the default scheduler *and* be used for all future system boots, you must enter both commands.

The FSS scheduling algorithm treats processes in the global zone the same way that it treats processes in non-global zones. To ensure that you can run programs in the global zone, including commands that manage the zones, you should ensure that the global zone has also been assigned a sufficient quantity of shares. The following command accomplishes that goal:

```
GZ# zonecfg -z global
zonecfg:global> set cpu-shares=100
zonecfg:global> exit
```

9.5.3 Create Zones

We will first create and customize one zone, then replicate it. After Oracle Solaris 11 is installed on the new system, the process of installing a zone begins with configuring it. Chapter 3, "Oracle Solaris Zones," describes the individual commands used in the rest of this section.

```
GZ# zonecfg -z web01
web01: No such zone configured
Use 'create' to begin configuring a new zone.
zonecfg:web01> create
zonecfg:web01> set cpu-shares=100
zonecfg:web01> add capped-memory
zonecfg:web01:capped-memory> set physical=1g
zonecfg:web01:capped-memory> set swap=2g
zonecfg:web01:capped-memory> set locked=100m
zonecfg:web01:capped-memory> end
zonecfg:web01: select anet 0
zonecfg:web01:anet> set allowed-address=10.1.1.101/24
zonecfg:web01:anet> end
zonecfg:web01> verify
zonecfg:web01> exit
```

Use `sysconfig(1M)` to create a system configuration profile for web01. Choose "None" for networking, because the network configuration is driven by the zone's configuration.

```
GZ# sysconfig create-profile -o /tmp

SC profile successfully generated as:
/tmp/sc_profile.xml

Exiting System Configuration Tool. Log is available at:
/system/volatile/sysconfig/sysconfig.log.6445
```

Install web01 with the following system configuration profile:

```
GZ# zoneadm -z web01 install -c /tmp/sc_profile.xml
The following ZFS file system(s) have been created:
    rpool/VARSHARE/zones/web01
Progress being logged to /var/log/zones/zoneadm.20160516T143228Z.web01.install
...
Log saved in non-global zone as /system/zones/web01/root/var/log/zones/
↳zoneadm.20160516T143228Z.web01.install
```

Boot the `web01` zone to have an opportunity to further configure the zone as a web server. First configure the zone to be an NFS client. The file `/etc/vfstab` will need an entry like this one:

```
nfsserver:/web   -    /webpages   nfs   -   yes   intr,bg
```

A new zone does not automatically mount NFS shares, but it is very easy to enable this service, and any services that it needs:

```
web01# svcadm enable -r nfs/client
```

Although Oracle Solaris includes the Apache web server software, it is not installed by default. The following command will perform this installation, adding any other packages that are required:

```
web01# pkg install apache-22
            Packages to install:  7
            Mediators to change:  3
            Services to change:  2
        Create boot environment: No
Create backup boot environment: No
...
Updating package state database                 Done
Updating package cache                          0/0
Updating image state                            Done
Creating fast lookup database                   Done
Updating package cache                          1/1
```

You can configure the web server software after installation is complete. For this example, we will simply tell the software the location of the static web pages, by editing the file `/etc/apache2/2.2/httpd.conf`. Using that file, you can enable the web server. This starts the web server now, and tells Solaris that the web service should be started automatically when the zone boots. Also, Solaris will automatically restart the web service if it fails.

```
web01# svcadm enable apache22
```

At this point, the zone `web01` is a functioning web server. Now we can replicate that zone and its configuration and customization, with two exceptions, to complete the project.

First, two preparation steps must be completed. The first command stops the original zone so that it can be replicated; the second saves its zone configuration in a file that can be used as input for the configuration of the other zones:

```
GZ# zoneadm -z web01 shutdown
GZ# zonecfg -z web01 export -f /tmp/web.cfg
```

The next few steps must be performed once per additional web server. The commands that following demonstrate the creation of one of these zones.

Using the zone configuration information from `web01` as a starting point, configure a new zone. The only difference is the IP address, so you can simply edit the file that you created earlier, `/tmp/web.cfg`. Then configure the zone with this command:

```
GZ# zonecfg -z web02 -f /tmp/web.cfg
```

You must also modify the system configuration information that you saved in `/tmp/sc_profile.xml`. The only change needed is the node name, which must be changed from `web01` to `web02`.

With that, we are ready for the final step: cloning the original zone.

```
GZ# zoneadm -z web02 clone -c /tmp/sc_profile.xml web01
The following ZFS file system(s) have been created:
    rpool/VARSHARE/zones/web02
Progress being logged to /var/log/zones/zoneadm.20160516T154210Z.web02.clone
Log saved in non-global zone as /system/zones/web02/root/var/log/zones/
↪zoneadm.20160516T154210Z.web02.clone
```

Using the `clone` subcommand replicates the configuration modifications that have been made to `web01`, including enabling the NFS client service and Apache web service, and their configuration files.

9.5.4 Testing

You should now be able to test the zones with a web browser, using their host names or IP addresses.

9.5.5 Summary

Solaris Zones make it easy to consolidate multiple workloads from separate systems into one system, as there is only one copy of the OS to manage. This section demonstrated a manual method of creating a few similar zones. If your situation calls for a large number of zones, use of the Solaris Automated Installer will simplify the entire process of zone creation by automating it.

9.6 Security Hardening with Oracle Solaris Zones

Previous sections in this chapter described the use of Oracle Solaris virtualization in Oracle Engineered Systems. Many simpler uses of virtualization exist. For example, server virtualization is commonly used to consolidate multiple workloads onto one computer.

Oracle Solaris Zones have subtle uses in addition to their application for general-purpose consolidation. These uses rely on a unique combination of features:

- Service Management Facility (SMF) services are configured separately for each zone, allowing you to turn off unneeded services in a zone such as Telnet, FTP, and even SSH, yet still allow secure access from the platform administrator's environment, called the global zone.
- Zones have a strict security boundary that prevents direct inter-zone interaction.
- You can prevent unauthorized modification of Oracle Solaris programs with the `file-mac-profile` feature. This yields an "immutable" zone.
- Privileges granted to a zone are configurable, enabling a platform administrator to further restrict the abilities of a zone, or to selectively enhance the abilities of a zone.
- Resource management controls can be assigned to each zone, allowing the platform administrator to limit the amount of resources that the zone can consume.

How can this combination provide unique functionality?

Solaris Zones can be configured to be more secure than general-purpose operating systems in many ways. For example, even the root user of an immutable zone cannot modify the zone's operating system programs. This limitation prevents Trojan horse attacks that attempt to replace those programs with malicious programs. Also, a process running in a zone cannot directly modify any kernel data, nor can it modify, add, or remove kernel modules such as device drivers. Zones lack the necessary privileges to modify the operating system and its kernel, and there is no mechanism to add privileges to a running zone from within the zone or anywhere else.

Even considering those measures, the ability to selectively remove privileges can be used to further tighten a zone's security boundary. Other features can easily disable network access except for specific network services. This feat is difficult to accomplish in most operating systems without rendering the system unusable or unmanageable. After all, without SSH or Telnet service, how would you log in to such a system?

You can combine all of those limitations to achieve *defense in depth*—a strategy conceived by the U.S. National Security Agency to defend computers against unwanted intrusion. Disabling services limits the external attack surface of the zone. An attacker who tries to take advantage of a weakness in the service being provided, such as web server software, will find that the *internal* attack surface is also very small, because so little of the zone can be modified. If the zone is configured appropriately, an intruder who somehow gains entry cannot access other systems via the network, or can access only a specific list of systems and services provided by those systems.

The combination of the ability to enforce those limitations and the resource controls that are part of the functionality of Solaris Zones is very powerful. Collectively, they enable you to configure an application environment that can do little more than fulfill the role you choose for it.

This section describes a method that can be used to slightly expand a zone's abilities, but then tighten the security boundary tightly around the zone's intended application. This section combines individual steps and knowledge from Chapter 3, "Oracle Solaris Zones." The example in this section uses the Network Time Protocol (NTP) service. Because this section is intended as a platform for a discussion of security, however, we do not provide a complete description of the configuration of NTP. You can visit `http://www.ntp.org` to obtain more information about the proper use of NTP. Note that many other services can be hardened by using this method.

The command examples in this section use the prompt `GZ#` to indicate a command that must be entered by the root user in the global zone. The prompt `timelord#` shows that a command will be entered as the root user of the zone named `timelord`.

9.6.1 Scenario

Imagine that you want to run an application on an Oracle Solaris system but the workload running on this system must not be accessible from the Internet.

Further, imagine that the application needs an accurate sense of time, which can be achieved without zones by using multiple systems and a firewall. With Solaris Zones, you can accomplish those goals with just one system, and offer additional protection as well.

In this scenario, you will need two zones. One zone provides a traditional environment for the application, and will not be discussed further in this section. The second zone has the ability to change the system's clock, but has been made extremely secure by ensuring that it meets the following requirements:

- The zone can make outbound network requests and accept responses to those requests.

- The zone does not allow any inbound network requests (even secure ones such as SSH requests).

- The zone can make outbound requests only to a specific set of IP addresses and port numbers associated with trusted NTP servers.

- The zone can set the system's clock, which is used by the global zone and most types of zones.

- The zone has minimal abilities beside the ones it needs to perform its task.

A Solaris zone can be configured to meet that list of needs.

Each zone has its own Service Management Facility. As with non-virtualized Solaris environments, network services provided by a zone do not accept remote connections by default, except SSH. The zone that will manage the clock can also be configured so that it does not respond to SSH requests. Likewise, configurable privileges enable you to remove unnecessary privileges from the zone. Typically, native zones share the global zone's system clock, but may not modify it. A configuration setting can be used to permit a zone to modify the shared system clock.

Figure 9.4 shows the zone named `timelord`, the NIC it uses, and the system's clock, which will be modified by the zone. It also shows a different internal network, plus the zone for the application. The application zone will share the `bge0` NIC with the global zone.

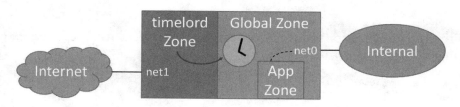

Figure 9.4 A Secure Network Service

9.6.2 Basic Steps

The following outline shows the steps to accomplish the goals described earlier in this section. It can be generalized to harden any service, not just an NTP client.

1. Configure and install a zone.
2. Boot the zone.
3. Install additional software.
4. Remove unnecessary privileges.
5. Reboot the zone to verify correct operation without those privileges.
6. Permit the zone to modify the system clock.
7. Lock down the system configuration.
8. Test the zone.

In most cases, the order of those steps is not critical, but occasionally it is necessary to remove privileges *after* the system has been configured because the configuration steps may require those privileges.

9.6.3 Implementing Hardened Zones

Chapter 3, "Oracle Solaris Zones," discussed the commands used to create and boot a zone. The commands in the current example assume that a separate network interface (net1) exists, and that the zone was configured with the following commands:

```
GZ# zonecfg -z timelord
zonecfg:timelord> create
zonecfg:timelord> select anet 0
zonecfg:timelord:anet> set lower-link=net1
zonecfg:timelord:anet> set allowed-address=192.168.5.5/24
zonecfg:timelord:anet> set defrouter=192.168.5.1
zonecfg:timelord:anet> end
zonecfg:timelord> exit
```

Additional configuration information can be provided with the sysconfig(1M) command:

```
GZ# sysconfig create-profile -o /tmp -g \
naming_services,location,users,identity,support,keyboard
```

You will be prompted to provide some system configuration information, after which you can boot the zone.

```
GZ# zoneadm -z timelord install -c /tmp/sc_profile.xml
GZ# zoneadm -z timelord boot
```

After the zone is running, you can disable unneeded Oracle Solaris services. By default, Solaris 11 and newly created Solaris Zones offer only one network service: SSH. We will access the zone from the global zone with the `zlogin` command, so we can disable that service as well. The service `rpc/bind` does not allow connections, but would show up in a port scan, so we will disable it, too. Finally, we will need the software related to time synchronization, so we will install that.

```
GZ# zoneadm -z timelord boot
GZ# zlogin timelord
timelord# svcadm disable rpc/bind
timelord# svcadm disable ssh
timelord# exit
GZ# zoneadm -z timelord shutdown
```

The next step is to modify the zone's set of allowed privileges, removing unnecessary privileges and optionally adding privileges that are not part of the default set, but are needed so the zone can achieve its goals. It can be challenging to determine the complete set of privileges needed by a program unless you can exercise all of the code in the program. However, the `ppriv(1)` command will report attempts to perform operations that require privileges not currently held by the process. Zones have all the privileges that they need to use NTP, so we do not need to add any.

We know that this zone will not be using NFS as a client or server, so we can remove the `sys_nfs` privilege. Also, we choose not to support system accounting, although we could use that service if we wished. With that choice, we can remove the privilege `sys_acct`. We can use `zonecfg` to remove those two privileges:

```
GZ# zonecfg -z timelord
zonecfg:timelord> set limitpriv=default,!sys_nfs,!sys_acct
zonecfg:timelord> exit
```

At this point, the zone is configured without unnecessary privileges.

For this example, we will use the Network Time Protocol service daemon, `ntpd(1M)`, to automatically synchronize the system's clock with time servers on the Internet on a periodic basis. To enable the zone to modify that clock, the zone's `global-time` setting must be set to `true`. The following command sequence permits the zone to set the system clock:

```
GZ# zonecfg -z timelord
zonecfg:timelord> set global-time=true
zonecfg:timelord> exit
```

After removing unnecessary privileges, and granting the ability to perform necessary operations that are not permitted by default, we can complete the configuration of the one service that this zone will perform:

```
GZ# zoneadm -z timelord boot
```

Wait for the zone to finish booting. Then, install, configure, and enable the NTP service:

```
GZ# zlogin timelord
timelord# pkg install network/ntp
timelord# cd /etc/inet
timelord# cp ntp.client ntp.conf
(Customize /etc/inet/ntp.conf for your site.)
timelord# svcadm enable network/ntp
```

The following command sequence prevents the zone from modifying its Solaris programs or configuration, beginning with the next boot:

```
GZ# zonecfg -z timelord
zonecfg:timelord> set file-mac-profile=fixed-configuration
zonecfg:timelord> exit
```

Reboot the zone and verify the immutability of the system configuration files:

```
GZ# zoneadm -z timelord reboot
GZ# zlogin timelord
timelord:# cd /etc/inet
timelord:/etc/inet# echo "# text" >> ntp.conf
-bash: ntp.conf: Read-only file system
timelord:/etc/inet# ls -l ntp.conf
-r--r--r--   1 root     root         4210 May 19 13:19 ntp.conf
timelord:/etc/inet# chmod 744 ntp.conf
chmod: WARNING: can't change ntp.conf
```

While isolating the zone, why not also limit the amount of resources that it can consume? If the zone is operating normally, the use of resource management features is unnecessary, but they are easy to configure and their use in this situation could be valuable. These limits could reduce or eliminate the effects of a hypothetical bug in `ntpdate` that might cause a memory leak or other unnecessary use of resources.

Further, limiting the amount of resources that can be consumed by the zone provides another layer of security in this environment. In particular, resource constraints can reduce or eliminate risks associated with a denial-of-service attack. Note that the use of these features is not strictly necessary. Instead, their use is shown here for completeness, to demonstrate the possibilities.

Chapter 3, "Oracle Solaris Zones," described the resource controls available for Solaris Zones. Here is a brief explanation of our choices. Note, however, that there are other reasonable choices for this situation.

After setting a RAM cap on the zone described previously, a few quick tests with `rcapstat(1)` might show that the zone needs less than 100MB of memory to do its job. We could cap the amount of RAM at 100MB to prevent this zone from consuming an unnecessary amount of RAM, but we also want to prevent it from causing excessive paging. We can prevent a zone from paging by setting the RAM and virtual memory (VM) caps to the same value. Of course, we do not want to set the VM cap below the amount that is really needed, so we will set a generous limit on both: 100MB caps for both RAM and VM. A cap on locked memory will further minimize the potential for the zone's processes to disrupt other legitimate activities without causing a problem for NTP.

NTP is not a compute-intensive activity, so we will limit its ability to use a CPU. Also, capping the number of processes limits the ability to exhaust a fixed resource: process table slots.

```
GZ# zonecfg -z timelord
zonecfg:timelord> add capped-memory
zonecfg:timelord:capped-memory> set physical=200m
zonecfg:timelord:capped-memory> set swap=200m
zonecfg:timelord:capped-memory> set locked=20m
zonecfg:timelord:capped-memory> end
zonecfg:timelord> add capped-cpu
zonecfg:timelord:capped-cpu> set ncpus=0.5
zonecfg:timelord:capped-cpu> end
zonecfg:timelord> set max-processes=100
zonecfg:timelord> exit
```

Additional restrictions can be placed on this zone, as mentioned later in this chapter.

9.6.4 Test

A simple method to test this zone in a lab environment includes stopping the zone, using the global zone to change the system clock with the date command, and then monitoring the clock while booting the zone. The clock should be synchronized with NTP servers within a few minutes.

9.6.5 Security Analysis

Many attacks on computers try to take advantage of a security weakness in software that listens to the network. The ability to turn off all such services greatly decreases the security risk posed by this kind of weakness. You can also use many of the other features of Oracle Solaris to enhance the security of a zone. Table 9.1 reviews the security features and capabilities used in the example described in this section.

Table 9.1 Security Controls

Security Control	Benefit
IP Filter	Prevents unwanted connection requests from reaching applications; prevents network attacks *from* this zone
Limited network services	Reduces the number of programs listening to network ports
Disabled SSH	Prevents network login
Network virtualization, `mac-nospoof`, `ip=nospoof`	Prevents ARP and IP spoofing attacks; prevents modification of Physical, Data Link, and Network Layer parameters
No device access	Prevents access to other networks via other NICs
No device access	Prevents attacks on other types of devices
No kernel access	Prevents attacks on the operating system and on other zones
`file-mac-profile`	Prevents modification of the operating system
Reduced privilege set	Reduces the set of actions that can be performed in the zone
Resource controls	Further limits the ability of processes in this zone to affect other zones

Before using a security method like the one described in this section, you should validate its ability to handle the types of attacks you want to prevent.

The method described in this section may or may not be suitable for your particular security needs.

9.6.6 Summary

Oracle Solaris Zones offer significant security capabilities not available with other virtualization technologies. An understanding of security issues and the features of Solaris Zones will help you to balance security and functionality needs.

9.6.7 Further Reading

This section focused on the process of fine-tuning the functionality of a Solaris Zone, by expanding on the default abilities and removing others. It was not intended to showcase all of the features that could have been used. Additional features that might be used in situations that require increased security are described in the Oracle Solaris documentation:

- Solaris Privileges, described individually in the `privileges(5) man` page
- Solaris IP Filter, to prevent any unwanted outbound network connections
- Encryption for network traffic and ZFS file systems
- Automated security compliance reporting tools

9.7 Customer Deployment 1

The preceding sections discussed Oracle architectures and products. In this section, we will briefly illustrate some anonymous (and blended) customer deployments that offer interesting examples of Oracle Solaris virtualization in practice. Several common deployment styles and use cases have proved successful and been deployed in multiple institutions in real-world applications.

One example involves a large financial institution that was scaling up core applications into logical domains on M-series servers. This company needed vertical scale for the applications, and it had stringent requirements for performance and availability. At the same time, it had applications that were certified for Solaris 10 and needed to continue to operate them.

To meet these requirements, the company deployed M6-32 systems using Oracle RAC across physical domains, which provides isolation and insulation from OS and processor faults, and across separate M6-32 systems, which provides additional protection. In addition to Oracle RAC, it deployed Oracle Solaris Cluster to maintain high-availability applications.

This financial institution used virtual I/O for many of its domains, but root domains and SR-IOV were used for the domains with the most critical performance. These choices maximized I/O performance without incurring the overhead of going through a service domain. Logical domains support SR-IOV for Ethernet, InfiniBand, and FibreChannel.

Another interesting choice was the use of logical domains dynamic resource management (DRM), which automatically adjusts the number of virtual CPUs in a domain based on its CPU consumption. This feature of Oracle VM Server for SPARC lets administrators set high and low thresholds for CPU utilization: When the domain's utilization rate is low and it has more CPUs than it needs, CPUs are removed until the CPU utilization rate exceeds the lower limit, or until a minimum CPU count is reached. When a domain's utilization rate is high, CPUs are added based on CPU threshold values until the maximum number of CPUs for the domain has been reached. This feature permits automatic CPU load-balancing for domains based on changing load conditions, without requiring further administrative intervention. This outcome was important for meeting the company's goal of deploying several hundred domains without acquiring enough resources for the peak capacity needed by each domain. For even higher consolidation density, the organization deployed zones within the same domain containing an application and the database containing its data—a multitier application environment in a single domain.

This deployment illustrates the use of logical domains for large applications on vertically scaled servers, as well as server consolidation to reduce operational expense and complexity.

9.8 Customer Deployment 2

Another popular deployment pattern is creation of pooled server farms as private clouds. This pattern was introduced long before the term "cloud" came into popular usage, and has been seen at multiple institutions.

One company set up a pool of more than 100 T4 servers, and used them as a consolidation target from older "legacy" SPARC servers. The firm moved existing applications through a combination of reinstalling applications in new domains and using the logical domains' physical-to-virtual (P2V) tool to rehost an existing physical Solaris instance in a guest domain. It also used standard Solaris techniques to create archives of existing Solaris systems running on older hardware.

As a consequence, the company could install these systems in domains using customized JumpStart methods. It was ultimately able to reduce its server footprint by hundreds of physical servers, while moving to a more modern platform that added performance and agility.

A similar implementation was done at another customer in the same business sector. In this case, the company established "built for purpose" virtual server farms for middleware applications and for databases, each configured and optimized for its specific application category.

9.9 Customer Deployment 3

As an additional example of a popular pattern, multiple customers have combined Oracle VM Server for SPARC and Oracle Solaris Zones, similar to the strategies used by the previously mentioned companies, but with additional elaborations.

One common pattern is to rehost old Solaris versions in new hardware, and many customers are hosting Solaris 10 even on new M7 and T7 servers by running it in guest VEs. Some of these Solaris 10 Zones are hosting legacy Solaris 8 and Solaris 9 environments in branded zones so that they can continue to operate even older applications. Other customers, which do not have this increasingly rare combination, host Solaris 11 domains with Solaris 10 branded zones—a scheme that permits them to run Solaris 10 certified applications while benefiting from the Solaris 11 kernel, which runs much more effectively on the newest hardware.

Another example using nested virtualization comprises logical consolidation for a single application that resided on separate physical servers in the past. While customers frequently accomplish this type of consolidation with multiple domains, some have found that they can get better hosting density and improved performance by hosting related applications in zones residing in the same domain. This approach leverages the in-memory networking stack, which then eliminates network I/O latency for multitier applications. Examples include middleware combined with the organization's database, and Oracle PeopleSoft and other layered applications combined with the database.

These examples illustrate how customers have leveraged Oracle virtualization technology to provide greater operational efficiency, increased performance, and reduced costs.

9.10 Summary

This chapter has reviewed use cases in which the unique capabilities of Oracle virtualization technologies are leveraged in Oracle product solutions, or exploited in customer deployments. The common theme is that these technologies can be combined to provide virtualization with near-zero overhead that permits high performance and high scale while providing the primary benefits of virtualization.

Appendix: History of Virtualization and Architectural Evolution

A.1 A Brief History of System Virtualization

This section describes the origin and evolution of server virtualization, and highlights design issues, problems, and solutions that still affect and influence today's systems.

A.1.1 Then and Now, Why and How

A 50-year-old overnight success in commercial use since the 1960s, server virtualization is now experiencing renewed interest. Available in different forms on every modern computer family, server virtualization permits multiple computing environments to coexist on a single computer, with each environment behaving as if it has its own dedicated computer. IT organizations use this approach to run multiple computing environments—even different operating systems—on the same server at the same time. Server virtualization is perhaps a misnomer, since virtualized environments can also be desktop or embedded systems, but virtualizing server systems is its most prominent use.

In today's data centers, server virtualization is primarily used to consolidate multiple low-utilization physical servers, thereby reducing costs for power, cooling, rack space, software licensing, and administrative effort. This differs from the original economic driver for virtualization—namely, to avoid high acquisition costs of expensive computer systems. Despite the different rationales, the effect is similar: multiple virtual computing environments on the same physical machine.

While server virtualization is now available on almost every computer product line and in multiple architectural forms, the original and most widely used form of server virtualization is the *virtual machine*, pioneered by early hypervisors that ran on IBM mainframes in the 1960s and 1970s. Virtual machines inspired and influenced many technologies that emerged in the following decades—most obviously the current mainframe hypervisor, z/VM, but also hypervisors for other system families such as Xen (including Oracle VM Server for x86), VMware and Oracle VM VirtualBox. They also influenced hardware/firmware solutions such as Amdahl's Multiple Domain Facility, IBM's PR/SM and LPARs, and Sun SPARC Enterprise M-Series Dynamic Domains and Oracle VM Server for SPARC (formerly known as Logical Domains), as well as OS-level virtualization such as BSD Jails, Oracle Solaris Zones, and Linux containers.

Challenges and issues faced in the early days still confront modern virtualization technologies, making an understanding of the early systems both valuable and relevant.

A.1.2 The Early Hypervisors

Virtualization has its roots in CTSS (the Compatible Time-Sharing System), which was created at Massachusetts Institute of Technology (MIT) in the mid-1960s. CTSS was the first operating system to time-slice a single computer between interactive users. It also introduced architectural features that would be central to subsequent virtualization environments—including address relocation to permit separate address spaces for each user, preemptive multitasking of user processes, and isolation of physical traps, devices, and interrupts from user processes.

Another major event in the 1960s was IBM's introduction of System/360, a family of architecturally identical computer systems with models at different price and performance points. IBM intended System/360 sites to run a batch-oriented operating system called OS/360. While this system became very successful in the commercial space, its lack of support for address relocation and time-sharing prevented its use for interactive applications.

This limitation led to the development of an experimental system called CP-40, which ran on a customized System/360 model 40 that used an associative memory to translate virtual memory addresses to real memory addresses. CP-40 introduced a concept that its developers named a "virtual machine," and was the parent of all subsequent hypervisor-based virtualization. CP-40 proved that a physical computer could concurrently run multiple virtual computers, each of which could run a different operating system. The hypervisor was also referred to as a "virtual machine monitor" or "host," while the virtual machines running under it were commonly referred to as "guests."

CP-40 was based on technical prerequisites for virtualization that have remained consistent in the intervening decades. These requirements were described by Popek and Goldberg (*Communications of the ACM*, Volume 12, Number 7, July 1974) as follows:

- *Equivalence*: Execution in a guest environment is "essentially identical" to execution running on bare metal.
- *Resource control*: Guest environments have access to only the physical machine's resources that are explicitly granted to it by the hypervisor.
- *Efficiency*: The majority of the instructions executed by the guest are executed directly by hardware at native speed, without intervention by the virtual machine monitor.

These properties are provided by hardware architectures that offer a system mode of execution in which all instructions can be executed, and a user mode in which privileged instructions are suppressed and generate a program trap. In non-virtualized environments, this approach protects system integrity by preventing malicious or buggy applications from issuing instructions that change machine state (such as enabling or disabling interrupts, or changing memory mapping) and potentially crashing the system or creating security exposures.

This mechanism works differently in virtual machine environments, since guest operating systems execute privileged instructions and need them to behave the same way as on the real machine. An attempt by a guest operating system to execute a privileged instruction generates a program trap to the hypervisor, which then emulates the instruction (in software) solely in the context of the virtual machine. This has performance implications that will be discussed later in this appendix.

The resulting paradigm supports the Popek and Goldberg properties and is still used by hypervisors. Note that the x86 architecture did not satisfy the "trap and execute" virtualization described by Popek and Goldberg. x86 virtual machines can tell that they have been "deprivileged," and some privileged instructions (such as `popf`) are suppressed but do not cause a trap. x86 hypervisors handle this in different ways: VMware performs binary translation to replace these instructions with code that manipulates guest state without privileged instructions, or with a call to the hypervisor. Xen uses paravirtualization to eliminate use of privileged instructions. Enhancements to the x86 platform have elaborated on the original concept.

A.1.3 Virtual Machines Emerge from the Laboratory

CP-40 was ported to the System/360 model 67, IBM's first production virtual memory computer, and renamed CP/67, and subsequently to the System/370 line under the name VM/370. VM/370, with a simple design based on virtual machines, began to be used for time-sharing using a simple interactive single-user OS originally called the Cambridge Monitor System (CMS), later renamed Conversational Monitor System with the same acronym.

Instead of a single OS instance shared by multiple users, as in CTSS, Multics, and UNIX, CMS provided a lightweight single-user OS instance for each user, and exploited a separation of functions with the hypervisor for resource management and access control. This permitted a very simple design: a flat per-user address space, a non-multitasking program model (multitasking was provided by overlapped execution of multiple CMS users), a minimal permission model (all security was implemented in the virtual machine monitor), and a basic, private file system. Each user had virtual disks called "minidisks," implemented by cylinder extents on physical disks.

This design—a simple OS leveraging services from the hypervisor—had a small memory footprint and short instruction path length that were well suited to providing short response times on the computers of the day. The idea of a lightweight virtualization environment can be seen in unrelated later systems such as Oracle Solaris Zones that shift "heavy lifting" to the underlying operating system kernel. This design pattern was also deployed for non-interactive users: CMS guests running disconnected from a terminal were used to implement "service virtual machines" (a precursor to UNIX daemons) for scheduled or event-driven work. This design pattern is now seen in lightweight container virtualization methods such as Docker.

It also became routine practice for many customers to run several incompatible operating systems (DOS/360, OS/360, and their descendants) at the same time. Institutions used VM/370 to run multiple guest OS instances on the same physical machine, so the same machine could be shared by different workloads. Many customers found virtual machines essential for operating multiple workloads or converting to new operating systems. There was no alternative, short of purchasing additional systems, to run a new operating system in parallel with the existing production environment. This use case is seen today in x86 virtualization environments running Linux, Microsoft Windows, or Solaris in virtual machines running on the same server.

While it might seem odd from today's perspective, in the 1970s very few people directly interacted with a computer. Those who did generally relied on time-shared multiuser computer systems in the style pioneered on CTSS. VM extended this concept, and anticipated the personal computer by giving each user a virtual personal computer with a private, lightweight CMS instance. The PC eventually made the time-sharing style of computing largely disappear, but interactive computing in the 1970s and 1980s was dominated by time-sharing on VM, UNIX, and VAX VMS. Time-sharing never completely disappeared, and it re-emerged with thin-client computing, such as Oracle's Sun Ray and Virtual Desktop Integration (VDI), which provides the economic advantages of shared infrastructure using modern user interfaces and application interfaces.

The division of functions between the VM hypervisor and the simple CMS guest was extended in non-time-sharing contexts by inter-user messaging APIs that presaged TCP/IP sockets. These APIs, which were implemented by a protocol that let a guest virtual machine request services from the hypervisor, permitted creation of interacting collections of daemon-style "service virtual machines." The applications were often implemented in scripts, which reduced difficulty and let a wider population of developers create services. It became common for applications to be implemented by communicating virtual machines, which were forerunners of the later client–server systems with applications implemented by physical machines.

A.2 Architectural Evolution and Influences

A.2.1 Performance and Manageability Challenges and Responses

VM systems pushed the limits of contemporary systems in hosting multiple workloads. Early implementations were particularly vulnerable to disappointing performance due to poorly understood causes. Some workloads took several times longer to run in a virtual machine than natively, even when there were no other users competing for resources. Solutions were slow to evolve, and a few problems remain for which there are still no complete answers. Some issues discovered in early virtual machine systems continue to affect today's systems, and current solutions to these issues are influenced by the early experiences. This section describes some of the most notable issues, the ways in which they were first handled, and current systems' solutions for handling them.

A.2.2 Performance Impacts of Instruction Emulation

The most obvious form of overhead in virtual machine environments is the cost of emulating privileged operations executed by a guest's OS, as described previously. Guest operating systems need to emulate such operations to execute correctly—for example, disabling or enabling interrupt masks to enter or exit a critical section, issuing I/O, marking memory pages as referenced, or changing memory maps when dispatching different processes. These instructions must not be allowed to run directly on the real machine, because they would break the integrity of the hypervisor and its guests. Instead, guests run in a mode where executing these instructions results in a hardware trap. The general (and greatly simplified) flow of execution is as follows:

1. The guest OS in the virtual machine executes a privileged instruction that generates a hardware trap.
2. A context switch to the hypervisor saves the machine state and determines the trap's cause.
3. The hypervisor emulates the instruction in software, in the context of the guest.
4. The hypervisor does a context switch back to the guest, if it is still runnable.

A similar effect occurred with the "system call" instructions that applications use to request OS services. These include the SVC ("supervisor call") instruction on IBM mainframes, the ta software trap instruction on SPARC, and the int $0x80 and sysenter instructions on Intel. When executed in a real machine, these instructions cause a context switch to a location pointed to by an interrupt vector in real memory, and a context switch into the OS. When executed in a virtual machine, they do the exact same thing, but the vector in physical memory is owned by the hypervisor (which uses it for its own purposes) and, therefore, points to a location in the hypervisor instead of the guest OS. The hypervisor's interrupt service routine determines if the trapped system call came from a virtual machine, and if so, it reflects the system call instruction to the guest OS by using the equivalent guest's virtual memory address. This inflates CPU path lengths because the execution time of a system call is roughly doubled.

A similar process occurs when reflecting an interrupt (timer or I/O event) to a guest. The program running at that moment is interrupted with a context switch to the hypervisor. The hypervisor determines the virtual machine with which the physical interrupt is associated, and then maps the interrupt into the virtual machine's state. Several context switches take place between hypervisor and guest, whereas a physical server environment would require only one.

Instruction simulation and interrupt reflection require thousands of instructions and may occur thousands of times per second. This is a substantial source of overhead, especially for I/O-intensive workloads that generate many system calls and many privileged operations, and is a challenge on most hypervisor-based systems.

Sometimes the emulated hardware capability is trivial and can be implemented with a few instructions. For example, simulating an instruction to mask off interrupt classes might take just a few instructions. In such cases, most of the added CPU time is spent on context switching—purely overhead—and very little time is devoted to emulating the instruction causing the trap. In other cases, the instruction to be simulated requires substantial processing. This is typical for I/O instructions, which may have complex semantics on real hardware, and can require substantial CPU time when emulated via software.

Early VM systems were seen to spend a majority of their CPU time emulating instructions rather than running user applications. One obvious means to streamline this process was to instrument and tune high-frequency code paths, but an alternative in the IBM mainframe implementation was to move privileged instruction simulation into "virtual machine assist" firmware. With these assists, privileged instructions caused a branch to a microcode routine in firmware rather than the original trap. The microcode determined if the interrupting instruction was one it could handle, since many privileged instructions were too complex to emulate in firmware, or if it involved guest state changes that required intervention by the hypervisor. If microcode could handle it, it would emulate the instruction entirely in firmware. This approach was faster than the original trap and software emulation, and reduced instruction simulation overhead. On a few hardware models, selected high-frequency code paths in the hypervisor were implemented in firmware as well. These assists made it possible to run guest VMs with near-native performance (exclusive of slowdown caused by competition for resources with other virtual machines running at the same time, of course).

Integrated design of software and hardware was not as straightforward in the x86 marketplace, where hardware designers (Intel, AMD) do not create hypervisors (VMware, VirtualBox, Hyper-V, Xen), or operating systems (Windows, Solaris, Linux). However, the importance of virtualization in the x86 marketplace led AMD and Intel to create architectural enhancements to their products that reduce "trap and emulate" context switches and make virtualization more efficient. Paravirtualization is now used by all available hypervisors to reduce or eliminate guest execution of privileged instructions.

Oracle's SPARC servers using the Oracle VM for SPARC hypervisor solve this problem differently. The hypervisor dedicates physical CPU strands to each domain rather than sharing them among all guests, so a guest does not have to be restricted from changing processor state. This strategy was made possible by defining a new `sun4v` CPU architecture (prior SPARC servers used the `sun4u` architecture) that controls hardware protection and resource visibility at the hardware level. Context switching has been moved into the processor, where it can be done much more quickly than in software, requiring only a single clock cycle. Oracle Solaris Zones solve this problem even more directly: There is only one kernel regardless of the number of virtual environments in zones. Application system calls invoke the kernel identically, whether they are issued in a zone or not. These architectures eliminate the complexity and overhead associated with instruction emulation.

A.2.3 The Question of Time (Does Anybody Really Know What Time It Is?)

A problem first faced by early hypervisors is "clock skew," in which time proceeds in a virtual machine at a different rate than on the real hardware. A guest operating system has no way of knowing that between two sequential instructions it may have been interrupted by the hypervisor and delayed for an arbitrary amount of time. Perhaps the hypervisor decided to run a different guest for a few milliseconds, or the guest suffered a page fault and stalled until a page was read from disk. In either case, real "wall clock time" will have advanced, even as virtual clock time has remained the same.

Clock skew between virtual and actual time has significant consequences. The time and date reported by a virtual machine might be wrong, or interval-based time-slicing within a guest may fail to work correctly.

On the original CP/67 hypervisor, the only timer mechanism was an interval timer based on a location in memory that was decremented on a periodic basis and caused a timer interrupt when it underflowed. Clearly, this solution could not scale, as it would have required the hypervisor to accurately update a location in each guest's memory many times per second. The next hardware architecture added hardware timers that were accessed by privileged instructions and maintained both the current time of day and the accumulated CPU time. The guest OS referred to these clocks via intercepted instructions, giving the hypervisor a chance to provide correctly adjusted time-of-day clock values, and updated CPU-usage timers that reflected the time that the virtual machine was dispatched and executing instructions.

This problem persists with current hypervisors. x86 has several hardware time facilities, and hypervisors such as VirtualBox, VMware, and Xen have provisions for dealing with clock skew. For example, VMware emulates the x86 CMOS Real Time Clock (RTC) and Programmable Interval Timer (PIT) and provides "apparent time" that can lag real time but catch up to it. Clock skew may occur because several operating systems (Windows, Linux) keep time by recording timer interrupts (ticks, or "jiffies") whose duration may be longer than the specified timer interval. VMware provides add-on tools for different hypervisors to compensate for clock skew. Modern operating systems can also use the Network Time Protocol (NTP) for coordinating time against an external standard.

Oracle Solaris Zones completely bypasses this problem, as each zone runs off the same clock and timer environment provided by the kernel. Clock skew is also avoided with Oracle VM Server for SPARC, as clock resolution is provided by the firmware and per-CPU hardware. The hypervisor additionally maintains a TOD offset for each domain.

A.2.4 Synthetic Instructions for Guest–Hypervisor Service Protocols

VM/370 introduced a private interface using a synthetic instruction for guest communication with the hypervisor and access to APIs it exports. The original name for this capability was DIAGNOSE (for the mainframe instruction being repurposed), but it is now generically referred to as a "hypercall." The trapping and emulation of a privileged instruction still occurs, but hypercalls permit shorter path lengths than the real-machine I/O and machine control instructions that they replaced.

Synthetic instructions made it possible to add services to make a virtual machine more functional than a real one. Different APIs provided a command interface to the hypervisor (virtual machines can issue commands to the hypervisor and see the message results), inter-user message passing, input/output services, timer management, and other useful functions.

This design pattern is now widely used in virtual machine systems, permitting cooperation between the guest OS and the hypervisor. It is a hallmark of the Xen hypervisor, in which a guest can use hypercalls to efficiently request services such as I/O and memory management. A variant method is provided by VMware, which supplies device drivers for virtual network devices for some guest operating systems, which can be emulated more efficiently than the highly specific aspects of different physical network cards.

A.2.5 The Nested CPU Resource Manager Problem

One largely unsolved problem is that of the nested CPU resource manager. VM/370 provided a "fair share scheduler" that permitted preferential CPU service to be delivered to important guests, similar to the ticket, share, or proportional weight schedulers such as Xen's credit scheduler used in Oracle VM Server for x86, the Oracle Solaris Fair Share Scheduler, and VMware's scheduler. These schedulers give virtual environments proportional access to CPU time based on relative shares assigned to them.

Such a scheme works well when a guest has only one purpose and one level of importance, but it can be problematic when the virtual machine is itself a multiprogramming environment with work having different priorities, or when the guest OS does non-performance-critical tasks in the background. Consider a modern virtual machine in a VDI implementation: It should have good response time for mouse and keyboard events and interactive applications, but it may also perform low-priority housekeeping work such as running a virus scanner or indexing a file system. In the original mainframe context, this problem occurred with guests that needed good service for network devices and interactive users, but also had low-priority CPU-crunching workloads.

Two types of problems can result from this situation in a resource-constrained environment: If the guest is given a share value high enough to provide preferential CPU access for both critical and unimportant work, it will have better-than-needed CPU access and may run its unimportant work with better service than other guests. If the preferred guests' CPU share is large enough to perform its important work but not all of its tasks, it becomes possible for a low-priority process to absorb the preferred CPU shares, causing the high-performance work to be starved when it runs later. Both cases can result in CPU starvation at unpredictable times, causing inconsistent response times. The root cause is that the hypervisor does not generally have visibility into the relative importance of the work the virtual machine is executing, and it cannot differentiate between the important guest's important work and its unimportant work.

An approach to addressing this problem was invented in the mid-1970s by Robert Cowles, then at Cornell University, who created an API to let his primary guest OS send hints to the VM hypervisor about the importance of the work it was preparing to run. The VM would not waste high-priority CPU access on the preferred guest's low-importance work, and the priority for the entire guest could be reduced to cover only its high-importance work. It was possible to run work with different priorities on the same guest and give each application its due level of service. The result was reduced CPU starvation for other guests and for the high-priority work of the preferred guest, with measurable improvements in response time and throughput for both.

Unfortunately, this approach has not been generally adopted, and the problem still remains. Most guest operating systems today are complex operating environments that sometimes give higher-than-necessary priority to background tasks that could tolerate being delayed. The approach with contemporary systems is to separate work of different priority classes into different single-purpose virtual machines. This approach increases the number of virtual machines needed, which increases overhead (as each guest has its own CPU and memory footprint) and can make it harder for them to share data. Another approach is made possible by environments like Oracle VM Server for SPARC, which avoid the entire issue because CPUs are dedicated rather than time-sliced subject to scheduler decisions. Finally, it is now more economically feasible to throw hardware at the problem by not consolidating as aggressively as was necessary when hardware was so much more expensive. The lower cost of CPU capacity means that fewer systems run at high levels of CPU utilization that risk CPU starvation due to nested resource priorities.

A.2.6 Memory Management: Controlling Thrashing

An even more challenging performance problem hindering virtualization efforts was learning how to efficiently provide virtual memories. This problem persists in current systems to some degree, but was especially problematic when computer memory was limited by price and architectural restrictions.

The implications of hosting virtual memories whose aggregate sizes exceeded physical memory was not well understood in the early days of virtual machines. The concept of a "working set" was still extremely new, and the separate research efforts by Lazslo Belady and Peter Denning on virtual memory had only just been published when CP/67 was written. One of the few operational virtual memory systems of the time was the Atlas Ferranti, which was known to suffer performance problems under high loads.

The main problem was "thrashing"—a state in which applications struggle to establish a working set of pages (the set of memory they will access in a small window of time) in real memory, so that they can operate without spending most of their time waiting for pages to be swapped to and from disk. The replacement algorithms and multiprogramming controls needed to prevent thrashing had yet to be developed.

In a thrashing system, an application briefly runs, and then experiences a page fault by referring to a virtual address that is not currently in memory. It stalls and waits for that page to be fetched from disk, which may take millions of instruction times. Most elapsed time is spent waiting for data to be retrieved from disk rather than running applications. In a thrashing system, a virtual environment spends its time slice page-faulting its working set from disk into memory, and in so doing evicts the pages of other applications from memory to disk, or even some of its own pages. At the end of the time slice, the next virtual environment runs and does the same thing to pages loaded by its predecessor. Applications continually evict each other's pages and try to reestablish their working sets, rather than accomplishing actual work.

Thrashing can happen on any virtual memory system, but was especially intense with virtual machines because guest operating systems have larger memory footprints than a single application, and because they exhibit poor locality of reference. An application program running in a virtual memory OS such as Solaris or a Linux distribution has a working set size based on its application needs. In contrast, most operating systems refer to as much RAM as is installed on the computer, typically for buffering file contents. If such an OS runs on a machine with 8 GB of RAM, it will use 8 GB of RAM, regardless of how much memory an application actually needs. When an OS runs in a real machine, this behavior makes perfect sense, as unused RAM is wasted and could have been used to reduce I/O delays. In a virtual machine, however, memory seen by the guest is virtual memory, backed by physical RAM shared by all guests. Thus, using extra virtual memory in one guest reduces the physical memory available for other guests. It is typical for the physical memory footprint of a guest to approach the virtual memory size of the guest. For example, a Solaris or Linux guest running in a virtual machine sized as 8 GB would tend to occupy 8 GB of RAM because it will touch all of the pages that it thinks it owns. A "best practice" for virtual machines is to reduce the virtual memory size as much as feasible to reduce this effect.

A pathological situation called "double paging" can occur when the guest operating system itself provides virtual memory, as most do. Consider a guest's application that suffers a page fault, causing the guest OS to write a least recently used (LRU) page to its swap disk to provide a real memory page frame to page-in the faulted location: a disk write and a disk read. Recall that what the guest considers to be "real memory" is actually "virtual memory" from the hypervisor's view. If that guest's page has already been swapped out by the hypervisor, an additional disk read (from the hypervisor's external swap/page space) will be necessary to bring in the page that the guest will immediately write to its swap/page space and then discard.

The algorithms used to implement virtual memory can work paradoxically in a virtual machine environment. Approximations of the LRU replacement algorithm are used in most virtual memory systems. LRU is based on the expectation that a page that has not been used recently is likely not to be used in the near future; hence it is the best page to "replace" by writing its contents to disk so that its RAM can be freed up and used for an active working set page. Most operating systems proactively write LRU pages to disk so there will be available pages when an application has a page fault and needs to have data paged in. However, when a guest selects its oldest untouched page for replacement, the act of doing so references the page from the point of the hypervisor, making it the most recently used (MRU) page. That has the effect of making the guest's actively used pages *older* in terms of actual memory access than pages that the guest has not used in a long time! Depending on the relative page pressure within the guest OS and among the hypervisor's various guests, a nested LRU system could wind up evicting the very pages it should retain. This behavior has, in fact, been observed under high load circumstances.

VM/370 ran in extremely memory-constrained environments, and developed a scheduler that ran only those virtual machines whose working sets fit in memory. Other guests were held in an "eligible" queue and occupied no RAM at all. As delayed applications "aged," they eventually reached a priority high enough to evict one of the running applications. Essentially, applications in a memory-constrained system took their turns running, but when they ran, they had enough RAM for their working sets and ran efficiently.

A "handshaking" mechanism enabled guest and host environments to communicate with one another. The VM hypervisor could tell a guest that it had incurred a page fault, so the guest could dispatch a different user process rather than be placed into a page wait state. This strategy was useful for guests running multiple processes, though it could have the undesired effect of inflating working sets, and it was unproductive if there was no other runnable process for the guest to run. A hypercall API let a guest tell the hypervisor that it no longer needed a block of memory, so pages in real memory and swap area backing it could be released. This reduced the guest working-set size and prevented double paging. If the guest subsequently referred to those pages, the hypervisor gave it new page frames with zeroed contents rather than retrieving the discarded contents from a swap file.

These methods anticipated the cooperative memory management and ballooning techniques available with VMware and Xen, in which the hypervisor can cause the guest OS to use a smaller working set during times of high load on real memory. Typically, a guest daemon allocates a memory buffer and maps it into the guest's RAM. When memory pressure in the hypervisor is low, the memory buffer is shrunk, so the guest has more pages that it can allocate to its applications. When memory pressure in the hypervisor is high, the daemon is told to increase the size of the buffer ("inflate the balloon"). This reduces the number of pages that the guest OS can allocate to applications, which decreases both its working set and its contribution to memory pressure on the hypervisor.

Another approach is exemplified by Oracle Solaris Zones, which uses a single resource manager for a Solaris instance with many virtual environments. Since there is only one memory manager, the problem is neatly and elegantly sidestepped.

Today, the economics of memory prices make it feasible to simply not over-subscribe memory, as was necessary in VM/370's day. This practice is used with Oracle VM Server for SPARC, which allocates to each guest as much real memory as the guest's virtual memory size. While this practice constrains the number of domains that can run at any moment in time, it eliminates this entire complex category of problems.

A.2.7 Memory Management: Multiple Address Spaces

Another expensive situation is efficiently providing virtual memory to guest operating systems that themselves provide virtual memory. The difficulty in this case is not providing enough RAM to support memory requirements for each guest, but rather efficiently translating their virtual addresses to the real RAM addresses in which they reside.

This can be explained by describing how most processors translate virtual addresses into real ones. One common scheme divides virtual memory addresses used by processes into segment, page, and offset components. The segment number is used as an index into an array (the segment table) of virtual address segments owned by the process, so as to point to the pages belonging to that segment. The page number is used as an index into this table, and points to an entry containing the address of the physical page in RAM containing the virtual address page. Finally, the offset part of the virtual address is added to the page address, producing the real memory address corresponding to the virtual address.

If this was implemented literally as described in the preceding paragraph, every application reference to memory would require at least two more memory references. Requiring three memory references for every user memory reference would impose an intolerable overhead. Instead, most processors cache recently translated virtual page addresses in a "translation lookaside buffer" (TLB), a fast associative memory that can be probed for a page table entry (PTE) with a matching segment and page address in a single cycle. The SPARC name for this associative table is the Page Descriptor Cache (PDC), but this appendix uses the generic term for it.

If a segment and page address has been recently used, it will be found in the TLB and the matching real memory address used. If the entry is not present, the slow table lookup is used, but the resulting address is stored in a PTE in the TLB for later reuse. If the TLB is full, the least recently used PTE is replaced. If the page is not resident in memory, a page exception trap is generated.

Normally this approach works very well. Indeed, contemporary processors have separate TLBs for instructions and data, just as they typically have separate on-chip instruction and data caches. SPARC processors keep statistics that Solaris can probe to determine the hit rate being achieved, and page sizes up to 16 GB can be used to reduce the number of TLB entries needed for a large memory application. This SPARC feature helps reduce TLB thrashing for vertically scaling applications such as Oracle Database.

Unfortunately, a serious complication arises in a virtual machine environment. The TLB translates from a virtual address to a real one—that is, there are two levels of addresses. In a virtual machine environment, however, there are typically three address levels:

1. The addresses of the machine's RAM, sometimes called the physical address, or "host real," which are visible to only the hypervisor.

2. The virtual addresses for each virtual machine's virtual memory, which appear to the guest OS as if they are physical memory addresses. Such an address is called a "guest real" or simply "real" address, or "host virtual," indicating that what the guest thinks is an address in RAM is actually a virtual memory address. The hypervisor maintains segment and page tables to map a guest's level 2 address to a level 1 address.

3. The virtual address spaces created by the guest OS for each guest application process. This type of address is called "guest virtual." Each guest OS maintains segment and page tables to map every process virtual address (level 3) to what it thinks is a level 1 address.

Non-virtualized systems perform one translation from virtual address to a real one, but two translations are needed in a virtual machine environment.

VM/370 bypassed this problem for its CMS time-sharing users because CMS runs only one program at a time and uses only a single address space. For guest operating systems that provided virtual memory (MVS, or VM/370 itself), the solution was to create per-guest "shadow page tables" that are indexed by the guest-virtual segment and page numbers, and contain the host-real addresses corresponding to those guest pages. This is conceptually the same method used today in virtual machine monitors such as VMware.

Maintaining these tables can be a resource-intensive endeavor. When the guest OS context switches between different processes, the hypervisor must intercept the change in guest address spaces, and switch to a different shadow page table. When the hypervisor context switches from one guest to another, it must purge the contents of the hardware-provided TLBs (so address references from the now-running guest do not point to memory in the recently running guest), and switch to the set of shadow page tables associated with the new guest. A substantial bookkeeping effort is associated with this activity, adding to the CPU overhead of virtualization. It also adds to the memory cost of virtualization: Shadow page tables can be quite large, and there must be enough of them to efficiently represent all the active processes of each virtual machine.

Modern systems from AMD and Intel use several methods to reduce the overhead of maintaining shadow page tables, using nested page tables and tagged page tables with hardware support for changing address mappings. Intel's VT-i provides tagged page tables that are marked with the virtual-processor identifiers (VPIDs) of the guest's virtual CPU that are operational when the VPID is running. This scheme eliminates the need to purge TLB entries on VM entry and exit. AMD's Nested Page Tables (NPT) provide a hardware-managed per-guest translation table, which contains each guest's address spaces and provides a hardware page table walk. Although the implementations differ, both Intel and AMD provide a hardware capability that dramatically reduces this virtualization overhead. To provide even better performance, hypervisors such as VirtualBox and VMware leverage these technology enhancements on the systems implementing them.

Oracle's virtualization technologies bypass this issue entirely. Oracle Solaris Zones do not run a virtual memory environment nested under another virtual memory environment, so there are only virtual and physical memory addresses. This scheme is just as efficient as running Solaris without zones. Oracle VM Server for SPARC addresses the issue of multiple memory spaces by binding guest real memory to physical memory on a one-to-one basis. Address mappings between host-real and host-physical addresses can be cached externally to the OS-visible TLB. Since each CPU strand on a SPARC server runs no more than one domain, and since each has its own memory mapping unit (MMU) and TLB, there is no need to purge and replace TLBs during context switching—CPU strands are not context-switched at all. The hypervisor manages TLBs that translate directly from virtual to physical memory addresses, bypassing the need to perform a double translation. These architectural innovations avoid the overhead of maintaining guest virtual address spaces.

A.3 Summary and Lessons Learned

This appendix has described the early hypervisors, their evolution, and problems and design choices that they addressed. While today's computers are far more powerful than their counterparts in the early days, the experiences with the early virtual machine systems continue to influence today's systems.

The economic incentives for virtualization have evolved since server virtualization was invented. Originally, virtualization was intended to help minimize mainframe acquisition costs by sharing a single computer among many virtual machines (or conversely, amortizing its expense over their combined workloads) in circumstances where an individual computer was extremely expensive. Today, server virtualization is used to reduce environmental and license costs resulting from server sprawl, and to consolidate the loads from underutilized computers whose individual costs are low. While these motivations might seem to be very different, they are actually opposite sides of the same coin. Both yesterday and today there are substantial benefits to be realized by reducing the number of physical servers, and virtualization is a powerful tool for making that possible.

Current virtualization technologies draw heavily on the concepts, architecture, and even the language invented in relation to the early hypervisors.

Index

REGISTER YOUR PRODUCT at informit.com/register

Access Additional Benefits and SAVE 35% on Your Next Purchase

- Download available product updates.

- Access bonus material when applicable.

- Receive exclusive offers on new editions and related products.
  (Just check the box to hear from us when setting up your account.)

- Get a coupon for 35% for your next purchase, valid for 30 days. Your code will
  be available in your InformIT cart. (You will also find it in the Manage Codes
  section of your account page.)

Registration benefits vary by product. Benefits will be listed on your account page
under Registered Products.

InformIT.com–The Trusted Technology Learning Source

InformIT is the online home of information technology brands at Pearson, the world's foremost
education company. At InformIT.com you can

- Shop our books, eBooks, software, and video training.
- Take advantage of our special offers and promotions (informit.com/promotions).
- Sign up for special offers and content newsletters (informit.com/newsletters).
- Read free articles and blogs by information technology experts.
- Access thousands of free chapters and video lessons.

Connect with InformIT–Visit informit.com/community

Learn about InformIT community events and programs.